Negotiating Urban Conflicts

Materialities | ed. by Gabriele Klein, Martina Löw and Michael Meuser | volume 1

Helmuth Berking, Sybille Frank, Lars Frers, Martina Löw,
Lars Meier, Silke Steets, Sergej Stoetzer (eds.)
Negotiating Urban Conflicts
Interaction, Space and Control

[transcript]

Bibliographic information published by Die Deutsche Bibliothek
Die Deutsche Bibliothek lists this publication in the Deutsche Nationalbibliografie;
detailed bibliographic data are available in the Internet at http://dnb.ddb.de

© 2006 transcript Verlag, Bielefeld

All rights reserved. No part of this book may be reprinted or reproduced or utilized in any form or by any electronic, mechanical, or other means, now known or hereafter invented, inlcuding photocopying and recording, or in any information storage or retrieval system, without permission in writing from the publisher.

Cover layout by: Kordula Röckenhaus, Bielefeld
Typeset by: Silke Steets, Sergej Stoetzer
Cover illustration by: Ilka Flora, www.obrigada.de
Printed and bound in Great Britain by Marston Book Services Ltd, Oxfordshire
ISBN 3-89942-463-8

Contents

Introduction: Negotiating Urban Conflicts   9

I   Politics of Space:
The Modern, the Postmodern and the Postcolonial

Postcolonial Cities, Postcolonial Critiques   15
ANTHONY D. KING

Contested Places and the Politics of Space   29
HELMUTH BERKING

The City as Assemblage. Diasporic Cultures, Postmodern Spaces, and Biopolitics   41
COUZE VENN

**Remapping the Geopolitics of Terror:
Uncanny Urban Spaces in Singapore**   53
LISA LAW

Cultural Homogenisation, Places of Memory, and the Loss of Secular Urban Space   67
ANIL BHATTI

II Spatializing Identities

The Politics and Poetics of Religion:
Hindu Processions and Urban Conflicts　　　　　　　　85
LILY KONG

Negotiating the City—Everyday Forms of Segregation
in Middle Class Cairo　　　　　　　　　　　　　　　99
ANOUK DE KONING

Negotiating Public Spaces: The Right to the Gendered City
and the Right to Difference　　　　　　　　　　　　113
TOVI FENSTER

On the Road to Being White: The Construction of Whiteness
in the Everyday Life of Expatriate German High Flyers
in Singapore and London　　　　　　　　　　　　　125
LARS MEIER

Prostitution—Power Relations between Space and Gender　　139
MARTINA LÖW/RENATE RUHNE

III Imageries of Cities

Between Refeudalization and New Cultural Politics:
The 300th Anniversary of St. Petersburg　　　　　　　155
ELENA TRUBINA

Reflections on a Cartography of the Non-Visible.
Urban Experience and the Internet　　　　　　　　　167
MARC RIES

Picturing Urban Identities　　　　　　　　　　　　　177
SERGEJ STOETZER

Communist Heritage Tourism and its Local (Dis)Contents
at Checkpoint Charlie, Berlin　　　　　　　　　　　195
SYBILLE FRANK

Earthquake Recovery and Historic Buildings:
Investigating the Conflicts 209
FATIMA AL-NAMMARI

IV Exclusion, Security and Surveillance

The Phenomenon of Exclusion 227
HEINZ BUDE

Orbit Palace. Locations and Cultures of Redundant Time 235
SILKE STEETS

Pacification by Design:
An Ethnography of Normalization Techniques 247
LARS FRERS

Violence Prevention in a South African Township 261
KOSTA MATHÉY

Homeland/Target: Cities and the "War on Terror" 277
STEPHEN GRAHAM

Terrorism and the Right to the Secure City:
Safety vs. Security in Public Spaces 289
PETER MARCUSE

Authors 305

Introduction: Negotiating Urban Conflicts

If city life is understood as a complex composition of strangers among strangers, difference, conflict, and compromise are not only—and inevitably—defining features of this particular place. They are also, and have to be, carried out in spatial terms based on and tied into a specific politics of space. It is above all in cities that the spatial practices of social actors and institutions —and thus highly divergent *spatial politics*—come up against one another.

Cities have always been arenas of social and symbolic conflict. As places of gender, class, ethnicity, and the myriad variations of identity-related differences, one of the major roles they are predestined to play is that of a powerful integrator; yet on the other hand urban contexts are, as it were, the ideal setting for marginalization and violence. The struggle for control of urban spaces is an ambivalent mode of sociation, one that cuts systematically across the whole of everyday life: In and by producing themselves, groups produce exclusive spaces and then, in turn, use the boundaries they have created to define themselves. In this way border control and politics of identity represent two sides of one coin. The spatial politics subscribed to by social actors at the same time shapes the contour of the city's inner order and the symbolic universes of the groups living in it.

These manifold lines of potential conflict run up against institutional regimes designed to guarantee urban security. What is paradox here are the effects engendered by attempts to 'domesticate' violence and the promise of security they imply, for they themselves are based on spatial politics and thus encourage the creation of new boundaries and renewed marginalization. Be it addressed as location policy or logic of segregation, as ghettoization or gentrification, invariably, it would appear, the underlying issue is the definition and production, the stabilization and maintenance of spatial arrangements and the way they are hierarchized.

Class, ethnicity, and gender, indeed all categorial identities, not only mark symbolic distances. They also unfold their distinctive (local) significance more in connection with the realization of spatial divisions that refer the categorial sense of orientation to strictly delimited, territorialized entities. "That's the ghetto over there"; "back there is where the new money lives"; "this is a safe part of town," etc.

The struggle for territorial control, spatial arrangements, and order focuses some of the motives—fundamental in nature though not always borne in mind by social policy and social theory—apparent in all types of urban conflict. Building on this premise, *"Negotiating urban conflicts"* centers on various mutually disruptive and reinforcing *spatial politics* with a view to pinpointing some of the major old and very new conflict potentials, but without losing sight of the need to identify altered negotiating processes. To put the main thread of this edition in a nutshell version means conceptualizing spatial politics from the perspective of a) actors, b) institutional regimes, c) constructions of difference with the processes of compromise which they entail.

Since urban conflicts, demarcations, and claims to space are played out in local contexts, though without being restricted by them in their scope, cultural frames take on particular significance here. Given that options of collective actors, configurations of institutional regimes, and possible compromises vary in cultural terms, the central question is: How can those specific and distinctive logics be grasped on which locality as a particular frame of knowledge, meaning and practice is built? Urban-sociological research designs have always tended not only to play down the role of the local as a just context driven site but to 'Europeanize' it as well. The background assumptions that have today merged to form the ideal type of the "European city" systematically obstruct our view of other modes of urbanization, of processes involved in staking out claims to and demarcating space(s) in Asia, Africa, eastern Europe, and Latin America. It is for this reason that theoretical interventions, in any case insufficiently grasped by the keyword "postcolonialism," are of particular interest in the present context. The latter have gone some way toward de-centering the supposed center and calling to memory the powerful geographies of colonization, linking the genesis of the urban centers of the West with the violent construction of colonial space. It is precisely because the discourse on the postcolonial city systematically thwarts any attempts to construct a clear-cut geographic delineation of "the West and the rest" by providing the tools needed to narrate the (hi)story of urbanization not "from the inside out" but from "the outside in" that this shift in perspective may be seen as a necessary corrective to the Eurocentric urbanization discourse. After all, what we have experienced since the end of the Second World War and the period of decolonization—the palpable presence of people from other cultures and continents in our midst—has for centuries been the usual case in the world that is not Europe. Given this geohistorical backdrop, the assumption that multiculturalism is neither a European invention nor deeply embedded in its past is hard to deny.

"Postcolonialism" and "spatial politics" constitute the two discursive frames of this edition. While the motives and motivations of postcolonialism ensure that the geographic trajectories and the power-political configurations of local cultures, stocks of knowledge, constructions of identity, etc. are reassessed, the issue of spatial politics provides the thematic focus needed to grasp cities, urban conflicts, etc. in terms of their own specific internal logic, but without reducing them to what might be termed local specificity. This approach makes it possible to recognize distances and specify differences that, if they do not radically alter our notion of urbanity and urbanization, at least go some way toward enlarging it, laying the groundwork for us to re-explore possibilities for social change as well as new political governance potentials.

This collection of essays is organized in four chapters. "Politics of Space" (I) assembles contributions on postcolonialism, diasporic cultures, and diverse processes of cultural homogenization with a main emphasis on theoretical efforts of how to conceptualize spatial politics. "Spatializing Identities" (II) presents case studies focusing mainly on the distinctive, territorialized significance of both the production and ascription of categorical identities. "Imageries of Cities" (III) examines various modes of institutional and everyday-life-related imagining and image engineering of the urban landscape. The final chapter, "Exclusion, Surveillance and Security" (IV), deals with the multiplicity of social effects strategies of spacing evoke and with the power in places.

Although, as the content as well as these sentences show, there is a certain arrangement of topics at work here, this is by no means meant as an organizational structure for advancing a single and all-inclusive theoretical approach. On the contrary: Situated in quite different geographical as well as theoretical landscapes, this book offers insights into the ongoing and polyphonic debate about the past, the present, and the future of the urban. Readers are invited to various border crossings. You will encounter the views of geographers, anthropologists, and urban planners, of sociologists, media theorists, and political scientists, and, of course, you are invited to make your own pathways through these politics of space, which constitute the urban condition. "Cities," Kofi Annan has noted, "are the collective future of humankind." But the future of cities depends on the people inhabiting, and thereby creating and changing, them.

Acknowledgments

This collection of essays came out of a three days conference of the same title held at the Darmstadt University of Technology on April 7-9, 2005, sponsored by the British Council, the Carlo und Karin Giersch Foundation at Darmstadt University of Technology, the City of Science, Darmstadt, the Darmstadt University of Technology, the Embassy of the United States of America, the Heinrich Böll Foundation Israel, the MAB Projektentwicklung GmbH, the Post-Graduate College 'Technology and Society', the TZ Rhein-Main, and the Westfälisches Dampfboot Verlag.

We want to thank all organizations and the persons whose generosity and commitment made this event possible. Our special thanks go to Professor Dr. Ing. Johann-Dietrich Wörner, President of the Darmstadt University of Technology. Special thanks go also to Prof. Dr. Ingrid Breckner, Prof. Dr. Bruno Arich-Gerz, and Prof. Dr. Hermann Schwengel who chaired and intellectually structured various sessions. We are deeply indebted to Heike Kollross and Meherangis Bürkle, who always kept a level head in the office. Caroline Fritsche, Andrea Gromer, Richard Händel, Regine Henn, Jochen Schwenk, Isabelle Speich, and Gunter Weidenhaus, our student staff, not only solved all kinds of problems but also set the stage for an ambience of hospitality and relaxation.

The Editors   Darmstadt, March 2006

I. Politics of Space:
The Modern, the Postmodern
and the Postcolonial

Postcolonial Cities, Postcolonial Critiques

ANTHONY D. KING

The chapter discusses recent postcolonial writing on cities outside and inside Europe, both in relation to revisionary interpretations of "the colonial city" and on the concept (and reality) of the contemporary postcolonial city itself.[1]

Introduction

The organizers of the conference on which this collection is based acknowledged two basic postcolonial premises. They refer to "the powerful geographies of colonization" linking the development of urban centers in the West with the genesis of colonial space, connecting this to "the palpable presence of people from other cultures and continents in our midst." This, "for centuries, has been the normal case in the world that is *not* Europe." Revising this paper six months after the conference, following "terrorist" bombings in London, the earthquake in South Asia, riots in French cities, and the continuing war in Iraq, it is apparent that the "postcolonial presence" assumes daily a new significance, the subtext of this paper.

In accepting these two premises, however, my aim in this essay is to discuss recent postcolonial writing on cities both outside and inside Europe. I first briefly address recent writing on the topic of colonial cities by postcolonial authors indigenous to those cities. I then address recent scholarship on the postcolonial city, understood, as it is, in different ways, and the cross-over between notions of the postimperial, postcolonial, and global city. While all these categories are inter-related, the obvious distinction between them is the political and historical framework within which each is conceived and repre-

---

1 Parts of this paper appeared in Soziale Welt 16, 2005: 67-85.

sented. The central issue concerns the question of representation, especially the power of representation to affect both the understanding of the city as well as policies adopted towards it.

Most urbanists would probably agree that the most influential representation of the city in recent years has been that of the "world" or "global city." Yet while the criteria for identifying "world cities" are clearly stated (Beaverstock et al. 1999; Keil/Brenner 2006), they are not particularly useful for addressing issues of global or local security posed by religious or other ideologically driven groups, or for policies of education or language conceived in relation to specific cultural histories and contemporary political identities. While acknowledging that "world city" populations are racially and ethnically diverse and frequently characterized by social and spatial polarization, the "world city" model ignores the religio-cultural origins of the city's populations and the geopolitico-historical conditions explaining their presence. While the concept of "postcolonial" would, in many cases, be analytically more useful, this is not its most important use. However, it does serve to illustrate that any city's "reality" is inseparable from its representation.

Until the early 1980s, "post colonial" simply meant "after the colonial" and referred to peoples, states, and societies that had experienced a formal decolonization process. Subsequently, "postcolonial" has come to mean "an attitude of critical engagement with colonialism's after effects and its constructions of knowledge" (Radcliffe 1997: 1331). Postcolonialism is "a critical politico-intellectual formation [...] centrally concerned with the impact of colonialism and its contestation on the cultures of both colonizing and colonized peoples in the past, and the reproduction and transformation of colonial relations, representations and practices in the present" (Gregory 2000: 612).

Postcolonial criticism also assumes a knowledge of colonial histories in the contemporary world, not only of major European imperial powers but also of the USA, Russia, and Japan. By the early twentieth century, Europe held a grand total of 85 percent of the earth as colonies, protectorates, dependencies, dominions, and commonwealths (Said 1993: 14). At the heart of much postcolonial critique is an assumption succinctly expressed in the title of Chakrabarty's book, *Provincializing Europe* (2000). In addressing the topic of postcolonial cities, therefore, both usages—a period following colonization and a critical conceptual position—need deploying.

Cities: Colonial and postcolonial

> Not only are the 'colonial city' and the 'imperial city' umbilically connected in terms of economic linkages as well as cultural hybridization, but their 'post-equivalents' cannot be disentangled one from the other and need to be analyzed within a single 'postcolonial' framework of intertwining histories and relations (Yeoh 2001: 457).

As Yeoh suggests, to write about the postcolonial city presupposes some minimum knowledge of its predecessor, the colonial city, including its historiography.[2] Though embracing, for geographers, "a variety of urban types and forms," it may nonetheless be generalized as "a distinct settlement form resulting from the domination of an indigenous civilization by colonial settlers" (Pacione 2001: 450–1), the focus here being on the colonial city established by Europeans mainly in the 19th and early 20th century in Asia and Africa.

Important here, and bringing the second meaning of "postcolonial" into play, we need to recognize that both the concept of, and most of the literature on, the colonial city comes from Euro-American scholars (principally English and American, some French and Spanish), and is written in these languages. Not only is the colonial city apparently a colonial product, so also is its representation.

Ethnic origin, geographical location, or political position alone should not, of course, be treated as an essentialism giving indigenous inhabitants of the one-time colonial city a privileged insight into its characteristics.[3] It is rather that these mainly "non-indigenous" studies—which might be described as the first critical "postcolonial" accounts of colonial cities, produced in the three or four decades following independence—locate the topic, understandably perhaps, within a European or Euro-American frame. As Indonesian scholar Abidin Kusno has written about these various studies of colonial urbanism (e.g. King 1976; Rabinow 1989; Metcalf 1989; Wright 1991 etc.), "to what extent have studies centered on European imperialism themselves 'colonized' ways of thinking about colonial and postcolonial space?" (2000: 6).

Similar views can be found in *Urbanism: Imported or Exported: Native Aspirations and Foreign Plans* (2003), where the editors refer to "a sense of unease" among young researchers regarding the "content, methods and tone" of much recent literature on the formation of modern cities, particularly in "developing countries," a feeling that "it often did not adequately convey the complexity of power relations and flows. In particular, the local elements are under-represented [. .] and where they are present they are often dealt with as recipients of actions rather than as actors [...] a significant part of the litera-

---

2   Cf. King (1985) and (1989).
3   While the location of an author is less important than the position from which she or he speaks—epistemologically, politically, culturally—it is statistically more likely that authors from (or with connections to) the one-time colonized society are not only fluent in the colonial as well as the national language, but possibly also in local and regional languages of the once colonized state. They may also have better knowledge of local sources. Given the contemporary movement of scholars between locations worldwide, *where* they work or write up their research is of less importance. Valid contributions can be made by anyone (cf. King 2003: 170).

ture on colonial urbanism has been written based on strictly metropolitan sources, rather than [...] local archival material" (Nasr/Volait 2003: vii–xx).

In what follows, therefore, I refer to recent revisionist writing on the colonial city as exemplary of what might be called an indigenous "critical postcolonial" perspective. Themes include the agency of the indigenous population in producing the colonial city, the indigenous appropriation of the city, and the larger narrative within which the city is framed.

When was the colonial city?

The stereotypical representation of the colonial city is best expressed by Frantz Fanon:

> The colonial world is a world divided into compartments. It is probably unnecessary to recall the existence of native quarters and European quarters, of schools for natives and schools for Europeans; in the same way we need not recall apartheid in South Africa. Yet if we examine closely this system of compartments, we will at least be able to reveal the lines of force it implies. This approach to the colonial world, its order and its geographical layout will allow us to mark out the lines on which a decolonized society will be organized (1968: 37–38).

Fanon's words were written over forty five years ago (1961). Whether in relation to the original, supposedly "decolonized" post-colonial city, or, alternatively, in the supposedly post-imperial city—are they still applicable? We do not know, because, in one sense, the goal posts have been moved.

Irrespective of changing conditions, at what point in historical time does the "colonial city" morph into a different category? Is its subsequent identity (and representation) destined to be either "postcolonial" or to be transformed (if so, by whom?) into a "world" or "global city," as suggested, for example, in regard to one-time colonial cities in Asia by Dick and Rimmer (1998) or Skeldon (1997)? As Cooper and Stoler point out, peoples' histories are made up "of more than the fact that they were colonized" (1997: 18). For Goh (2005), Singapore remains a paradigmatic example of a city that occupies both identities and exploits them to its advantage. What is not considered here, however, fifty years after independence, are the persistent social and spatial maldistributions of resources (schools, jobs, transport, income) among the population in some postcolonial cities (King 2004). But are such inequities "postcolonial" through neglect, are they the result of oppressive, neocolonial regimes following independence, or has the nature and conditions of the debate changed, as in postcolonial, postapartheid South Africa (Murray/Shepherd 2006)?

The colonial city revisited: "Indigenous" postcolonial critiques

Different perspectives, interpretations, and representations of the colonial city result from the use of different sources, frameworks, and methods. Yeoh's study *Contesting Space: Power Relations and the Urban Built Environment in Colonial Singapore* is based on a detailed study of local archives. It is perhaps the first account challenging the notion of the colonial city as being simply a product of "dominant" (Western) "forces" and representing the city as the product of indigenous agency (1996: 9–14). Two other examples are worth citing because they address what is perhaps the most central feature said to characterize the colonial city, namely, the racial, social, and spatial divide between the indigenous city and European colonial settlement.

Hosagrahar's study of "old Delhi" between the 1850s and 1950s examines transformations in the indigenous city during a century of colonial presence, this latter first represented by a "typical" colonial urban settlement of "civil station" and military cantonment and, from 1911, the new colonial capital of New Delhi. Eschewing binary classifications between colonial/indigenous, new/old, European/native, "modern"/"traditional," she investigates the spatial development of Delhi over a century using an array of different source materials, including contemporary interviews. "Beneath the apparent opposition," she writes, was a charged interconnection between the two spaces. The residents of Delhi responded to the new model of urban life by "disdaining and rejecting, mocking and mimicking, participating and conniving, and learning and accepting" from the colonial Western lifestyle. The new colonial settlement offered opportunities for some Indian residents to construct new identities, a way of identifying with the new by rejecting the old, and, on occasion, moving between the two spaces (2005). Chattopadhyay's *Representing Calcutta: Modernity, Nationalism and the Colonial Uncanny* (2005) brings yet another perspective to the "colonial city" and its supposedly defining attributes. She reads the city primarily as the cradle of Bengal nationalism, subverting its colonial representation as a space marked simplistically by the Manichaean division between the "European city" and the "black town." While such labels certainly exist in European maps and the Anglophone colonial literature, in Bengali accounts of the city she examines, Chattopadhyay finds no evidence of these or comparable terms.

What these studies show is the contested and ambiguous space of "the colonial city" represented in these recent accounts, postcolonial in both senses of the term (see also Glover, forthcoming). It was, and is, a space too complex and unpredictable for easy classification. While these latest studies might be based on previously unexamined indigenous language sources, or the interrogation of official colonial accounts, they also frame the "colonial city" within a different narrative. Most commonly it is the discursive space of "modernity," or the role of the city's inhabitants in the emergence of a collective (and resistant) national, regional, or perhaps gendered identity. In Kusno's study of Jakarta, he states "(m)odern architecture and urbanism in the colonial and postcolonial world have generally been understood in relation to European domination." Instead, he "explores the theme from another perspective: as a colonial gift inherited by the postcolonial (society and) state" (Kusno 2000: cover). He takes the Western obsession with (oversimplified) "east-west" antagonisms and redirects his focus to political relations within the region. Regarding Indonesia, he foregrounds the persistence of colonial oppression in the supposedly "postcolonial" regimes themselves.

Postcolonial cities: Postcolonial criticism

Compared to colonial cities, postcolonial cities have received far less academic attention.[4] There are some obvious explanations.

As stated, postcolonialism is concerned with colonialism's after effects, including its constructions of knowledge. Depending on the author, its politico-intellectual formation can be informed by poststructuralist, feminist, psychoanalytic and other perspectives. It is also an intellectual position that has been criticized from different viewpoints. The most trenchant criticism suggests that it "re-orient(s) the globe once more around a single, binary opposition: colonial/postcolonial … (such that) Colonialism returns at the moment of its disappearance" (McClintock 1992; King 2004).

Resistance to representing "fully independent" states and cities as largely uninfluenced by their colonial past is one explanation why "postcolonial" does not figure as an analytical category. For other (and not just "Western") urbanists, the "world space" in which they operate, prior to the imagined "global" of the late 1980s, is the (obsolescent?) one of the "three worlds," conceived in 1953 (Wolff-Phillips 1987). Though the "third world city" concept was probably in circulation before Tinker's *Race and the Third World City* (1971), representation of many postcolonial cities has been subsumed within this ideological framework. Here, postcolonial cities are viewed through the lens

---

4 Googling "postcolonial city/cities, postkoloniale stadt/staedte, ville/villes postcoloniale," brings up numerous references, mostly book titles. Themes addressed include representation in the arts, sites of tension and citizenship, their role in "Westernization" and in flows of capital, migration, and terrorism, their shaping by imperial legacies and tradition, questions of subjectivity, multiculturalism, hybridity, nationalism, modernity, globalization, etc. Specifically mentioned cities include Bombay/Mumbai, Cairo, Calcutta, Chandigarh, Dakar, Delhi, Jaipur, Jakarta, Lagos, London, Melbourne, Rabat, San Francisco, Sao Paulo, Tunis. Apart from one article on Bombay/Mumbai, I found no reference to religion.

of "third world problems": air pollution, megacity size, traffic management, "slums," and water scarcity. Questions about religious or cultural identity and subject formation do not figure here. What Venn (2006) refers to as "the neglected interface between urban studies and development studies" (cf. also Robinson 2005), means that cities in different continents are not only represented through different theoretical and methodological frameworks, but also that their interconnections are ignored. While a postcolonial perspective does make this connection, it is clear that "world," "global," "colonial/postcolonial," and "first/third world" cities are all labels invented in the West.

Postcolonial cities

How is the postcolonial city recognized? This depends on how the term is understood. Cities are not necessarily postcolonial in the same way.

Yeoh suggests that "for some, postcolonialism is something fairly tangible" (2001: 456). In one interpretation of this "tangibility," Bishop et al., referring to Singapore, argue, "*post* (after) doesn't necessarily indicate either that the colonizers have gone away [...] or that the conditions of postcolonialism have necessarily changed much from those of colonialism, despite appearances" (2003: 14). Here, postcolonialism is seen as the failure of decolonization.

Elsewhere I have referred to "actually existing postcolonialism" (King 2003), particularly as manifested in the spatial environments of one-time colonial urban landscapes used to help institutionalize (and also symbolize) social relations of exclusion, segregation, and privilege based on race, class, and power, and which, fifty years after independence, continue to do so, albeit in modified form.

Yeoh (2001) provides an extensive review of literature on the geography of postcolonial cities focusing on themes of identity, heritage, and encounters. Depending on our viewpoint, these may (or may not) be seen as belonging to a more positive interpretation of "postcolonialism," one adopting a non-Western "occidentalist" perspective, and viewing the one-time colonial city as "a gift" (Kusno 2000).

The postcolonial city is "an important site where claims of identity different from the colonial past are expressed and indexed, and, in some cases, keenly contested" (Yeoh 2001: 458). This is seen especially in regard to matters of space, architecture, and urban design, the public signs of which are often fiercely contested political and social positions. Many studies detail the various ways in which postcolonial states and cities have both engaged with and simultaneously distanced themselves from their colonial past, aiming to construct new citizen identities with a consciousness of national culture. States have built new capitals or capitol complexes (Perera 1998; Vale 1992); toponymic reinscription aims to reclaim the cultural space of city streets (King 1976; King 2004; Yeoh 1996); modernist design attempts to create new images for the nation (Kusno 2000; Holston 1989). Constructing "the world's tallest building" has become an essentially competitive strategy for postcolonial nations to make claims on others' definitions of modernity, or establish them as "global players" (King 2004). A recent contender, a 710 meter skyscraper planned for Noida, near Delhi, according to the architect, aims "to show the world what India can do" (Guardian, 29 March 2005). Such projects are thought to provide a nation's leaders, and perhaps its people, with a new, more positive identity.

An increasing number of authorities have argued for the preservation of the architecture, urban design, and planning of one-time colonial cities, including UNESCO's International Committee on Monuments and Sites (ICOMOS). Unprecedented rural migration and what are seen as overdependence on state-led development projects imposing Western urban models are behind attempts to prevent "the disappearance of the Asian city," including its colonial history (Logan 2002; Lari/Lari 2001). In this perspective, fifty years after independence, the symbolic significance of colonial buildings has lost its old political meaning. New generations see colonial urban design as generating tourist revenue rather than prompting memories of colonial oppression.

Yet few such reports represent buildings and spaces not just as aesthetic but also as cultural, social, and political phenomena. The elite Dutch colonial suburb of Menteng, outside Jakarta, with its Art Deco houses and spacious tree-lined boulevards, continues, as in colonial days, to house the rich and powerful elite (including ex-President Suharto). In Korea's capital, Seoul, the neo-baroque Japanese Government-General headquarters building, constructed in 1926 from the designs of a German architect, and, after 1945, used as the City Hall and subsequently the National Museum of Contemporary Art, was ceremoniously demolished in 1995—significantly, on the 50th anniversary of Korea's liberation from Japan. It restored the appearance of Korea's Gyeongbok Palace, "the most important symbol of (our) national history," and the seat of the 500-year-old Korean Choseun Dynasty (Kal 2003).

Cities: Postcolonial or postimperial?

So far I have assumed that "postcolonial" refers only to those cities in formerly colonized societies and "postimperial" to those one-time imperial capitals such as Paris, Lisbon, or London. However, the distinction between postcolonial and postimperial can be ambivalent. Labeling London as (technically) postimperial foregrounds its earlier imperial role. Yet for postcolonial migrants from South Asia, London may also (like them) be postcolonial. And as the one-time metropole has been powerfully influenced by postcolonial forces, "postcolonial" is now used to describe it, particularly in regard to its ethnic and racial composition. Whether we live in a postcolonial world, or more accurately, in *The Colonial Present* (Gregory 2003), colonial and post-colonial histories of migration and memory not only distinguish the population, politics, and public culture of one postcolonial city from another, but also from other "world" or "global cities" such as Frankfurt or Zurich.[5]

For example, over half of the almost 30 percent foreign-born population of New York are from the Caribbean and Central America, with significant proportions from Europe, South America, and South and Southeast Asia (Salvo/Lord 1997). Any explanation for the presence of, for example, English-speaking migrants from the Caribbean, or South and Southeast Asia[6] must recognize colonial and postcolonial histories. This is equally so with the Spanish-speaking migrants from the Caribbean and Central and South America. In London, of the roughly 25 per cent of 'foreign born' population, the large majority are principally from postcolonial countries, particularly South/Southeast Asia, Ireland, East, West and South Africa, the Caribbean, North America, and Australia, as well as from continental Europe (Merriman 1993; Benedictus 2005). In Paris, the more than 15 percent of foreign-born residents are primarily from postcolonial North Africa (Algeria, Morocco, Tunisia), Armenia, or Mauritius (Ambroise-Rendu 1993).

These distinctively postcolonial migrations clearly have major influences on the economy, society, culture, politics, spatial environments, and, in some cases, security, of the city. They bring to the so-called "global city" a variety of vibrant but also very specific post-colonial cosmopolitanisms. Powerful postcolonial minorities bring their influence to bear on government policies, both domestic (immigration, employment, educational, press freedom or welfare) or foreign (international disputes, disaster relief, and the conduct of war).[7] Multiple temporalities coexist in urban space, as do multiple spatiali-

---

5   How postcolonialism impacts these and other European cities is still to be explored.
6   South Asia (India, Pakistan, Bangladesh) accounts for some fifty percent of cab-drivers in New York City, and (Anglophone) Indians are prominently represented in the information technology and medical professions in the USA.
7   Media coverage of the four July 7 suicide bombers in London focused almost exclusively on their British citizenship and "Islamist fundamentalist" identity. Yet the specific motivation of the bombings, widely believed by a majority of the public (though not, Prime Minister Tony Blair) to be Blair's complicity in the US-lead attack on Iraq, was also seen as a response to the decades-long history of British and US colonial oppression in the Middle East, including Britain's colonial role in early twentieth century Iraq (cf. Gregory 2003). The shift in media sentiment towards Pakistani-born residents in the UK in the three months between the July bombings and early October, when Pakistan and Indian

ties, extending the real and the virtual space of the city and its inhabitants to other urban and rural locations around the world (Venn 2006).

The growing outsourcing of employment from North America and the UK to the large Anglophone labor market in Indian cities (especially call centers), generating employment and a boom in office building, cannot be understood without a postcolonial frame (King 2004). In Paris, as the riots of November 2005 have exposed, most postcolonial minorities are in the *banlieues*, which, already "in the 1990s, have become a byword for socially disadvantaged peripheral areas of French cities" (Hargreaves/McKinney 1997: 12). Structurally equivalent to British and American inner city areas, and seen as ghettoes, the *banlieues* provide a space to develop "a separatist cultural agenda marked by graffiti, music, dancing, and dress codes" with which the *banlieusards* (suburb-dwellers) reterritorialize the "anonymous housing projects" (ibid). In Britain, the inner suburban landscapes of postcolonial London are regenerated and transformed by South Asians, who, "though united by belief, are nonetheless divided along national, ethnic and sectarian lines" (Nasser 2003: 9). In Britain's "second city" of Birmingham, the largest group of 80,000 South Asian Muslims is from Pakistan, comprising 7 percent of the city's population (ibid. 2003:9). Leicester, with 28 percent of its 280,000 population from South Asia, is said to be "the largest Indian city in Europe." Though Vietnamese scholar Panivong Norindr writes, "policies of colonial urbanism help to explain race and class divisions in Western metrocenters of today" (1996: 114), we need to recognize that individual urban authorities have their own distinctive policies regarding housing, planning, and education. In multicultural societies, members of particular communities (like the British overseas) frequently stay together, with their own shops, social centers, and places of worship.

Long after the formal end of empire, postcolonial memories continue to affect the use of space. Jacobs (1996) shows how the continuity of discourses over historic sites in the City of London, remembered as "the economic center of the Empire," have influenced decisions about urban design. Yet consciousness of the postcolonial multicultural is also powerfully celebratory. It signifies a changing, vibrant future, a new kind of intellectual milieu created by unique ethnicities, hybridities, and diasporas. New and distinctive cultures develop in geographically and culturally specific "postcolonial cities." Whether in the one-time metropole or the one-time colony, postcolonialism creates

---

Kashmir were struck by the most disastrous earthquake in their history, with tens of thousands of victims, was palpable. With over 700,000 residents of Pakistani birth/ descent in Britain, mostly from the Kashmir region, and many British nationals, the mood of the tabloid media shifted from suspended suspicion to one of sympathy and shared loss, followed by a major fund-raising campaign for survivors.

conditions for both the split, as well as the suture between "traditional" and "modern" identities.

Attributes that distinguish postcolonial populations—a language in common with the host society, a shared, if contested, history, some familiarity with the culture, norms, and social practices of the metropolitan society, the presence of long-established communities, are features among others which distinguish postcolonial communities and migrants from those of non-postcolonial origin. In this way, "multicultural" Berlin differs from multicultural London or Vancouver.

I have not addressed here the more metaphorical uses of the terms, yet clearly colonial/postcolonial are also relevant in describing the processes of urbanism in contemporary Europe. Today, newly colonized populations in cities—migrant labor, legal as well as legal, arrives from all over the world, including Eastern Europe, filling the lowest paid slots in an ever increasingly globalized economy. Labor is colonized by capital.

Sidaway (2000) and Domosh (2004) show how the postcolonial paradigm has now expanded to cover many historical and geographical instances. Though not sufficient in themselves, postcolonial histories, sociologies, and geographies are nonetheless key to understanding a plethora of issues, and not only in the multicultural, postcolonial/postimperial global cities of Melbourne or Toronto. "Postcolonial vision" results from postcolonial migration and globalization (Hopkins 2002). It is a comparative, cross-cultural, and cross-temporal perspective. Despite its ambiguity, the paradigm provides one among many ways of reading the contemporary city.

References

Ambroise-Rendu, Marc (1993) "The Migrants who Turned Paris into a Melting Pot". Guardian Weekly, June 27, p. 14.
Beaverstock, Jonathan V./Smith, R.V./Taylor, Peter J. (1999) "A Roster of World Cities". Cities 16/6, pp. 445–58.
Benedictus, Leo (2005) "The World in One City". The Guardian, 21 January.
Bishop, Ryan/Phillips, John/Yeo, Wei-Wei (eds.) (2003) *Postcolonial Urbanism: Southeast Asian Cities and Global Processes*, New York and London: Routledge.
Chakrabarty, Dipesh (2000) *Provincializing Europe: Postcolonial Thought and Historical Difference*, Princeton NJ: Princeton University Press.
Chattopadhyay, Swati (2005) *Representing Calcutta; Modernity, Nationalism and the Colonial Uncanny*. London and New York: Routledge.
Cooper, Frederick/Stoler, Ann L. (1997) *Tensions of Empire: Colonial Cultures in a Bourgeois World*, Berkeley: University of California Press.

Domosh, Mona (2004) "Postcolonialism and the American City". Urban Geography, 25/8, pp. 742–54.

Fanon, Franz (1968) *The Wretched of the Earth*, New York: Grove.

Glover, William R. (forthcoming) *Making Lahore Modern: Constructing and Imagining a Modern City*. Minneapolis: University of Minnesota Press.

Goh, Robbie B.H. (2005) *Contours of Culture: Space and Social Difference in Singapore*, Hong Kong: Hong Kong University Press.

Gregory, Derek (2000) "Postcolonialism". In R. Johnson/Derek Gregory/ D.M. Smith (eds.) *The Dictionary of Human Geography*, Oxford: Blackwell.

Gregory, Derek (2003) *The Colonial Present*, Oxford: Blackwell.

Hargreaves, Alec G./McKinney, Mark (1997) *Postcolonial Cultures in France*, London and New York: Routledge.

Hopkins, Anthony G. (ed.) (2002) *Globalization in World History*, London: Pimlico.

Hosagrahar, Jyoti (2005) *Indigenous Modernities: Negotiating Urban Form*, London and New York: Routledge.

Jacobs, Jane M. (1996) *Edge of Empire: Postcolonialism and the City*, London and New York: Routledge.

Kal, Hong (2003) *The Presence of the Past: Exhibitions, Memories and National Identities in Colonial and Postcolonial Korea*, PhD dissertation. Binghamton University.

Keil, Roger/Brenner, Neil (2006) *The Global Cities Reader*, London and New York: Routledge.

King, Anthony D. (1976) *Colonial Urban Development: Culture, Social Power and Environment*, London and Boston: Routledge and Kegan Paul.

King, Anthony D. (1985) "Colonial Cities: Global Pivots of Change". In R. Ross and G. Telkamp (eds.) *Colonial Cities: Essays on Urbanism in a Colonial Context*, Dordrecht: Martinius Niehoff.

King, Anthony D. (1989) "Colonialism, Urbanism, and the Capitalist World Economy: An Introduction". International Journal of Urban and Regional Research, 13/1, pp. 1–18.

King, Anthony D. (1990) *Global Cities: Postimperialism and the Internationalization of London*, London and New York: Routledge.

King, Anthony D. (2003) "Actually Existing Postcolonialism: Colonial Architecture and Urbanism after the Postcolonial Turn". In R. Bishop et al. (eds.) *Postcolonial Urbanism: Southeast Asian Cities and Global Processes*, New York and London: Routledge.

King, Anthony D. (2004) *Spaces of Global Cultures: Architecture, Urbanism, Identity*, London and New York: Routledge.

Kusno, Abidin (2000) *Behind the Postcolonial: Architecture, Urban Space and Political Cultures in Indonesia*, London and New York: Routledge.

Lari, Yasmeen/Lari, Mihail S. (2001) *The Dual City: Karachi During the Raj*, Karachi: Oxford University Press and Heritage Foundation Karachi.

Logan, William S. (2003) *The Disappearing "Asian" City: Protecting Asia's Urban Heritage in a Globalizing World*, New York: Oxford University Press.

McClintock, Anne (1992) "Angel of Progress: Pitfalls of the term 'Postcolonialism'". Social Text 31/32, pp. 84–98.

Metcalf, Thomas R. (1989) *An Imperial Vision: Indian Architecture and Britain's Raj*, Berkeley: University of California Press.

Merriman, Nick (ed.) (1993) *The Peopling of London: Fifteen Thousand Years of Settlement from Overseas*, London: Museum of London.

Murray, N./Shepherd, N. (2006) *Desire Lines: Space, Memory and Identity in Postapartheid South Africa*, London and New York: Routledge.

Nasr, Joseph/Volait, Mercedes (eds.) (2003) *Urbanism: Exported or Imported? Native Aspirations and Foreign Plans*, London: Wiley.

Nasser, Noha (2003) "The Space of Displacement: Making Muslim South Asian Place in British Neighborhoods". Traditional Dwellings and Settlements Review, 15/1, pp. 7–21.

Norindr, Panvivong (1996) *Phantasmic Indochina: French Colonial Ideology in Architecture, Film and Literature*, Durham NC and London: Duke University Press.

Pacione, Michael (2001) *Urban Geography: A Global Perspective*, New York and London: Routledge.

Perera, Nihal (1998) *Decolonizing Ceylon: Colonialism, Nationalism, and the Politics of Space in Sri Lanka*, New Delhi: Oxford University Press.

Rabinow, Paul (1989) *French Modern: Norms and Forms of the Social Environment*, Cambridge MA: MIT Press.

Radcliffe, S.A. (1997) "Different Heroes: Genealogies of Postcolonial Geographies". Environment and Planning D: Society and Space, 15, pp. 1331–33.

Robinson, Jenny (2005) *Ordinary Cities: Between Modernity and Development*, London and New York: Routledge.

Said, Edward (1993) *Culture and Imperialism*, London: Vintage.

Sidaway, James (2000) "Postcolonial Geographies: An Exploratory Essay". Progress in Human Geography, 24/4, pp. 591–612.

Skeldon, Ronald (1997) "Hong Kong: Colonial City to Global City to Provincial City?" Cities, 14, pp. 265–71.

Tinker, Hugh (1971) *Race and the Third World City*, Oxford: Oxford University Press.

Vale, Lawrence (1992) *Architecture, Power and National Identity*, Princeton: Yale University Press.

Venn, Couze (2006) "The City as Assemblage". (Present volume)

Wright, Gwendolyn (1991) *The Politics of Design in French Colonial Urbanism*, Chicago: Chicago University Press.
Yeoh, Brenda S.A. (1996) *Contesting Space: Power Relations and the Urban Built Environment in Colonial Singapore*, Kuala Lumpur: Oxford University Press.
Yeoh, Brenda S.A. (2001) "Postcolonial Cities". Progress in Human Geography, 25/3, pp. 456–68.

Contested Places and the Politics of Space

HELMUTH BERKING

This article deals with certain problems related to efforts to conceptualize the spatial dimensions of urban conflicts. Since it is no coincidence that urban conflicts are so intimately interwoven with territorial claims, I will focus on the peculiar interplay between agency and territoriality using the still fuzzy conceptualizations of the global-local interplay as a prime example.

Fierce debates about space and place run deep in the social sciences today. Attempts to spatialize social theory go hand in hand with a far-reaching critique of well-established sociological concepts, and this dramatic change of perspective seems to be establishing a new and quite revolutionary paradigm of social theory. The historical distance between banalizing, or even negating, and negotiating space has been an amazingly short one. Two decades ago the British sociologist Peter Saunders was just expressing common sense when he stated that "social theory has been quite right to treat space as a backdrop against which social action takes place [...] Space does not enter into what we do in any meaningful sense, because mere space can have no causal properties and is quite incapable of entering into anything. It is passive; it is context." And, he concludes, "that there is nothing for theory to say about space" (Saunders 1989: 231f.).

This was, of course, only moments before globalization discourse finally took off, forcing social scientists to come to terms with a phenomenology of the social, basically evoked by processes of socio-spatial reconfigurations and new modes of the spatial organization of social relations. To realize the radical shift to space-related theorizing, one only needs to bear in mind that the global is first and foremost nothing other than a socio-spatial scale that, while relationally differentiated, is also tied into the logic of scale: of the local, the regional, and the national. If one eliminated this relationality of scale, the story of globalization could not be narrated at all.

In outlining this background, I will use quotidian conceptualizations of the global-local nexus as a point of departure to offer some critical comments on the—thus far—neglected question of the local. Reflections on the global production of locality, so the thesis goes, might not only change the dominant representation of the global. They might also redirect theoretical attention to the power of places. But before I take a closer look at the different stages of globalization discourse to characterize the particular state of space representations, I will briefly summarize some of the guiding premises of this undertaking.

First, it has now become almost conventional wisdom to conceptualize space as a social construction that simultaneously structures and is structured by social action. Human agency itself has to be looked at in its space-producing and space-consuming qualities. It was Emile Durkheim (1965) who, in his famous book *The Elementary Forms of Religious Life*, formulated the idea that the spatial organization of groups serves as a prime model for the mental organization of the world. If the focus is placed on the spatial nature of identities, meanings, classifications, world-view structures, etc., this could prove to be an analytically promising way to conceptualize all kinds of social action—from the most intimate face-to-face interaction to global conflicts—as distinctive variants of a "politics of space."

Second, two general modes of spatiality, or more precisely, of the spatial organization of social relations, can be distinguished. Social relations can be territorialized relying on a well-defined and forcefully maintained territorial unit which clearly marks inside and outside and gives meaning to legitimacy, rule enforcement, and collective identity. Or they can be organized in a deterritorialized way that does not depend on borders and territorial enclosures, but on far-reaching networks. The former space-as-container theory is attributed to the territorial nation-state and its dominant epistemology, which sees social relations being both organized and reproduced exclusively in territorially defined and spatially isomorphic entities. The later space-as-flows ontology (Castells 1996; 1997) is usually imagined with reference to the space-transcending strategies of global capital as well as to the particular space-related politics of translocalities and global diasporas.

Third, there appears to be an intimate and quite disturbing relationship between space production and identities. Just as space is always a relational product of multiple trajectories, interactions, practices, conflicts, and struggles between social groups (cf. Löw 2001), so are identities, be they ascribed to places and/or to individuals and collective actors. Categorical identities, however, have a tendency to become territorialized. Territorial identities fuel the politics of space. A similarly complicated relation exists between space production and knowledge production. The now famous Foucauldian power-knowledge nexus may have to be extended and transformed into a power-knowledge-space relation. On a quite simple level, it is important to realize that if the production of space goes hand in hand with the evocation of knowledge, then knowledge is space-related. Certain spaces and places do not only contain distinctive stocks of cultural knowledge; they also limit the scope of what might be perceived as legitimate knowing. "Placing" categories give meaning to categories like gender, class, ethnicity, etc., just as categories give particular meaning to places. The postcolonial decentering of Eurocentric worldview structures is just one—albeit important—case in point. Common references to "local cultures" might be another.

Fourth, if spatial patterns, from the physically built environment to symbolic landscapes and categorical identities, can—and probably have to—be discerned as place-related, then the shift of theoretical attention from the global to the logic of locality might be indeed not only feasible but necessary.

Since all these issues are negotiated under the header of globalization as a new spatial order, I will briefly describe some of the basic controversies within this field.

It is not by accident that in a first round of globalization studies the nation-state served as a privileged point of departure to depict the "global" as its opposite. And it is not by accident either that urban studies, and especially world- and global-city models became the prime examples for identifying alternative modes of spatial organization. The notion of a world consisting of a multiplicity of territorially fixed, hermetically sealed, culturally homogeneous entities for which "territoriality" is the only and exclusive model of spatial organization—aptly characterized as "methodological nationalism" by Anthony Smith (1979)—was abandoned by multiple deterritorialization approaches that revealed globalization to be an ongoing process of production of spaces of flows against which the now traditional spaces of place are bound systematically to loose momentum. The thesis of the end of the nation-state was grounded in the thesis of the end of territoriality. And this theorizing paved the way for both a highly generalized, powerful image of the "global" as an unfettered, free, and unbounded space, and a highly generalized, paling image of the local as relict of the past.

All strands of globalization theories claim that the global has become the most important frame for organizing socio-spatial relations. Standard definitions, which depict globalization as all those "processes by which the peoples of the world are incorporated into a single world society, a global society" (Albrow 1996), however, are underestimating, or even neglecting, the context-generating potentiality of the local by reducing this spatial scale to a traditional and territorialized form of socio-spatial relations. The question of what the global actually is has tended as a rule to be answered by referring rather vaguely to the disappearance of the local. As a cumulative effect of globalization—flexible accumulation, global migration, deregulation, media-generated images of the world, new communication technologies, and so forth—processes of space formation could be discerned, which for some authors seemed to support images of cultural homogenization. Whether it was depicted as a totally Americanized, McDonaldized culture (Ritzer 1993), or as a generalized consumerist culture exploited by transnational corporations and ruled by a new emerging transnational class (Sklair 2001), in these views the global, "world society," and so forth derived from and represented first and foremost the geographic expansion of the West. Fettered by an unreflected technological determinism—globalization is as inevitable as technological change—such narratives represented, at least to a certain extent, continuations of the old functionalist modernization approaches (cf. Massey 1999; Wimmer 2001).

It was during the second stage of the globalization discourse, looking beyond mere economic globalization, when social scientists began to reject the homogenization paradigm. Instead of conceptualizing globalization as an ongoing process of economic, political, and cultural homogenization—the story of the outward expansion of European modernity—analytical attention was directed to the emergence of new societal forms, the mixing of local and global under the headers of "glocalization" (Robertson 1995), "creolization" (Hannerz 1996), and "hybridization" (Pieterse 1995; Hall 1991; Tomlinson 1999; Urry 2000). Attempts to criticize methodological Eurocentrism went hand in hand with forceful debates on "global modernities" (Featherstone et al. 1995), "multiple modernities" (Eisenstadt 2000), or "uneven modernities" (Randeria 2002). New key concepts like "cosmopolitanism" (Learmount/Vertovec/Cohen 2002; Beck 2000; Hannerz 1996) and "diaspora" (Clifford 1997; Hall 1990; Gilroy 1993; Cohen 1997; critically: Anthias 1998; Mitchell 1997) promised to capture the impact of these global-local interplays on worldview structures, cultural knowledge, and identity constructions. But even though particular emphasis was placed on cultural syncretism and the crucial global-local nexus, a kind of overblown representation of the global as a free, unbounded, and deterritorialized space of flows still remains in place. The pitfalls of this representation of the global seem to be at least threefold.

First, contrary to conceptualizations of globalization as an inevitable process of deterritorialization and state erosion, territoriality in general, and territorial states in particular, seem destined to remain powerful organizational modes of socio-spatial relations. If what we identify as global is still "grounded in national territories" (Sassen 1996: 13), then theoretical attention has to be directed to processes of spatial reconfiguration which do not necessarily end up in deterritorialized flows but also include powerful tendencies toward re-territorialization. The fact that "capitalism," the "nation-state," or the "daily newspaper" have gained global presence does not imply that *India Today, the Boston Globe,* and the *Darmstädter Echo* are becoming indistinguishable. Poverty is contextualized differently in Poland than it is in Zambia; migrants are confronted with different institutional regimes in England and in Saudi Arabia; and even average Americans may have a media-transmitted view of the Arab world which is significantly different from the one held by a German. In short, the constraints which local cultures impose on global flows are and will remain quite considerable.

Second, it is, in analytical terms, not convincing to connect socio-spatial scales like the local and the global with modes of socio-spatial organization. For what reasons should the local be conceptualized as a territorial mode of sociation, while the global is perceived exclusively as a deterritorialized space of flows?

Third, there is a strong tendency toward categorical confusion in the way that the global and the local are incessantly used as synonyms for space and place and vice versa. "Opposing global with local," states Robert Latham, "is quite intuitive since the former term ultimately refers to some kind of claim about the range of forces operating across space. Typically, the local is either a discrete element within that global range or simply a site or phenomenon subject to global forces that are external to it" (Latham/Kassimir/Callaghy 2001: 6). If one, just for the sake of the argument, follows Bruno Latour's thought experiment concerning the Eurasian railway system (Latour 1993), the dilemma involved becomes obvious. Not really global, though of considerable reach, this system stretches from Gibraltar to Vladivostok, from Hanoi to Bergen. But at every point on our imagined journey we will find people, huts, villages, stations, and so forth. Most important, however, nobody, neither the traveler nor the conductor, ever crosses the magic border that separates the local from the global. And is this not equally the case with transnational corporations, whose global networks are composed of local branches designed to exploit local conditions as effectively as possible? And those global flows: of people, images, cultural artifacts? Do they not unfold their social and symbolic potential only at the moment in which they are regrounded and reembedded locally? Or as Doreen Massey strongly insists: "Could global finance exist without its very definite groundedness in that place, the city of London, for example. Could it be global without being local?" (Massey 2004: 8).

Yet representations of the global opposing the local still remain in place, feeding a power matrix for which the global is closely associated with capital, progress deterritorialization, and unbounded space, while the local is linked to place and tradition, inhabited by the usual suspects: the poor, minorities, women entrapped in local cultures and generally victims of outside forces (Massey 2006). The devaluation of the local parallels the devaluation of place

(Agnew 1989). To imagine the local as a product of the global is to imagine place as the product of relations from elsewhere, implying that place has no agency since all that matters has to be placed outside of place. But the very fact that places are also the moments "through which the global is constituted, invented, coordinated, produced," in short: that places, as Doreen Massey states, are "agents *in* globalisation" (2004: 11) must be seen as quite incontestable if one looks for example at London or New York City as places for which nobody would willingly assume the status of pure victims of global forces.

Given these insights, a provisional subtotal of three decades of globalization discourse supports the impression that a major shift of theoretical attention is under way. After the discovery of the global it is now the revaluation of the local, or more precisely: explorations of place and locality that have to be foregrounded. In a phenomenological tradition locality refers to the construction of that peculiar horizon of closeness, familiarity, and knowing by which individuals and groups (re)produce themselves. The production of locality as a daily effort of everyday life practices implies the thesis that local settings and places are not just context-driven spatial units but have a context-generating potential as well.

This search for the relatedness of agency and space has had a profound impact on urban studies, especially on the mode in which the "city" is constructed as an object of scientific knowledge. I only exaggerate slightly in stating that since its emergence/inception as a scientific object, the city has been dealt with primarily as a subcategory of such concepts as society, modernization, market economy, and so forth. This logic of subsumption, paired with an unenlightened functionalism, has a longstanding tradition that goes back to the Chicago school of urban studies, for which not the city of Chicago, but the city as a field of experience, a laboratory of social change, deviance, segregation, etc. was of prime interest. It continues with the new urban-studies approach, which analyzes the systemic function of the city within the transformation processes of capitalist sociation. And even global-city research was blamed for reducing the city to its geostrategic position and role within economic globalization—and thus not only for neglecting but for systematically missing the cultural and discursive strategies of constructing the particularity of a city. The critique, aptly formulated years ago by John Friedman, that global-city models miss the locality of their objects, "their rootedness in a politically organized life space with its own history, institutions, culture and politics" is still topical (1995: 34). Berlin is not Prussia, but without Prussia, Berlin would not be Berlin.

Another quite noteworthy strand in urban studies is the position certain cities hold as kind of showcases within the historical geography of urban thinking (cf. Crang/Thrift 2001). For decades Chicago served as an uncontested model for urban growth. Nineteenth-century Paris became a metonym for urbanity and modernity, Los Angeles represented the postmodern *sans phrase*, and New York seemed to be the archetypical global city.

In all these cases the undercurrent that place has no agency seems to be taken as a given. But is it not time to redirect analytical attention to the particularity of a particular city? Is it not time to conceptualize the various modes of the production of locality in a comparative perspective with a view to identifying local classification systems, stocks of knowledge, and the role they play in constituting, contesting, receiving, and changing whatever is meant by the global?

Cities are more than nodal points within the global space of flows, more than locations of a headquarter economy of global capitalism, more than touchdown areas for various globally circulating artifacts. They belong historically and systematically to that space of places for which territoriality, habitus and habitat, place-making, and politics of space, in short: all those efforts that go into the production of locality, are quintessential (cf. Berking 2002).

One of the major obstacles encountered in conceptualizing locality is opposing space and place, associating place with groundedness, concreteness, authenticity, and territorial enclosure. But as long as the global is not the outside-of-the-local, space is not the outside-of-place. Following the line of argument advanced by Henry Lefèbvre (1991), namely that social groups, classes, or factions of classes cannot constitute themselves or recognize one another as subjects unless they generate or produce a space, the production of space must always been seen as embedded in processes of place-making. To analyze the concreteness of a place, however, does not necessarily mean focusing solely on local preconditions and falling into the trap of buying into the idea of territorial enclosure. The question, then, is whether social sciences should not make use of the geographic concept of scale to avoid any romanticized notions of place. Socio-spatial scales do structure and order perception. They are socially constructed by individuals and groups who, via this politics of spatial distance, create borders, mark belongings, and territorialize identities. If one takes the body-related space of proximity, the local, the regional, the national, the global, as typical relational socio-spatial scales, the theoretical challenge would be not to limit concepts of place and locality to the local but to use all socio-spatial scales from the local to the global to depict the reach and deep structure of this particular place.

On the surface, it is easy to describe the politics of space. When the city council of Chicago, for example, decided years ago to give leeway for ethnic minorities to rename their residential areas in keeping with their origins, Devon street became Indhira Ghandi Boulevard at the heart of the Indian community, changing to Golda Meir Street only two blocks away, while simply remaining Devon for the rest of the population. The interesting point here is that even though the majority of Indians do not live on Indhira Ghandi Boulevard, this place has not only become an attractive tourist site for ethnic food and fashion, but also a highly contested space used by Bangladeshi and Pakistani youth movements to protest against whatever they find amiss in politics in India. This example demonstrates both: that place-making has a territorializing aspect and that the agency of place can not be fully understood as exclusively confined to the local.

But the question of the production of locality runs much deeper inasmuch as its aim is to depict the very particularity of cities. In an impressive comparative study covering New York, Chicago, and Los Angeles, Janet Abu-Lughod addressed the logics of the production of locality in an attempt to unveil the "unique personalities" of these cities. What started out as an incisive critique of the ahistorical and overgeneralized character of global-city research, and is then followed by an exemplary historical reconstruction of the natural, the spatial and climatic preconditions and an in-depth analysis of the interactive relatedness to the world, the migration-related changes in the economy, politics, and culture of these cities finally leads to a precise description of three distinct local cultures whose spatial forms, logics of incorporation, life styles, and local politics could not be more different. That the very construction of urban space plays a major role in constituting the biography of these cities is beyond doubt. "Spatial patterns are deeply associated with variations in social life and the relationships among residents, and it is these social relations that yield differences in the patterns of urban living that give to each city its quintessential character" (1999: 3). Although Abu-Lughod is of course aware of the problem that much of what has happened within these cities is placed in quite different and distant geographic spaces, she nonetheless is able to demonstrate the extent to which answers and solutions are locally contextualized. That the end of Fordist reconstruction affected Chicago in a quite different way than it did L.A. or New York, that the socio-spatial concentration of Latinos in L.A. places constraints on ethnic coalitions and the politics of identity, while New York, thanks to its ethic diversity, is still doomed to play the ethnic poker game and Chicago remains entrapped in its longstanding racist color line—these are only some of the local structurations which determine the atmosphere, but also the action and problem-solving capacities of the three cities. Even individuals seem to be forced to adapt habitually to the particular style of a particular city. "Space in New York," Abu-Lughod claims, citing journalist Joseph Giovannini, "collects people; in Los Angeles it separates them." And: "If you drop any New Yorker other than Woody Allen in Los Angeles, he will eventually become acquisitive about cars ... if you drop any Angelo other than the Beach Boys in New York, he will eventually choose his neckties for their coded social meanings" (Giovannini, quoted after Abu-Lughod 1999: 423).

If we transferred into the field of sociology Ulf Hannerz' critique of urban anthropology as anthropology *in* the city that needs to be complemented by an anthropology *of* the city, we might be more than tempted to contemplate a concept of a sociology of cities.

British cultural geographer Doreen Massey has suggested conceptualizing places as products of social relations, as "meeting places." "This is a notion of place where specificity (local uniqueness, a sense of place) derives not from some mythical internal roots nor from a history of relative isolation […] but precisely from the absolute particularity of the mixture of influence found together there" (1999: 22). If one attempts to describe the particular character of a place with a view to the way in which the world is represented here as compared to there, one might be able to uncover the cumulative structure of local cultures, the physical and symbolic sediments of a city, as those decisive materials which give particular meaning to action orientation and future opportunity structures. Focusing on the production of locality might offer not only an alternative perspective on cities as an object of scientific knowledge but also a prospect for producing a knowledge that, beyond global talk, could contribute significantly to clarifying the still fuzzy problem of the global-local interplay.

References

Abu-Lughod, Janet (1999) *New York, Chicago, Los Angeles*, Minneapolis: University of Minnesota Press.
Agnew, John (1989) "The Devaluation of Place in Social Science". In John Agnew/Peter Duncan (eds.) *The Power of Place,* Boston: Unwin Hyman, pp. 9–29.
Albrow, Martin (1996) *The Global Age. State and Society beyond Modernity,* Cambridge: Polity Press.
Anthias, Floya (1998) "Evaluating 'Diaspora': Beyond Ethnicity?" Sociology 32, pp. 557–580.
Beck, Ulrich (1997) *Was ist Globalisierung?* Frankfurt am Main: Suhrkamp.
Beck, Ulrich (2000) 'The Cosmopolitan Perspective". British Journal of Sociology 51, pp. 79–106.
Berking, Helmuth (2002) "Global Village oder urbane Globalität". In Helmuth Berking/Richard Faber (eds.) *Städte im Globalisierungsdiskurs,* Würzburg: Königshausen & Neumann, pp. 11–25.
Castells, Manuel (1996) *The Rise of the Network Society,* Cambridge: Blackwell.

Castells, Manuel (1997) *The Power of Identity,* Cambridge: Blackwell.
Clifford, James (1997) *Routes. Travel and Translation in the Late Twentieth Century,* Cambridge, MA: Harvard University Press.
Cohen, Robert (1997) *Global Diasporas: An Introduction,* London: UCL Press.
Crang, Mike/Thrift, Nigel (eds., 2000) *Thinking Space,* London: Routledge.
Durkheim, Emile (1965) *The Elementary Forms of Religious Life,* New York: Free Press.
Eisenstadt, Samuel (2000) "Multiple Modernities". Daedalus 129/1, pp. 1–29.
Featherstone, Mike/Lash, Scott (1995) "Globalization, Modernity and the Spatialization of Social Theory: An Introduction". In Mike Featherstone/Scott Lash/Roland Robertson (eds.) *Global Modernities,* London: Sage, pp. 1–24.
Friedman, Jonathan (1995) "Where we Stand: A Decade of World City Research". In P. Knox/P.J. Taylor (eds.) *World Cities in a World System,* Cambridge: Cambridge University Press, pp.21–47.
Gilroy, Paul (1993) *The Black Atlantic,* London: Verso.
Hall, Stuart (1990) "Cultural Identity and Diaspora". In John Rutherford (ed.) *Identity: Community, Culture, Difference,* London: Lawrence and Wishart.
Hannerz, Ulf (1996) *Transnational Connections, Culture, People, Places,* London & New York: Routledge.
Latham, Robert/Kassimir, Ronald/Callaghy, Thomas (2001) "Introduction. Transboundary Formations, Intervention, Order, and Authority". In Thomas Callaghy/Ronald Kassimir/Robert Latham (eds.) *Intervention & Transnationalism in Africa,* Cambridge: Cambridge University Press, pp. 1–20.
Latour, Bruno (1993) *We Have Never Been Modern,* London: Harvester Wheatsheaf.
Learmount, Simon/Vertovec, Stephan/Cohen, Robin (eds., 2002) *Conceiving Cosmopolitanism – Theory, Context, and Practice,* Oxford: Oxford University Press.
Lefèbvre, Henri (1991) *The Production of Space,* Oxford: Blackwell.
Löw, Martina (2001) *Raumsoziologie,* Frankfurt am Main: Suhrkamp.
Massey, Doreen (1999) *Power-geometries and the Politics of Time-space.* Hettner Lecture II, University of Heidelberg.
Massey, Doreen (2004) "Geographies of Responsibility". Geografiska Annaler 86/B: Human Geography, pp. 5–18.
Massey, Doreen (2006) "Keine Entlastung für das Lokale". In Helmuth Berking (ed.) *Die Macht des Lokalen in einer Welt ohne Grenzen,* Frankfurt am Main: Campus, pp. 25–31.
Mitchell, Katharyne (1997) "Different Diasporas and the Hype of Hybridity". Environment and Planning D: Society and Space 15, pp. 533–553.

Pieterse, Jan (1995) "Globalization as Hybridization", in: Mike Featherstone/Scott Lash/Roland Robertson (eds.) *Global Modernities*, London: Sage, pp. 45–68.

Randeria, Shalini (2002) "Entangled Histories of Uneven Modernities". In Yehuda Elkana/Iwan Krastev/Elísio Macamo/Shalini Randeria (eds.) *Unravelling Ties – From Social Cohesion to New Practices of Connectedness*, Frankfurt am Main: Campus, pp. 284–311.

Ritzer, George (1993) *The McDonaldization of Society*, Newbury Park, CA: Pine Forge Press.

Robertson, Roland (1995) "Glocalization: Time-Space and Homogeneity-Heterogeneity". In Mike Featherstone/Scott Lash/Roland Robertson (eds.) *Global Modernities*, London: Sage, pp. 25–44.

Sassen, Saskia (1996) *Losing Control? Sovereignty in an Age of Globalization*, New York: Columbia University Press.

Saunders, Peter (1989) "Space, Urbanism and the Created Environment". In David Held/John Thompson (eds.) *Social Theory of Modern Societies*, New York: Cambridge University Press.

Sklair, Leslie (2001) *The Transnational Capitalist Class*, Oxford: Blackwell.

Smith, Anthony (1979) *Nationalism in the Twentieth Century*, Oxford.

Tomlinson, John (1999) *Globalization and Culture*, Cambridge: Polity Press.

Urry, John (2000) *Sociology beyond Societies*, London: Routledge.

Wimmer, Andreas (2001) "Globalizations Avant la Lettre". Comparative Studies in Society and History 43/3, pp. 435–466.

The City as Assemblage. Diasporic Cultures, Postmodern Spaces, and Biopolitics

COUZE VENN

The paper focuses on the emergence of the megacity/postmodern city and argues that its conceptualisation as space must break with notions of linear development and homogenous temporality in the analysis of urban socialities and in the application of centralised forms of governance to the regulation of such spaces. I draw attention to diasporic settlements, the co-habitation of different temporalities and spatialities, the emergence and the co-existence of discrepant imaginaries and ways of being. There are implications for issues of identity, biopolitics, and for cultural analysis.

Problematizations

In what follows, I want to focus on what the postcolonial recognition of the ubiquity of diasporas and the emergence of a new problematic about transcultural processes mean for rethinking the questions of culture and identity from the point of view of the heterogeneity of spatiality and temporality. One of my aims is to challenge some long-standing assumptions in the discourse of modernity about temporality, spatiality, and social imaginaries, although Lefebvre (1991) already opened up a theoretical space for such an undertaking. In particular, I will argue that the idea that the ordered community is ideally ethnically homogenous and developmentally "progressive," an idea central to occidentalism, is fundamentally incompatible with the mutant, creolised, and "vernacular" cosmopolitanisms (Hall 1999) that have now become the norm in the megacity/postmodern city.

A displacement is therefore necessary at the level of theory, informed, on the one hand, by the fact that the current phase of globalisation has seen a massive intensification and extension in the scale of displacement and migration of people, both at the transnational and the national levels, mostly to urban spaces throughout the world (Papastergiadis 2000; Sassen 1999). Whilst the figures themselves—for instance 140 million in 2000, which is far greater than in any other period (Castles 2000)—give an indication of the change in scale, the problem is not just about quantities. Rather, the problem is that the imagination of both the urban and the diasporic, especially with regard to governance, has largely remained circumscribed by reference to the model of the state as nation-state, supported by the idea of the nation as ideally ethnically homogeneous. The foundations of this conceptual framework continue to haunt postcolonial thought (Cheah 2004). Notions of hybridity and multiculturalism entertain an ambivalent relationship with this framework, appearing to undermine it, yet open to recuperation by the disciplinary strategies of governance.

On the other hand, social theory needs to take into account the range of concepts that have emerged to address problems relating to issues of change, determination, the nature of the living, historicity, and memory, namely, concepts of complexity, flow, turbulence, emergence, indeterminacy, multiplicity, poiesis. I shall draw from them to propose the standpoint of the city as an assemblage, and point to the implications for cultural analysis, specifically in addressing issues of diasporas, the postmodern city, the biopolitics of governance, and the theorisation of mutations in cultures. One of my aims is to use this new work to problematize the approach in cultural theory that remains circumscribed within the conceptual framework of governmentality and governance, thus within the purview of knowledge/power that inscribes a particular imagination of the social world as one amenable to the exercise of a regulating and securitising power.

A related assumption within that problematic of the social is that of the subject as the rational, autonomous, unitary agent, incarnated in liberalism's idea of the self-centered individual. This subject not only doubles as the paradigm for the citizen of the modern nation-state, but functions as the normative standard in relation to which all other subjectivities and identities are categorised as lacking in some fundamental way: underdeveloped, or primitive or lagging behind, or exotic, that is, as "other," or as deviant. The idea that cultures and identities are fundamentally heterogeneous and mobile, the result of a history of encounters, exchanges, grafts, borrowings, and admixtures, cannot find a place within the logic of the older paradigms of identity and social order.

The point is that the interest of the nation-state from the point of view of governance has been precisely to constitute itself in the form of a homogeneous population, for example, the French, the English—though hierarchised in terms of class, race, and gender. Or at least, this interest has overdetermined cultural homogeneity as both the desired goal of its intervention in the domain of the social and as a condition for its rule. The normalising strategies which the nation-state has invented in the post-enlightenment period have tried to achieve this goal through the standardization of language and public conduct; the normativization of the norms of the normal on the basis of rational knowledges (as science, as Foucault has argued); the democratisation of its system of authority by founding it in the general will or will of the people; a state-oriented political economy; and the planned unification of the nation as a single community, with the discourse of race and culture playing a key role in this. It makes sense within these parameters to categorise difference and resistance as pathology, deviance, dysfunction, exoticism, or underdevelopment, that is, as problems that a disciplinary apparatus could address through the constitution of specific groups and their allocation to different regimes of formation and technologies of surveillance.

This form of governmentality and its disciplining strategies were applied to urban as much as to other spaces, for example the post-revolutionary Hausmannian redesigning of Paris, or the post-war remaking of cities within the concept of welfare and insurance, addressing questions dealing with education, health, security, employment. These devices were also part of the technology for (re)constituting the citizen in the modern city, in the attempt to homogenise, or at least to subject to the same legal regimes, the plural and mobile groups that have been characteristic of the profile of populations in cities generally, for instance, in early modern Europe, as Engin Isin (2002) has established. These apparatuses have been at work in colonial cities, and continue to operate, if unevenly, in postcolonial conditions. They have come to be seen as the instruments of modernisation and the signs of progress, so that implicitly the conceptual coordinates of the state as the nation-state, and its inscription of ethnic and cultural homogeneity and the point of view of governance in constituting populations, have become part of the invisible taken-for-granted, i.e. acting as "doxa" for planners and the social sciences alike.

Underlying the strategies of development and planning, one finds the assumption of linear temporality and the idea that "progress" or "modernisation" is a matter of stages of development that imply the erasure or conversion of the previous state of affairs in favour of more efficient and rational stages. Both modern governance, and town planning as an instance of it, are premised on this thinking. Within this perspective, the co-habitation of different spatialities and temporalities is seen as a sign of dysfunction, or a side-effect to be managed by translating discrepant environments either into the idiom of "heritage," refigured as an aspect of the "culture industry," or into the idiom of a "multiculturalism" that tolerates difference—the "stranger within"—so long as they do not challenge existing relations of power and the goals of rationalization. In the present climate of "war against terror," discrepant and counter-hegemonic ways of being are now thought of as inimical to good order and thus to be countered by a policy of total surveillance and, at the limit, "zero tolerance."

One should bear in mind that the model of the "imagined community," constituted in relation to print technology and modern governance, already made invisible, or marginalized the presence of non-Western people in Europe, but also the fact that cities everywhere have been, for a long time, the sites of transcultural exchanges amongst migrant populations. This is particularly true of imperial centres, for instance Rome, Constantinople, Baghdad, London. The tendency to see cultural and identity difference as a problem rather than as a normal feature of the urban cultural milieu is an aspect of this occidentalist epistemology. I am arguing that in order to move away from the older framework of analysis, theory today must recognise two related problematics: on the one hand, the complex interrelations between mobility and settlement, uprootedness and groundedness, being and territory (Ahmed 2003), and on the other hand, the recognition that the intertwining and heterogeneity of cultures is far more endemic and of longer duration than many analyses of diaspora, hybridity, multiculturalism, migrancy recognise (Said 1993). Cross-cultural and transcultural encounters and exchanges are precisely the mechanisms whereby cultures change, although conflict often attends these encounters, as in the case of invasion and conquest, or in the case of exclusion.

In other words, cultures are inescapably polyglot. This is even clearer today because the interpenetration of the global and the local at all levels means that the material and the virtual, roots and routes, are now correlated in terms of different spatialisations and temporalities constituted in relation to new technologies of communication and travel, new spatial technologies, and, alongside this everyday reality, in terms of new imaginaries that pluralise belonging in quite new ways (Sassen, 1999; Ong 2003; Shohat 1999).

It is worth bearing in mind too that the process of migration and settlement, whilst it is now differently grounded by reference to territorialization, nevertheless follows a pattern of deterritorialization and reterritorialization, which is driven by a search for settlement and ontological security that has long roots into the emergence of forms of sociality, as Deleuze and Guattari (1988) have argued. This perspective brings into view the fact that the ontological and the affective dimensions of being-in-the-world are correlated in the everyday. At the theoretical level, an agenda around diaspora and migrancy has surfaced in the wake of these developments that itself needs to be rethought in terms of the longue duree, going beyond the parameters of the hegemonic discourse of modernity. A displacement is therefore needed at the level of theory with implications for policy, and for the invention of new apparatuses that would support the new forms of diasporic cosmopolitan socialities that are appearing in cities across the world.

This displacement shifts the emphasis onto the importance of spatiality and temporality, namely, geography, architecture, and place, considered in terms of the imbrication of memory and history in the objects and environments that constitute the lifeworld of people and the investments that one makes in the material world. The spatio-temporal location of identity and subjectivity in regimes and "realms/lieux" of memory (Nora 1984–93), draws attention to the presence of the past in the present and the co-existence of the different rhythms and temporalities that inscribe existential belonging in the everyday (Lefebvre 2003). Such lifeworlds function as the habitus in relation to which people make sense of their lives. The constitution of such worlds and the constitution of social imaginaries and identity are correlated processes, that is to say, it is not possible to analyse the one without making visible the effects of the other processes.

Another displacement relates to the point of view of governmentality as elaborated in the work of Foucault, and thus the focus on the apparatuses and knowledges that constitute norms, authorise specific forms of power, and generate the technologies of the social concerned with forming, disciplining, and regulating populations (Foucault 1979). Contemporary conditions in the emergent megacity lead one to question the ability of state-based disciplinary regimes of power/knowledge to constitute socialities that conform to the norms it seeks to determine. The question that comes to mind is whether the co-presence of global and local effects—regarding social imaginaries and new identities—poses a fundamental challenge for state-based interventionary programmes. It can be argued that the model of governance premised on homogenous populations and temporality and on territorial exclusivity—with its own assumptions and myths or imaginaries about national and ethnic authenticity, cultural value, administrative efficiency, the space of belonging, the norms of the normal and so on—is obliged to impose ways of being and technologies of control that intensify conflict. The attempt in France in 2004 to use legislation to impose conformity to norms, as in the case of the wearing of the veil in school, has demonstrated the problems with such local mechanisms when dealing with processes that respond to geo-political and geo-cultural forces.

It should be noted that there exists a different discourse about the urban lifeworld for which flux and mobility, the evanescent, and the indeterminate are intrinsic features of modernity, intensified in the pleasures and dislocations that make the city the site of transient populations and speedy lives, as expressed in Benjamin's (1995) work. This view accords with the standpoint of assemblage that I will develop later. It is important to point out too that against this celebration of a certain "nomadism" and of particular creative and radical groups, one must remember the insecurities and hardships of those, mostly the poor, whose displacement is driven by the exigencies of survival in a world constantly transformed by forces outside their control. These forces operate across the new "contact zones" and "scapes" that are in fact correlated according to capitalist calculations and forms of ownership. Today, all these pressures and tendencies make the city a place of stabilities and instabilities, of de- and re-territorializations that play out a diversity of ends. This means that the analysis of the culture of cities must foreground the standpoint of its diasporic configuration and the interpenetration of the global and the local at all levels of social reality, challenging the dichotomies of here and there (Cairns 2004).

The megacity as new problematic

Let me note two research projects that take account of the problematizations that I have summarised in addressing the question of the city today. Bishop, Phillips, and Yeo (2003) explore the neglected interface between urban studies and development studies, proposing a new approach that brings into view features of urban realities that have not been adequately recognized because of the way disciplinary inscription has so far cut up the world. A salient feature is the fact that multiple temporalities co-exist within the urban space, temporalities that are colonial, postcolonial and geopolitical, more intensely experienced now, but present in other periods too, as postcolonial studies has shown regarding the invisible presence of non-white populations in the metropolitan cities of Europe in imperial times (Fryer 1985). The authors argue that global urbanism and postcolonialism are concomitant phenomena, shaped by interdependencies that are obscured by the conceptual framework which divides the colonial, the postcolonial, the cold-war and post-cold-war into a series of distinct periods succeeding each other. They point to the hybrid and mobile character of the identities that co-habit the urban space, a plural spatiality which is punctuated by different rhythms of existence and by the diversity of experience and social relations that are lived in it (Pile/Thrift 1995; Yuval-Davis/Werbner 1999; Lefebvre 2004; Grosz 2001).

The work of Koolhaas (2002) and others (Chung et. al 2002; Simone 2001; Sassen 2001), with their focus on the postcolonial city and the megacity, adds concrete support for the (Lefebvrian) view about co-habiting spatialities and temporalities, detecting the process in the discrepant urban life-worlds that are theorised in terms of dysfunction or failure from the point of view of a western instrumental modernity or occidentalism. Looking at Lagos as exemplar, Koolhaus notes that what appears to be signs of decay and failure turns out to be complex systems of survival operating through recycling, trading, and networks of mutual exchange and relations. These enact sophisticated strategies for sustaining non-"Western" forms of existence for populations of millions of people in poorly resourced environments. Such activities are what conventional theory categorises as "informal," that is, as elements of the "black" or shadow economy that escape the regulatory and disciplinary gaze of state agencies. Such activities exist to a degree in all cities anyway, for instance in favelas, bidonvilles, ghettos, and so on. They are the object of a biopolitics aimed at either containment or rehabilitation. What is clear is that postcolonial cities are set to increase in size and number globally—from Hong Kong to Shanghai, to Mexico City to Delhi—and that existing forms of governance cannot control these so-called dysfunctional areas that are not just by-products of displacements occurring both transnationally and from the rural to the urban (for instance already 40 % of the African population live in urban areas): they are constituent elements of postmodern urbanism and global capitalism. What is equally clear is that the effects of geopolitical power and transnational corporate activities reproduce inequalities at both the local and global levels, so that the analysis of the urban must be informed by wider theoretical perspectives developed in dissident and counter-hegemonic theorizations of the global, as in some postcolonial and cultural theory (Hardt/Negri 2000; Sassen 1999).

I would like to point to another perspective that throws additional light on the processes that sustain spatio-temporally plural and diasporic environments. It proceeds from the view that the lifeworld as living space is a territory appropriated by marking it in some way with marks that are culturally significant, that is, marks that constitute and reconstitute particular imaginaries. This activity, evidenced in the everyday in the décor and style of houses and buildings, or indeed in graffiti, and, generally, in the translation of place through their reiteration (their repetition with-and-in difference) in a new spatiality—say, China Town in Los Angeles, or Little India in Singapore, New England in the New World—is a form of memorialisation and socialisation of living space. It is a signifying practice that inscribes the material world with an affective economy and with historicity, so that it can be performatively appropriated as living space conceptualised in terms of such signifying practice. The fact that many people cannot appropriate the place they inhabit because of power relations that make them invisible or subaltern—say, women in some circumstances, the incapacitated, the elderly, the refugee, the "outsider" (Grosz 2001)—needs to be stressed when one thinks about the actualization of virtual spaces, the architecture of living space as well as attempts to intervene in these situations.

The reference to historicity is meant to bring into view the continuities as well as the shifts at the level of the imaginary when one considers displacement and settlement, de- and re-territorializations, in terms of the identities and diasporic socialities that inhabit urban places. For one thing, it makes visible what the discourse of modern governmentality makes invisible, namely, the fact that the urban space has been plural and diasporic for a much longer period than it acknowledges. Besides, it enables one to interrogate the plurality of spaces by reference to the effects of power at the level of subjectivity and culture. Issues about assimilation and multiculturalism must be located within this perspective, so that the remaking of identities and communities can be understood as strategic responses to perceived power relations, taking the form of accommodation, or resistance, or coping strategies, or creative artistic practice (Enwesor 2002). A question about agency surfaces here that would require more space to develop than I have in the context of this paper.

The problematic of assemblage

In the rest of the paper, I would like to sketch a different analytical apparatus for addressing the range of issues I have noted, organised around the concept of assemblage. This concept has emerged as one of a series of new concepts, alongside those of complexity, chaos, indeterminacy, fractals, string, turbulence, flow, multiplicity, emergence, poiesis, and so on, that now form the theoretical vocabulary for addressing the problem of determination and structure, of process and change, and of stability and instability regarding social phenomena. As with the previous set of concepts in the social sciences, notably the notion of structure, they derive from developments in the natural sciences and mathematics. Their introduction signals an important shift at the level of theorisation and methodology, opening analysis to the recognition of the complexity of cultural, social as well as "natural" phenomena, for instance concerning sociality, the organism, mind, and culturally plural spaces.

Structure in conventional paradigms in the natural and social sciences grounds causal determination within a logic of stability and linear causality. It is a central epistemological element in the work of the grand theorists of social science such as from Marx to Parsons. The notion of discrete and nomological determination, which positivism and some forms of structuralism support, has clear pay-offs from the point of view of categorising and predicting social phenomena, and thus for the possibility of intervention and rational governance. However, the limitations of approaches based on this notion of determination have been demonstrated in their failure to account adequately for the dynamics of change, resistance, agency, mobility, the event, the irruption of the unexpected or unpredictable, that is, complexity. The limitations relate also to their inadequacy from the point of view of co-relating phenomena across different fields, for example between the psychic and the social, the affective and the cognitive, and between matter and form. The problem for theory is that of re-thinking structure as well as multiplicity and indeterminacy within the same theoretical framework.

The concept of assemblage has appeared in the wake of questions about the relationship of structural determination to indeterminacy and emergence. In the recent literature it is mostly associated with the work of Deleuze and Guattari and clearly explained in Delanda (2002). One can also retrace its emergence by reference to developments in the physics of small particles, in topology, in molecular biology and generally in the interface between the theorisation of emergence and becoming (say in ontogeny and phylogeny), adaptation or autopoiesis and cybernetic systems (Maturana/Varela 1980), and post-structuralist mathematics. They all emphasise adaptivity rather than fixity or essence, the formal properties of the system rather than the specific instance, the spatio-temporal dimension rather than quantities, the relational, that is, co-articulation and compossibility, rather than linear and discrete determination, the multilinear temporality of processes such that emergence and irreversibility are brought to the fore (Prigogine/Stengers 1984).

In the light of the foregoing, assemblage can be seen as a relay concept, linking the problematic of structure with that of change and far-from-equilibrium systems. It focuses on process and on the dynamic character of the inter-relationships between the heterogeneous elements of the phenomenon. It recognises both structurizing and indeterminate effects, that is, both flow and turbulence, produced in the interaction of open systems. It points to complex becomings and multiple determinations (Ong/Collier 2004). It is sensitive to time and temporality in the emergence and mutation of the phenomenon; it thus directs attention to the longue duree. Whilst Deleuze and Guattari (1988) suggest desiring machines as exemplar, one could instead refer to weather formation and the genome, or for that matter, to the formation of identity and diasporic cultures, that is, to the (post-Deleuzian) question of emergence and becoming generally.

In relation to the latter, one must point to the fact that the translation of cultures through the diasporic displacement of people occurs mostly in urban environments. Cities are already technological and social assemblages, operating in the form of coordinated networks of sub-systems relating to buildings, transport networks, commodity exchange, productive practices, apparatuses of training, regulation and communication, artistic practices, and so on. All these sub-systems are open systems, coherent in terms of their own rules and routines and flows, yet open to the effects of contiguous systems, that is to say, they are dynamic, complex, processual, and autopoietic in their operation. Change and turbulence in one part of the assemblage has effects for the other parts, often with indeterminate consequences.

The conceptualisation of the city as assemblage has the advantage of enabling theory to recognise the degrees of freedom that enable the urban spatiality to adapt to change; another advantage is the ability to envisage disequilibrium as normal. Contemporary patterns of migrancy and settlement enable one to see this process of mutation in action, for example, in the case of the effects of mass migration such as Turks to some German cities. Such movements appear as event, that is, as an irruption that results in the emergence of innovation through adaptation, graft, invention, the mobilisation of potential capacities, new combinations, and changes in configuration.

In the idiom of assemblage, emergence is processual, it occurs according to a pragmatics of becoming. With regard to diaspora, one could take the case of the category of music called "urban," which has developed out of particular combinations of hip-hop, rock, jazz, indie and other musical forms from around the world, recombined to express the specificity of urban living in different locales, using new technologies of music production. This music belongs to the complex set of signifying practices that inscribe and shape diasporic identity. Its meaning and effects need to be located in relation to the range of teletechnologies that now form or mediate contemporary social imaginaries. Their functioning relates, on the one hand, to their imbrication in global corporate capitalism and in strategies of subjectification and subjection, and, on the other hand, to their deployment as the visible and audible technics for establishing and supporting networks of social relations operating transculturally to sustain plural belongings and habitations. Teletechnologies, as a constitutive element of contemporary cultures, sustain cultural spaces where both virtual and real co-habit, a space open both to mediatised capitalism and to "flexible citizenship" (Ong 1999) and alternative becomings. It is clear that the recognition of the centrality of migration and diasporas for an understanding of spatiality and culture, together with the standpoint of cultures as unavoidably intertwined and recombinant, entails a break with the epistemological framework that legitimates strategies of normalization, assimilation, exclusion and enfortressement in urban and national spaces, and the power relations played out through them.

I wish to thank Rob Shields, Ryan Bishop, and John Phillips for their invaluable comments on an earlier draft of this paper.

References

Ahmed, Sara (2003) *Uprootings/Regroundings*, Oxford: Berg.
Benjamin, Walter/ Tiedemann, Roy (eds.) (1999) *The Arcades Project*. Trans. Howard Eiland/Kevin McLaughlin. Cambridge: Belknapp Press.
Bishop, Ryan/Phillips, John/Yeo, S. (eds.) (2003) *Postcolonial Urbanism*, New York: Routledge.
Brah, Avtar/Hickman, Mary/Mac an Ghaill, Mairtin. (eds.) (1999) *Global Futures: Migration, Environment and Globalization*, Basingstoke: Macmillan.
Cairns, Stephen (2004) *Drifting: Architecture and Migrancy*, London: Routledge.
Castles, Stephen (2000) *Ethnicity and Globalization*, London: Sage.
Cheah, Pheng (2004) *Spectral Nationality*, New York: Columbia University Press
Chung, Chuihua Judy/Inaba, Jeffrey/Koolhaas, Rem/Leong, Sze Tsung (eds.) (2002) *Great Leap Forward*. Harvard Design School Project on the City, Cologne: Taschen.
Delanda, Manuel (2002) *Intensive Science & Virtual Philosophy*, London: Continuum.
Deleuze, Gilles/Guattari, Felix (1988) *A Thousand Plateaux*, London: Continuum.
Enwesor, Ekwui et al. (eds.) (2002) "Under Siege: Four African Cities. Freetown, Johannesburg, Kinshasa, Lagos". In Documenta 11/4, Ostfildern-Ruit: Hatje Cantz.
Foucault, Michel (1979) "On Governmentality". In Ideology & Consciousness. No. 6, pp. 5–22.
Fryer, Peter (1984) *Staying Power*, London: Pluto.
Grosz, Elizabeth (2001) *Architecture from the Outside. Essays on Virtual and Real Space*, Cambridge: MIT Press.
Hall, Stuart (1999) 'Thinking the diaspora: home thoughts from abroad,' in: Small Axe, 6, pp. 1–18.
Hardt, Michael/Negri, Antonio (2000) Empire, Cambridge: Harvard University Press.
Koolhaas, Rem (2002) "Fragments of a Lecture on Lagos". In O. Enwesor et al. (eds.) *Under Siege: Four African Cities. Freetown, Johannesburg, Kinshasa, Lagos*, Ostfildern-Ruit: Hatje Cantz.
Lefebvre, Henri (1991) *The Production of Space*, Oxford: Blackwell.
Lefebvre, Henri (2003) *The Urban Revolution*, Minneapolis: University of Minnesota Press.
Lefebvre, Henri (2004) *Rhythmanalysis. Space, Time and Everyday Life*, London: Continuum.

Isin, Engin (2002) *Being Political: Genealogies of Citizenship*. Minneapolis: University of Minnesota Press
Maturana, Humberto/Varela, Francisco (1980) *Autopoiesis and Cognition*, Dordrecht: Reidel.
Nora, Pierre (1984–1992) *Les Lieux de mémoire* (seven volumes), Paris: Edition Gallimard.
Ong, Aihwa (1999) *Flexible Citizenship*, Durham: Duke University Press.
Ong, Aihwa (2003) *Buddha is Hiding: Refugees, Citizenship, the New America*. Berkeley: University of California Press.
Ong, Aihwa/Collier, Stephen (eds.) (2004) *Global Assemblages. Technology, Politics and Ethics as Anthropological Problems*, London: Blackwell.
Papastergiadis, Nicos (2000) *The Turbulence of Migration: Globalization, Deterritorialization, and Hybridity*, Cambridge: Polity.
Pile, Steven/Thrift, Nigel (eds.) (1995) *Mapping the Subject: Geographies of Cultural Transformation,* London: Routledge.
Prigogine, Ilya/Stengers, Isabelle (1984) *Order out of Chaos*, London: Flamingo.
Said, Edward (1993) *Culture & Imperialism*, London: Chatto & Windus.
Sassen, Saskia (1999) *Guests and Aliens*, New York: New Press.
Sassen, Saskia (2001) *The Global City*, Princeton: Princeton University Press.
Shohat, Ella (1999) "By the Bitstream of Babylon: Cyberfrontiers and Diasporic Vistas". In Hamid Nificy (eds.) *Home, Exile, Homeland: Film, Media and the Politics of Place*, London: Routledge, pp. 213–232.
Simone, Abdou Maliq (2001) "The Worlding of African Cities". African Studies Review 44/2, pp. 15–41.
Yuval-Davis, Nira/Werbner, Pnina (eds.) (1999) *Women, Citizenship and Difference*, London: Zed Books.

Remapping the Geopolitics of Terror: Uncanny Urban Spaces in Singapore

LISA LAW

This paper considers urban conflicts as embedded in a range of geopolitical scales. Using post-9/11 Singapore as a case study, it is argued that the barricading of spaces deemed vulnerable to terrorist attack summons layers of historical division, connection, and affiliation—but these do not always include Washington at their geopolitical centre. Instead, urban tensions in Singapore are shaped by the uncanny return of the ghostly past, raising questions about belonging in the multicultural state.

On 28 November 2002, a text message threatening a bomb explosion in the expatriate enclave of Holland Village[1] caused widespread apprehension across Singapore. According to police, who isolated the source of the message within days, a 20-year-old man had initiated the panic. The young man's sister had apparently overheard a conversation about the discovery of a bomb amongst a group of expatriates in a Holland Village restaurant. She reported the conversation to her brother, who then circulated a text message warning his immediate friends. Given the seriousness of the message, and the technological ease of spreading the rumour, it circulated widely—eventually to hundreds of people. When a nearby school alerted police after receiving it, a news release was issued warning against such acts. The release found fear in a

---

[1] Holland Village was established sometime between the late 1930s and 1945 as a military village and served the recreational needs of British soldiers and their families (Chang 1995). When the British repatriated thousands of personnel between 1971 and 1976, it had already become a mainstay for Singaporeans and a new expatriate population.

community still reeling from the Bali blasts of a month earlier, and from government allegations that the Jemaah Islamiyah—an allegedly Al-Qaeda-linked organization with networks across Indonesia, Malaysia, Thailand, and the Philippines—had been targeting key sites across Singapore for terrorist activities. Despite knowledge that the young man had been mistaken, by the end of the month barricades had been put up along two streets in the area, which were closed to traffic from 6:30pm to 4:00am daily (*Figure 1*). As the months passed, Holland Village became a model for how to protect other sites "catering to Westerners," such as entertainment districts and hotels.

Figure 1: Barricading of the streets in Holland Village (Photo: © Lisa Law)

Did the bomb hoax represent a collective fear of the possible return of violence to the streets of Singapore? Was it possible that Muslim radicals would attack Western-oriented entertainment districts in capitalist Singapore that had also pledged support for America's war on terrorism? In a government White Paper released during 2003, details of potential terrorist activities in Singapore were elaborated (Republic of Singapore, 2003). According to "official sources[2]," the Jemaah Islamiyah (JI) intended to assault a series of American-

---

2   I use this term cautiously as it is difficult to have confidence in official sources when much of their information is obtained from subjects in detention. For an excellent review of how sources have been cited in academic and related debate, cf. Hamilton-Hart (2005). She argues that "fantasy" and "myopia" characterize much of the field of terrorism studies, and that certain fantasies about Southeast Asian terrorism are based on "uncertain conjecture posing as reliable information" (p. 304).

related interests across the island, including the American, Israeli, and British embassies, commercial buildings housing American companies, and a shuttle bus service used to ferry American military personnel to the Sembawang naval base. The remaining sites focused on Singapore state interests, and included the mass rapid transit system, Changi International Airport, the Ministry and Defence building, and the highly politicized water pipeline between Malaysia and Singapore. By September 2002, the government had arrested 31 persons suspected of being connected to the JI; more would be detained under the Internal Security Act, or placed under restriction orders (National Security Coordination Centre 2004). Their confessions, while in detention, unsurprisingly revealed links to the JI. Detainees also expressed commitment to a vision of Daulah Islamiyah Nusantara (an Islamic state or archipelago) stretching from Indonesia to Thailand and the Philippines, and into which Singapore would ultimately be absorbed.

Holland Village was not mentioned as a potential site of terrorist interest, although the area had recently been touted in the popular press as a "little Bohemia" where lifestyles outside the usual structures of Singaporean society could flourish. Fear of its bombing reflected many ongoing concerns, including a perceived Westernization of Singapore and the erosion of "Asian Values." Asian Values are a geographically and culturally specific state-sponsored ideology, where the family, community, and broader social order are privileged over individual liberty (Wee 1999). This ideology both enables a distinctive sense of Asian-ness in the postcolonial period, while at the same time decentring the role of religion in a multicultural state. Holland Village represented a site where Asian Values might be compromised, though with potentially contaminating effects. It was for this reason that an entertainment district not specifically targeted for terrorist attack, and where only hearsay fueled fears of danger, became a site of intervention and potential urban conflict.

The last time bombs exploded in Singapore was during the Indonesian Confrontation, or *Konfrontasi*, in the 1960s. During this time, Indonesian radicals infiltrated the streets of Singapore (then part of Malaysia), setting off bombs to generate alarm and stir up latent racial tension. The Confrontation was Indonesian President Sukarno's initiative to disrupt the new state of Malaysia, which was being crafted out of the remains of the colonial epoch. Many Indonesian leaders regarded the new state as a front for continued British presence in the region and a neo-imperialist plot to expand Malaysia's borders to include northern Borneo. But President Macapagal of the Philippines and President Sukarno of Indonesia, each conceiving Borneo as belonging to their own territories, had a different vision of a less rigid association of states across the Malay archipelago, which was detailed but never realized in the Manila Accord of 1963. That region was to be called Maphilindo—an amalgam of Malaysia, the Philippines, and Indonesia—and would symbolize the development of a self-reliant, free, and independent Malay region in Southeast Asia. Maphilindo was doomed to failure, however, as its conception was also embedded in a larger struggle between the superpowers of Britain (Malaysia), America (Philippines), and China (Indonesia). These visions of an allied archipelago would recede for the next decades as the post-colonial boundaries of Southeast Asia took shape.

The recent wave of terrorist detentions, threats of bombings, and dreams of a pan-Islamic state all bear an uncanny resemblance to this tumultuous period of post-colonial history. In 2002, Indonesian President Megawati and Philippine President Arroyo were both in power (and were the daughters of Sukarno and Macapagal, respectively). A modified and more explicitly Islamic version of Maphilindo was being articulated in fresh forms. Suspected terrorists were being detained under Internal Security Acts created during the Cold War to detain what were then understood as communist terrorists, and renewed American interest in the region saw the return of troops in the Philippines and a hasty thawing of relations with Malaysia. This appeared to be an uncanny era in Southeast Asian history: Was America's war on terrorism similar to its earlier war on communism, and thus another imperial project in the region? Or is this resemblance uncanny, in Freud's (1919) more particular sense, in that these eras inhabit each other in recognizable and foreign ways?

The "uncanny," according to Freud (1919), is resistant to definition, but represents a liminal state between what is familiar (*heimlich*) and unfamiliar (*unheimlich*)—an unstable moment that problematises order. What makes the uncanny unique is not that something familiar suddenly becomes strange, however; it is the way in which the two terms inhabit each other, making one feel "at home" and "unhomely" simultaneously. Because this produces a sense of being involuntarily repetitious, it can also be frightening. Mike Davis (2001), for example, draws on the uncanny to explain the American experience of 9/11, where the threat of global terrorism had been long dreamt about and imagined in Hollywood action films. Images of terrorism, death, and destruction recognizable to American audiences returned to the small screen in disturbingly unfamiliar ways—bringing fear to the streets of American cities. The uncanny also helps explain the experience of terrorism in Southeast Asia, where the contours of being "in place" and "out of place" became unsettled after 9/11. The resurgent vision of an Islamic archipelago introduced old questions of unity and disconnection across postcolonial nation-states, as well as new questions about the role of transnationalism in constructing pan-Islamic identities. These issues of national boundaries and geographies of ethnic and religious identity receded somewhat with the demise of Maphilindo—much as they did when advocated by the Darul Islam during anti-colonial struggles in the 1940s. Their return in familiar/unfamiliar ways raised specific issues for multicultural, but nevertheless Chinese-dominant, Singapore at a variety of scales. Was Singapore in or out of place in a Muslim archipelago? Could the postcolonial map of Southeast Asia be redrawn by Muslim radicals? Despite decades of official multicultural policy, did Singaporean Muslims identify with the nation or with a pan-Islamic identity? Did Holland Village represent a site where "Asian" and "Islamic" values were in conflict?

Perhaps this moment better represents what Gelder and Jacobs (1998) have characterized as the "postcolonial uncanny," in that it articulates the uneasy place of the sacred in the postcolonial nation-state. Gelder and Jacobs' (1998) analysis of Australian Aboriginal land claims enhances our understanding of the uncanny, where notions of belonging/not belonging and "sacredness-in-the-midst-of-modernity" help explain some of the tensions produced in the postcolonial moment. Their work parallels Freud's own concern with one's sense of place in a modern world, and examines uncanny experiences arising from the return of spiritual beliefs in the modern, Australian nation-state. Freud himself conceded that the latter were much more frequent, and that many people experience uncanny "feeling[s] in the highest degree in relation to death and dead bodies, [and] to the return of [...] spirits and ghosts" (in Gordon 1997:51). The uncanny thus represents a "quality" of feeling, an unsettling recurrence, and, as Gordon (1997:50) suggests, these are often haunting experiences. In Australia it is the return of the ghostly past— i.e. an Aboriginal Australia constructed out of sacred sites—that profoundly unsettles who is "in place" and "out of place" in the contemporary nation. Gelder and Jacobs examine how this remapping of national space overwrites postcolonial boundaries, producing tensions at local, regional, and national scales.

Although Singapore and Australia are very different sites with different issues and colonial histories, the "postcolonial uncanny" helps explain some of the tensions in post-9/11 Southeast Asia. For it is the possibility of a Malay Muslim geopolitical entity, with weighty historical roots, that haunts postcolonial Singapore. This is made all the more real by fragmentation in Indonesia, where there are struggles for greater autonomy in regions such as Aceh and Irian Jaya, and by separatist movements in Thailand and the Philippines. Fears about regional association have been apparent since the Confrontation and Sino-Malay racial riots in the 1960s, which were essentially struggles over the position of Malays (who are still unable to hold sensitive positions in the military, as it is thought their loyalty might be "compromised" in regional disputes). The war on terror has given these fears renewed veracity through media commentary (*Figure 2*), government reports of the JI's regional vision (Republic of Singapore 2003), and policy pronouncements that have created Inter-Racial Confidence Circles to encourage inter-communal harmony (Goh

2002). Since independence, the state has devoted enormous political effort to create a multicultural Singapore, whose origins are professed to be rooted in its discovery by Sir Stamford Raffles in 1819. Yet in Malay folklore, Singapore was founded in the 14th century by Sang Nila Utama, a Prince of supernatural origins (Miksic and Low 2004). The ruins of the Prince's palace, where his descendants resided until the beginning of this century, have been renovated and made into a museum celebrating Singapore's varied ancestry. In a controversial essay about race relations, Alfian bin Sa'at (2002:386) suggests that the museum erases this royal history, encouraging Malay Singaporeans to surrender their memories for the benefit of racial harmony.

Figure 2: Jemaah Islamiyah in the media[3]

It is the return of this spectre—a Malay world with its own history, geography, and "values"—that is more frightening than the fear of violence itself. It unsettles the boundaries of postcolonial states, raising uncertainties about multicultural coexistence and the place of Singapore's capitalist modernity in Muslim Southeast Asia. In this sense, fears about a Holland Village bombing are as much about a reworked regional vision as they are about the presence of Western expatriates. The remainder of this paper thus chronicles the unset-

---

3   This photo appeared with an article titled "JI Reloaded: Could it happen?" in The Straits Times, 13 December 2003. It depicts Abu Bakar Bashir, spiritual leader of the JI, together with Singaporeans arrested under the Internal Security Act (many photos are repeated). The article expresses the resilience of the network and how "it will try to penetrate Singapore again ... as its goals are long term ... terrorists are eminently patient creatures."

tling of now established geopolitical entities, as regional knowledge is crucial to understand the barricading of a space not explicitly deemed vulnerable to terrorist attack. First, I explore the "enduring fiction" of Southeast Asia, placing its coherence within a broader context of colonial and imperial aspiration. I examine the uncanny resemblances between the Cold War and the post-9/11 moment, charting the different ways Southeast Asia has been "produced" as a region since the end of WWII. While parallels can be drawn between constructions of the region as "potentially communist" and "radically Islamic," Washington's war on terrorism is not really a familiar imperial project in the region. Moving away from Anglocentric versions of Southeast Asia, I then consider broader questions about transnational connections and the hybridity of Southeast Asian capitalisms to illuminate recent events. The resurgent vision of a pan-Islamic archipelago represents one political alternative in a region experimenting with Christian, Islamic, and Confucian traditions. Engaging different regional visions helps explain a more complex global juncture, rather than an era over-determined by the Bush doctrine. It also helps illuminate the encounter with terrorism in the region, and the spectres haunting urban spaces.

The enduring fiction of Southeast Asia

The attacks on America on 9/11, and the subsequent war with Afghanistan, ushered in a new era of terrorist threat in Southeast Asia, as elsewhere. Although Southeast Asian nations universally condemned the horror of 9/11, and expressed this conviction by joining the global campaign against terrorism, American suspicions that the region might become the new "theatre" of transnational terrorist activities were pervasive. Surveillance and intelligence activities initially revealed that the JI had been developing military and economic links with Al-Qaeda since the Soviet-Afghan war in the 1980s. Moreover, the JI was alleged to have been planning attacks on American interests in places like Singapore, as well as visioning a pan-Islamic state. Before 9/11, terrorist activities had largely been homegrown, religion-based sectarian conflicts directed towards gaining autonomy or independence. Most of these movements found sustenance in the economic and political marginalization of large segments of the population. The discovery of plans to attack the US embassy and other American interests in Singapore, when combined with the shock of the Bali bombings in Indonesia, suggested that new tactics involving Western interests and civilian casualties were being incorporated into the JI agenda. Furthermore, the JI were not the usual suspects: their members, although small in number, were from the educated middle classes.

The unfolding of world events post-9/11 initiated a renewed American interest in the region, heralded by some as the "second front" in Washington's war on terrorism. The Bush administration sent several hundred troops to the Philippines, softened relations with Malaysia, and some pundits declared Indonesia the next Afghanistan. Southeast Asia is home to the world's most populous Muslim country, Indonesia, the two Muslim-majority states of Malaysia and Brunei, as well as nations, such as Singapore, Thailand, and the Philippines, that have significant Muslim minorities. Although the threat of radical Islam has been evident in Indonesia since President Suharto's fall in 1998, the suggestion of a more wide-ranging peril is difficult to disentangle from America's frenzied response to the tragedy of 9/11. Ethnic and religious diversity, comparatively democratic polities, the lack of pan-regional constituencies for radical Islam, and the JI's own limited ties to other broad-based Islamic groups, have all thwarted the development of a fundamentalist hegemony by any one group in the region (Gershman 2002; Hamilton-Hart 2005). Nevertheless, Southeast Asia emerged in the American geopolitical imagination as a volatile and potentially dangerous Muslim territory in the post-9/11 moment. States such as Singapore, fearing the economic repercussions of not responding to this image, initiated their own anti-terrorist campaigns.

American fears of terrorism, and suspicion of Muslim activities, are reminiscent of the Cold War "domino theory" that led to decades of American involvement in the region. The installation of military bases, the propping up of military dictatorships, and the war in Vietnam were all justified in the name of preventing communism from spreading south, domino style, to nations such as Thailand, Malaysia, and Indonesia. Communist obsessions helped to shape establishment of ASEAN in 1967, for example, which essentially divided up Southeast Asia into "communist" Indochina, "socialist" Burma, and "capitalist" ASEAN nations (Emmerson 1984). The latter, perhaps unsurprisingly, were "beneficiaries" of American military and economic assistance. In any case, Southeast Asia emerged more in relation to Anglo-American power and interests during and after WWII than to some indigenously defined and experienced regionalism. The region, produced through economic and military activities, was made all the more real and legitimized through area studies research that undertook projects on cultures, economies, and politics in largely national terms.

As the communist threat subsided there was a drastic change in the way the US engaged with nations in the region. American policies shifted from "compulsory" to "selective" engagement, and interests shifted to sites that were more consistent with neo-liberal economic development (cf. Bishop et al. 2003: 26). Aid and investment became more linked to mutually beneficial economic arrangements, and the American military bases in the Philippines withdrew. Tiger economies, with their networked nodes of capital, production, and labour, garnered much more attention than the fledgling economies of countries such as Cambodia, which lapsed into civil war. But the 1990s also saw ASEAN accept Vietnam, Cambodia, Laos, and Myanmar as members, and over the past decade have placed emphasis on regional economic and political cooperation both in the region and beyond. In a post-Cold War Southeast Asia that has grown more confident about East Asian futures, it would be difficult for America's desire to contain radical Islam to be realized in ways commensurate to its Cold War dominance. Although economic and military cooperation remain important to countries such as Singapore and the Philippines, and Southeast Asian nations do aim to present themselves as responding to the threat of terrorism for economic gain, reducing these examples to exemplify American hegemony in Southeast Asia is to downplay the sovereignty of local agendas and politics. It also serves to equate America's dominance in one arena with dominance in all spheres.

It is difficult to point to the limits of thinking in terms of American dominance in Southeast Asia without feeling somewhat uncomfortable. America's aggression in the Middle East seems to have revived the terminology of "imperialism" and "empire," and some suggest that recent events mark a moment in the re-territorialization of a dominant American capitalism (Smith 2001). Prior to 9/11 Southeast Asian nations would have more easily been depicted as negotiating relations with the US in a post-imperial, globalist world composed of more than one centre of power, and where events in Beijing, Tokyo, and Singapore were just as significant as those in Washington. Multilateral organizations such as APEC, transnational business networks, and the growth in intra-Asian cultural and intellectual traffic could have been marshalled to provide evidence of this claim. Since 9/11, however, states in the region have been anxiously looking at America in anticipation of an altered geopolitical map. Arrests have been made, trials are underway, and public protest has been carefully managed. Yet an emphasis on American dominance fails to appreciate the more subtle meanings that permeate a range of embedded scales—from urban spaces to the nation-state and region.

Re-mapping the Southeast Asian archipelago

It is with these ideas in mind that I return to different conceptions of Southeast Asia, ones that foreground different histories and imperatives, and place urban spaces within historical contexts that help explain Singapore's encounter with terrorism. This approach articulates the radical questioning of the ways area studies can now be conceived, given a range of critiques that have exposed the complicity of area studies with colonial, imperial, military, economic, or other ideological interests. Willem van Schendel (2002), for example, stresses the limits to understanding Southeast Asia as a meaningful term, as this presupposes stable and bounded states. His invented region of Zomia, formed at the convergence of Central, South, East, and Southeast Asia, did not make the world geopolitical map after WWII "because it lacked strong centres of state formation, was politically ambiguous, and did not command political clout" (2002: 647). Knowledge about the region thus fell into decline, creating geographies of ignorance. Van Schendel argues that attention to borderlands can be used to reinvigorate area studies, and to "imagine other spatial configurations, such as cross-cutting areas, the worldwide honeycomb of borderlands, or the process geographies of transnational flows" (2002: 647). In other words, different geographical networks that combine political, economic, and cultural flows that fall outside bounded nation-states offer new ways to imagine "areas." The resurgent vision of a pan-Islamic archipelago is one cross-cutting configuration.

Although reports of the history of the JI offer a variety of perspectives, it is generally alleged that the roots of the organization can be traced back to Darul Islam struggles against Dutch colonial rule in the 1940s (Republic of Singapore 2003, International Crisis Group 2002a, 2002b; Desker 2003). The Darul Islam itself was preceded by various tumultuous periods in Indonesian history, and anterior intellectual movements that had likewise struggled with ideas of Islamic nationhood (Laffan 2002). After Indonesia gained independence in 1949, the Darul Islam continued the struggle for the establishment of an Islamic state, staging a number of rebellions in the 1950s. In the 1970s and 1980s, the grouping gained new membership and became known as the JI. In the late 1970s, the Iranian Revolution and the availability of Indonesian translations of Middle Eastern writings on political Islam were stimulating unrest. In the 1980s, some JI members travelled to Afghanistan to solicit financial support for their activities and to acquire new tactics to fight the Indonesian state. An inner core of the network—including its spiritual leader Abu Bakar Bashir—also fled to Malaysia in the mid-1980s to avoid arrest by Suharto's secular dictatorship. This latter group did not return to Indonesia until the fall of the regime in 1998, but in exile had formed networks with Malaysians that are now portrayed as aiding in the planning attacks on targets in Singapore.

This condensed history highlights the problems with assuming that Southeast Asia can be framed in a linear trajectory that details its various engagements with colonialism, postcolonialism, the Cold War, and post-Cold War neoliberalism. It is precisely this narrative that constructs Southeast Asia as a region, making the war on terrorism difficult to understand locally, as it does not contextualize historical links to the Middle East—links that have been ongoing for centuries and are responsible for bringing Islam to the region—nor does it explain cross-cutting relations across the archipelago that existed prior to, within, and beyond the colonial period. While analyses of terrorism do scrutinize these connections, they are not historicized and/or are represented in the essentialist language of "terrorist cells." In so doing, these representations are able to eschew "significant challenges to the political and intellectual hegemonies of the West [...] located in the Middle and Far East" (Chan/Mandaville 2003: 3). Foregrounding these connections, and placing them within a context of a volatile geopolitical order, raises different questions about terrorism and its relation to Islamic movements.

As Southeast Asian nations struggle to find an identity and place in a postcolonial, post-Cold War globalist order, there are few examples of Islamic states that have brought peace and prosperity to their populations. It is thus important to place recent regional tensions within a context of the success of those nations that have developed and adopted Confucian capitalism, such as Singapore, reformulating prior models of economic development in hybrid ways that combine capital with the nation-state within a general framework of Asian values. Moreover, in a world guided by Christian and Confucian capitalist modernities, Muslim Southeast Asia has proposed "moderate Islam," a secular state embracing and inculcating Muslim values. This was most developed in Malaysia under Prime Minister Mahathir's leadership, and can be placed within the broader project of re-imagining how Islam's declined civilization might be reconstructed. Indeed, the war on terror might do well to consider enriching concepts and values from Islam, and how they might be inserted into discourses of modernity and globalization. Rather than place Southeast Asia within narratives that stress American imperialism, or conceive the region's connections to the Middle East in essentialist terms, perhaps it is more useful to contemplate the issues raised by the hybridity of postcolonial Southeast Asian modernities—a hybridity challenged by radical Islam.

Postcolonial hauntings

Understanding fears in public spaces in Singapore, especially those not specifically besieged by terrorist attack, requires nuanced accounts of how urban spaces are being remapped in the contemporary moment. For it is the potential redrawing of national boundaries that creates apprehension in places like Holland Village, raising uncertainties concerning belonging/not-belonging in postcolonial Singapore, or the region more generally. It is this instability that troubles both the state and public, and fragmentation in countries such as Indonesia, Thailand, and the Philippines only helps to shape a sense of unease. Traces of prior urban conflicts such as the bombs and riots of the 1960s, make these fears palpable. Add to this the application of Cold War government legislation—such as Internal Security and Sedition Acts—and the creation of post-9/11 policies to foster "racial harmony," and we witness an uncanny era of Singapore's history. It is an unstable moment that problematizes geopolitical "order," but is not reducible to Washington's "war on terror." It is the return of the ghostly past, with its militant geography, that produces trepidation in the streets.

Recent events in the Middle East have inspired a host of urban conflicts around the globe. Whether these debates are about Muslim dress in public spaces in Europe, the profiling of Muslim men in US cities, or the fortification of Singapore's expatriate enclaves, the colonial epoch has returned to haunt the present in a manner not witnessed since decolonization in the 1950s. Theorizing conflict in these spaces is not a simple task, as it entails understanding the multiple scales within which urban spaces are embedded, and the complex historical dynamics shaping conflict. As the example of Singapore shows, urban conflicts summon layers of historical divisions, connections, and affiliations that do not always include Washington at its geopolitical centre (although events in America are important). Decentring dominant narratives of "terrorism" enables a remapping of the politics of terror, taking into consideration other critical geographies and histories that profoundly shape urban tensions.

References

Bishop, Ryan/Phillips, John/Yeo, Wei Wei (2003) *Postcolonial Urbanism: Southeast Asian Cities and Global Processes*, Routledge: New York.

Chan, Steven/Mandaville, Peter (2001) "Introduction". In Steven Chan/Peter Mandaville/Roland Bleiker (eds.) *The Zen of International Relations*, London: Palgrave Macmillan, pp.1–14.

Chang, Tou Chuang (1995) "The 'Expatriation' of Holland Village". In Brenda S.A. Yeoh/Lily Kong (eds.) *Portraits of Places: History, Community and Identity in Singapore*, Singapore: Times Editions.

Davis, Mike (2001) "The Flames of New York". New Left Review 12, pp. 34–50.

Desker, Barry (2003) "Islam in Southeast Asia: The Challenge of Radical Interpretation". Cambridge Review of International Affairs 16/3, pp. 415–28.

Emmerson, Donald (1984) "Southeast Asia: What's in a Name?". Journal of Southeast Asian Studies 15/1, pp. 1–21.

Freud, Sigmund (1919) "The 'Uncanny'". In *The Standard Edition of the Complete Psychological Works of Sigmund Freud*, 24 vols., Hogarth Press: London, pp.217–252.

Gelder, Ken/Jacobs, Jane M. (1998) *Uncanny Australia: Sacredness and Identity in a Postcolonial Nation*, Melbourne University Press: Melbourne.

Gershman, John (2002) "Is Southeast Asia the Second Front?" Foreign Affairs 81/4, pp. 60–68.

Goh, Chok Tong (2002) "Opening remarks". Dialogue with Community Leaders on the Arrest of the Second Group of Jemaah Islamiyah Members, Ministry of Home Affairs, Singapore (available at http://www2.mha.gov.sg/mha/).

Gordon, Avery (1997) *Ghostly Matters: Haunting and the Sociological Imagination*, Minneapolis and London: University of Minnesota Press.

Hamilton-Hart, Natasha (2005) "Terrorism in Southeast Asia: Expert Analysis, Myopia and Fantasy". The Pacific Review 18/3, pp. 303–325.

International Crisis Group (2002a) "How the Jemaah Islamiyah Terrorist Network Operates". Indonesia Backgrounder, Asia Report 43, Jakarta/Brussels.

International Crisis Group (2002b) "Al-Qaeda in Southeast Asia: The Case of the 'Ngruki Network' in Indonesia". Indonesia Briefing, Jakarta/Brussels.

Laffan, Michael Francis (2002) *Islamic Nationhood and Colonial Indonesia: The Umma Below the Winds*, London: Routledge-Curzon.

Miksic, John N./Low Mei Gek, Cheryl-Ann. (2004) *Early Singapore: 1300s-1819*, Singapore: Singapore History Museum.

National Security Coordination Centre (2004) "The Fight Against Terror: Singapore's National Security Strategy". Singapore: MINDEF.

Republic of Singapore (2003) "White Paper on the Jemaah Islamiyah and the Threat of Terrorism". Ministry of Home Affairs, 7 January.

Sa'at, Alfian Bin (2002) "The Racist's Apology". Forum on Contemporary Art and Society (FOCAS) 4. pp. 385–393.

Smith, Neil (2001) "Scales of Terror and the Resort to Geography: 9/11, October 7". Editorial, Environment and Planning D: Society and Space 19, pp. 631–637.

Van Schendel, Willem (2002) "Geographies of Knowing, Geographies of Ignorance: Jumping Scale in Southeast Asia". Environment and Planning D: Society and Space 20, pp. 647–668.

Wee, C.J. Wan-Ling (1999) "'Asian values,' Singapore and the Third Way: Re-working Individualism and Collectivism". Sojourn 14/2, pp. 332–58.

Cultural Homogenisation, Places of Memory, and the Loss of Secular Urban Space

ANIL BHATTI

Postcolonial India's myth of secularism assumed that the planned evolution of the good society would be accompanied by the gradual marginalisation of contradictions between religions, languages, and cultural specificities. Bombay became symptomatic of this myth in film and folklore. Against this background, cultural homogenisation and identity-based politics occupy places of memory and heritage sites leading to the contestation of heterogeneous and homogeneous views of culture.

I

Conflict and violence have become an integral part of the city in India. Instead of becoming an urban space of liberation, the postcolonial city is the locus of disaster. Whether it is the hopelessly inadequate infrastructure, the slums, or the social tensions and communal violence, the city has become a patched-over space of catastrophe. There is a historical background to this. Much of the social tension in Indian cities today derives from the contradiction between a secular inclusivist idea of India and an exclusivist version of the homogeneous social order. The Bombay film, ever sensitive to the social mood suitable for its success, was responsible for reflecting these themes in the troubled history of the sub-continent from Independence and Partition in 1947, through the dictatorial Emergency in 1975, the Bombay textile strike and the rise of a fundamentalist right wing after the 1980s, the destruction of the Babri Masjid in 1992, and the Bombay riots of 1992-93. It may therefore be helpful to begin by referring to *the* Indian City, namely Bombay, its favoured artistic genre, the film, and its relationship to the project of constructing a secular postcolonial India against other restricted versions of the postcolonial order.[1]

In the 1950s the popular Hindi film from Bombay had started disseminating what might be called the secular, international, and yet quintessentially Indian, vision of post-independence India associated with India's first Prime Minister, Jawaharlal Nehru (cf. Nehru 1999; Khilnani 1997; Chatterjee 1998; Kapur/Rajadhyaksha 2001; Kaarsholm 2004; Patnaik 2003; Kaarsholm 2002). This helped to sublimate embarrassing questions of caste/class and make them bearable through the aesthetics of popular social drama and comedy.

Raj Kapoor's film *Shri 420* (*Mr. 420*, 1955) became paradigmatic for this view, and its famous, often quoted song, written by Shailendra and Hasrat Jaipuri, sums up this post-independence mood of Nehruvian secularism:

Mera juta hai japani/yeh patloon englistani
Sar peh laal topi roosi/phir bhi dil hai hindustani
(My shoe is Japani (Japanese)/these pants are Englistani (English)
The red cap on my head is Russi (Russian)/yet my heart is Hindustani (Indian))

These lines may well be read as an early example of complex cultural encoding and a comfortable affirmation of multiple identities in pluricultural societies before the postcolonial discussion popularised the term (cf. Csáky/Kury/Tragatschnig 2004). But the main theme of *Shri 420*, which was scripted by Khwaja Ahmed Abbas, is the loss of secular innocence through capitalist corruption. The number 420 in Raj Kapoor's film refers to the paragraph concerning cheating in the Indian penal code. The hero of the film, appropriately and allegorically named Raj,[2] succumbs to the lure of money and becomes a cheat, someone who can be booked under section 420 of the Indian Penal code, and this is significant for it consolidates Bombay's reputation as the richest and most corrupt of Indian cities, a perpetual threat to innocence and honesty. It is the perennial capitalist Other to the ideals of austerity, honesty, self-sacrifice, and service inherent in the freedom struggle. Raj, the hapless victim of avarice, appropriately pawns the honesty medal, which had been his only prize possession before he was appropriated by the world of money. He is, in a sense, a victim of money, modernity, and the metropolis, which classic writings on the city have emphasized (cf. Simmel 1958; Müller 1988: 18). But it is important to emphasize that the opposition to the Bad City is not some village idyll. The symbolic overdetermination in the film makes this clear. Raj himself is an educated migrant with a B.A. degree. His journey to Bombay in

---

1 Cf. the contributions in Patel, Sujata/Thorner, Alice (1996), and Kaarsholm (2002) for further literature on the theme of Bombay/Mumbai.
2 Raj Kapoor's first name "Raj" also means "rule." It also is synonymous with the British Raj or "rule."

search for work starts from the north Indian city of Allahabad, which was Nehru's birthplace. We see that, among other things, this film is also about the struggle between rapacious finance and secular idealism for the soul of independent India.

All this was, however, in the realm of popular social drama and comedy, which also made it bearable for large audiences. The Bombay film (irreverently called Bollywood today) had in its repertoire a sufficiently entertaining view of colonial/postcolonial/modern/postmodern Bombay. *Bombay meri jaan*, Majrooh Sultanpuri's song from the film *C.I.D.* (1954), sung against a background of Bombay's Victorian architecture echoed the ludic irreverence of the age of entertainment.

Aay dil hai mushkil jeena yahan,
Zara hattke, zara bachke,
Yeh hai Bombay meri jaan...
(O heart, its tough living here
Watch out, move aside this is Bombay my dear...)

"Jaan" literally means life and "meri jaan," which for the sake of an elusive rhyme I have rendered as "my dear," is a term of endearment common in northern India, which puns on Life and Love. Meri jaan is my life/love (cf. Pinto/Fernandes 2003; Kaviraj 2004). Bombay as a lifeline is also the love in which the vagabond is irrevocably implicated.

The combination of innocence abroad and streetwise behaviour became part of the filmic formula in the Bombay idiom. In a complex urban world the good ultimately did triumph so that a nascent nation had sufficient ground to believe in a tolerable and tolerant road towards non-aligned, third-world self-sufficiency, self-reliance, and industrial modernity with retention of flexible cultural moorings. In those days, one could indeed be pan-Indian and international.

This mood will be replaced by the emergence of a confident globalised Indian diaspora after the 1990s, which then need not enact internationalism on Indian soil but can look upon the world as its stage, which seems only to exist together with its icons Michael Jackson and Elvis Presley in order to bring out India and its film stars' celluloid uniqueness more effectively:

London dekha, Paris dekha, aur dekha Japan
Michael dekha, Elvis dekha, doosara nahin Hindustan
Eh duniya hai dulhan, dulhan ke maathey ki bindia
I love my India
(London seen, Paris seen, and also Japan
Michael seen, Elvis seen, nothing like Hindustan
The world is a bride, the bride has a bindia 9 [dot] on the forehead
I love my India) (Ray 2004: 173).

This is from a 1998 film, *Pardes* (*Abroad*). The itinerary of tourism is ticked off, as it were to reaffirm the smug self of a comfortably globalised indigenous urban bourgeoisie using English naturally to convey patriotic sentiments to the world without seeming odd now, because urban India uses such markers as signs of its urban multilingual semiotics. This is already a far cry from the romantic Raj who is recognisably part of a politically defined postcolonial world order in which India is placed as a perhaps poor but honourable participant. Ultimately this phase did not last for long, and appropriately the collapse of the Nehruvian Age of Innocence and the transition to the globalised age of dependency is summed up with the seismic sensitivity of the Bombay film by another film lyric which clearly alludes, in a parodistic manner, to the song from Raj Kapoor's *Shri 420*:

Aslam Bhai ...
Dubai ka Chashma, Cheen ki Chaddi, aur Irani Chai...
(Brother Aslam...
Spectacles from Dubai, Underwear from China, Irani tea....)

The movement from Raj's song to Aslam Bhai's song[3] is the movement from secular internationalism to rapacious globalisation. Spectacles from Dubai, underwear from China replace the Chaplinesque garb worn by Raj. The tea will be Indian, but served to Brother Aslam, a self-confident, streetwise Muslim denizen of globalised urban Bombay where drinking tea (chai) in one of Bombay's cafes run by members of the Irani community signals urban living. The Muslim innuendo is of course intended to refer to fundamentalism, the involvement of the Bombay film world with a mafia underworld controlled from the Gulf, and so on ("Never get involved with the mafia" is a line in the song). But more significantly, the demarcation of religious communities and marking them out of a secular totality becomes apparent through this song. Retrospectively, the Muslim tag reminds us that Raj is a Hindu name and Raj's song from *Shri 420*, which was supposedly pan-Indian now suddenly seems revealed as the fragile secular construct that it clearly was.

What concerns us here is the locale of the city as the place (*Ort, lieu*) of the secular dream and its loss and destruction (Prakash 2002: 2). For one thing, the foil to Bombay is not necessarily the idyllic village. The inability of the innocent migrant worker to live up to ideals is not necessarily linked with some myth of a village arcadia versus a brutal and anonymous city. The first encounter scene between the migrant and the city does of course lead to bewilderment and disorientation, but the genre sees to it that the hero gets to know the code very soon. In any case, the vision of India did not necessarily

---

3 From the film *Love ke liye kuch bhi karega* (2001). The website www.raaga.com is a useful source for information on Bombay film.

oppose the village to the city as substantive categories or life worlds, as there was usually enough feudal oppression in the village community to escape from. The myth of Bombay as the city of migrants and as "a heterogeneous mix of races, religions, and linguistic groups" (Singh 2003: 24), was always also coupled with problems of survival within the context of the uneven development in Indian industrial development and economy (cf. Acharya 2002).

But perhaps Bombay's main fascination lay in the fact that it was different. It did not carry the weight of cultural tradition like Calcutta; nor did it labour to live up to myths of Imperial grandeur like India's perennial political capital Delhi. Bombay was unabashedly the commercial capital of India, and by accepting the anonymous quality of money as the universal general equivalent of all values, Bombay too became the place where the tensions in the two competing visions of India could be played out the secular and the fundamentalist.[4]

II

Some of the above remarks may become clearer if we look at the international level, where we are witnessing social transformations that are characterised by two moments. Relatively homogeneous societies are developing into more complex social formations. On the other hand, existing complex societies are being subjected to tensions that seem to announce their break up (cf. Bhatti 2005).

The process of European integration may be looked upon as an example of the first type of transformation process. Large-scale migrations and globalising processes are leading to long-term societal transformations and relatively monolingual and homogeneous societies are opening up to the possibilities (both good and bad) of greater pluralism. On the other hand, in a counter process, traditionally pluricultural[5] countries like India, which seemed to have muddled through to an uneasy systemic balance exemplified by the slogan of "unity in diversity" characteristic of Nehruvian secularism and pluriculturalism, are now increasingly being subjected to fundamentalist pres-

---

4 The writer Sa'adat Hasan Manto, who lived and worked in the Bombay film world for twelve years and migrated to Pakistan after the Partition of India in 1947, was perhaps expressing this when he wrote: "That strip of land which is Bombay had taken me, a footloose young man rejected by his family, into its vast lap and said to me, 'You can be happy here on two pennies a day or on hundreds of thousands of rupees... Here you can do what you like; no one will speak ill of you. And no one will tell you what to do or moralize to you'" (Manto 2001: 17).
5 I use the term "pluriculturalism" rather than "multiculturalism," which can encourage rigid demarcations.

sures, which would logically lead to more rigid forms of homogeneous organization of socio-cultural and political units. In this context, we could remember the historical paradigm of the collapse of the Habsburg Empire. The end of Yugoslavia would be a more drastic contemporary reminder of this second type of process.

As a result of a questionable extrapolation of the European process of nation formation in the 18th and 19th centuries, fundamentalist thought today favours organisations that are as homogeneous as possible with regard to language, ethnicity, and religion. This in itself is not the explosive point. What is important is the assumption that this is the "natural" form of organisation of nation states. The concept of minorities results from this. And thereafter the negotiation of minority rights (civil rights, religious rights) is established.

It is worth remembering that Johann Gottfried Herder, in his seminal *Ideas on the Philosophy of the History of Humanity* (1784), assumed that drastic migrations and intermingling of peoples had characterised the pre-history of Europe, and without this process of amalgamation the "General Spirit of Europe" (*Allgemeingeist Europa's*) could hardly have been awakened (Herder 1989: 705). But the whole point of Herder's thought was then to go on to affirm that the historical retention of this diversity would be unnatural, and therefore wrong. Diversity for him becomes the pre-condition for homogenisation in both temporal as well as categorical terms. Assimilation and amalgamation are therefore the necessary and natural part of the pre-history of a historical process leading to increasing orders of complexity. But this is precisely why organisational solutions have to be found to deal with this process as one enters the modern age. In Herder's thought the most natural social order would be one that corresponds to a divine plan of nature. Since nature produces families in order to ensure the survival of the species, the most natural order was that of an organic family. Since the modern nation was to mirror this order, the most natural state would be an organic state in which one Volk with one national character would exist. It is this perspective that also leads to Herder's anti colonialism and his espousal of cultural mixing. Because colonialism led to an un-natural expansion of states and an unnatural and "wild" intermingling of the human species and nations under one sceptre, colonialism in Herder's eyes was, in the modern era, against the plan of nature. If there is such a thing as an enlightened and liberal philosophy of segregation, Herder's thought would lead to it. Multiculturalism as distinct from pluriculturalism (cf. Bhargava 1998; Chatterjee 1998; Thapar 2000) seems to me essentially to go back to this principle of liberal and distancing segregation. I need not point out here how fraught with problems multiculturalist perspectives are and how vulnerable they are to a distortion through notions of racial hegemony and ghettoisation, especially against the background of our contemporary experience.

It is against the background of the ideology of natural order that we can understand the nineteenth-century colonial drive towards classification and schematization in order to achieve something like a "colonial competence" (similar to a linguistic competence) in order to be able to control the material world now so suddenly at the disposal of the colonial powers.

The model that dominates seeks to proceed from chaos to order. Complexity is viewed as chaos that does not admit of administrative regulation. India's complexity for instance was viewed by colonialism as a chaos that required domestication. It was domesticated under colonialism by an extraordinary development of classificatory and taxonomic energy (cf. Cohn 1985). In learning to speak as a colonial power and developing a colonial competence, the systematic codification of modern Indian language practices was necessary. Since language and translation are important instruments of power, a certain type of language ideology developed that ignored overlapping and real forms of communication in favour of abstract linguistic classification mixed up with religion. A colonial bureaucratic order destroyed pluralities of social communication and replaced it with lexicographic classification. Languages as classified systems became autonomous and therefore negotiable among classes and communities of people who claimed to represent them. It then became part of the self-interest of the representatives of the new classified order and its beneficiaries to sustain the autocratically imposed system of classification and impart to it the status of being real and natural. In principle this holds good for the classification of the caste systems and the generation of subsystems of caste too.

III

Sa'adat Hasan Manto's short story *Toba Tek Singh* (1955), which, like the film *Shri 420*, has become a foundational text for the contemporary discourse on the beleaguered state of Indian secularism, would be pertinent here (Manto 1993; Ravikant/Saint 2001). The story has the bleak simplicity and logic of a Kafkaesque parable. Manto takes the problem to where it belongs, namely to the realm of madness: A few years after the Partition of the Indian subcontinent (1947) it occurs to the governments of India and Pakistan to complete the exchange of populations based on religious criteria by also exchanging the inmates of lunatic asylums. Insane Muslims remain in Pakistan and insane Hindu and Sikh inmates go to India. The logic of Partition dictated this (Hasan 2000). Accordingly, the inmates of the asylum in Lahore (Pakistan) are slated for exchange. One of the inmates, the Sikh Bishan Singh from the Punjabi town Toba Tek Singh, has been standing on his feet for fifteen years in the Asylum, speaking only in a gibberish constructed out of the three languages of Punjab's continuum of linguistic communication: Hindustani (Hindi-Urdu), Punjabi, and English. He refuses to be deported, and, after standing on his feet for fifteen years, collapses in the no-man's-land between the barbed wires of India and Pakistan, the creation of which he has cursed in his own private language, his own gibberish. The piece of land he collapses on becomes, in Manto's story, the surrealistic fusion of the man Bishan Singh and his home Toba Tek Singh. The piece of land between two barbed wires becomes the geographical placement of this town and the ultimate home of the man, thus negating the logic of Partition and the creation of hard arbitrary boundaries cutting across systems of cultural praxis.

Bhishan Singh's act of resistance can be seen as an act of resistance against Partition, seen as the final outcome of a complex colonial process, which, among other things, led to the destruction and reconfiguration of a pluricultural sphere of communication in North India (cf. Bayly 1996; Rai 2001). This public sphere was by no means a utopian, pacified area. It had its own system of power, repression, and domination. But, as result of a non-hermeneutic emphasis on praxis rather than on the hermeneutic strategy of creating difference in order to understand it, this public sphere functioned in many ways as an "ecumene" cutting across hard boundaries. Colonialism changed the configuration of the system of power and domination, of course, and privileged identities that could form coalitions of power through negotiation; or they could exterminate each other.

IV

Fundamentalism in India has inherited this drive from colonialism. Today, India's complexity is threatened by the fundamentalist ideological drive towards religious homogeneity. Fundamentalisms seeks to replace the pluralist praxis of Hinduism, which has many diverse forms, by creating a monolithical block, which then marginalises or patronises other religions in India like Islam or Christianity by stamping them as foreign and therefore implying that they are unauthentic. In the invidious logic of this "therefore" lies the threat to a secular India, which means a threat to its pluralistic form of loose diversity. In a sense, what we are witnessing is the replacement of historically evolved diversity by the ideologically posited naturalness (*Naturwüchsigkeit*) of monochromatic forms. The logic of homogenisation was perhaps propounded most succinctly by Carl Schmitt, whose influential study of constitutional law—*Verfassungslehre* (1928)—treats homogeneity of the *Volk* (not of humanity) as the basis for the relationship between ruler and ruled (Schmitt 1965: 229f.). The ground for homogenisation may vary, and race, colour, and religion are the usual candidates, but homogenisation establishes substantial equality as the basic precondition of Schmitt's conception of democracy, which was influential in formulating the ideology of the fascist German state. It also forms the basis for the distinction between clearly marked and defined systems of "friend" and "enemy" in Schmitt's political philosophy. Fundamentalisms today have inherited this dubious legacy of inclusion and exclusion.

As against the ideology of the "natural," homogenised order, the consciously secular postcolonial state dispenses with its legitimatization through the appeal to any transcendental "natural" order. Secularism is a conscious utopian construct. It is a fuzzy, diffuse notion, an ideal projected towards the future as against the hard contours of right-wing ideology based on resentments derived from interpretations of the past. Secularism dispenses with the tribal principle that bonds through race, religion, and language, which explains its "vulnerability" and its fragility. It is highly dependent on the success of modern democratic institutions functioning in an intact manner. It is the political way of dealing with and sustaining pluriculturalism. This also marks the attempt to construct a pluriculturalist society of choice (*Gesellschaft*) as against a community (*Gemeinschaft*) defined by religious bonding, to use a distinction made in 1887 by the sociologist Tönnies (Tönnies 1991). Secularism is a project of the postcolonial Indian state, which is directed against linear processes of religious homogenisation.

Jawaharlal Nehru tried to capture the linguistic and cultural complexity of India, its diversity, and unity by using the image of a palimpsest that negates the essentialisation imposed by authenticity and origins. As he wrote, while in jail from 1942-45 during the Freedom Struggle, India seemed to him to be an

ancient palimpsest on which layer upon layer of thought and reverie had been inscribed, and yet no succeeding layer had completely hidden or erased what had been written previously. All of these exist together in our conscious or subconscious selves, though we may not be aware of them, and they had gone to build up the complex and mysterious personality of India (Nehru 1999: 59).

This image of the palimpsest, which Victor Hugo also used for Europe (Lützeler 1982: 442), is admittedly idealistic, but it corresponds in many ways with the notion of the simultaneity of non-synchronous worlds in any historical formation (*Gleichzeitigkeit des Ungleichzeitigen*) that Ernst Bloch formulated in the context of his study of fascism (Bloch 1979). The validity of a palimpsest lies in its totality and not in any particular layer, for the layering can be seen as a form of enrichment that leads to the dominance of the multiple. Any attempt to ascribe authenticity to any particular layer or to some mythical *Urtext* of culture or history leads to an impoverishment because it destroys the totality of the process of inscription and the simultaneity of the latent presence of its multiple layers. Homogenisation is a form of cultural appropriation that seeks to give exclusive authenticity to a particular layer or section of a cultural palimpsest. Strictly speaking, however, the *Urtext* of a palimpsest would be a blank surface. The drive towards authenticity in a pluralistic society is a drive towards a *tabula rasa*, an obliteration of complexity. The destruction inherent in our contemporary wars is this obsession with the power of erasure.

But if we continue to use Nehru's idealistic perspective in an affirmative manner today without looking at the erosion of Indian pluralism through the rise of fundamentalisms, we lose sight of the utopian content of the ideal of the palimpsest. Salman Rushdie's novel *The Moor's last Sigh,* which is also an allegory of India and its iconic city Bombay, therefore withdraws Nehru's liberal vision and varies the aporetic possibilities of the figure of the palimpsest by resituating it negatively. Contemporary Bombay's contradictions lie now in the contradictions between a fictive appearance and a phantom-like reality, and this is perhaps true of the whole of India. In the novel, the protagonist, Moor, can comprehend the corrupt soul of his father, Abraham Zogoiby, only through a negative interpretation of the palimpsest of the city, now corrupted by the interwoven worlds of politics, crime and money, and communal violence. India and the city have become a grotesque palimpsest and a parody of cultural complexity:

> The City itself, perhaps the whole country, was a palimpsest, Under World beneath Over World, black market beneath white; when the whole of life was like this, when an invisible reality moved phantomwise beneath a visible fiction, subverting all its meanings, how then could Abraham's career have been any different? How could any of us have escaped that deadly layering? How, trapped as we were in the hundred per cent fakery of the real, in the fancy-dress, weeping-Arab kitsch of the superficial, could we have penetrated to the full, sensual truth of the lost mother below? How could we have lived authentic lives? How could we have failed to be grotesque? (Rushdie 1996: 184f.).

In the novel, the recovery of the utopian dimensions of a palimpsestic India is no longer possible through the politics of the present, and thus is located in artistic praxis. Moor's mother, Aurora Zogoiby's ironic project of painting pictures fuses the memory of the destruction of Europe's pluriculturalist potentials in the Spain of 1492 with independent India's potentials in 1947. The fusion of these two potentials seeks to *reconstruct* a heterogeneous, pluralistic India threatened by the forces of homogenisation. And this Utopia of reconstructed heterogeneity could then be called "Mooristan" or "Palimpstine" (Rushdie 1996: 226).

In Rushdie's novel, Palimpstine can be realised only as a dying vision. This is a realistic perspective because the destruction of palimpsestic perspective is the bleak reality of India's recent history. I conclude by referring to the monopolisation of tradition through fundamentalism. In the North Indian city of Ayodhya, birth place of Lord Ram, there is a mosque ascribed to the Mogul emperor Babur (15th century). The Babri Masjid, as it is called, has supposedly been erected on Hindu temple foundations devoted to Lord Ram. Hindu fundamentalist destroyed the mosque in 1992. If we adhere to the idea of a palimpsest, then it is in no way surprising that one religious monument should stand on the foundations of an older and different religious monument. This is part of the bloody history of the sub continent that we have inherited as a shared, historical, pluricultural result (Noorani 2003).

V

If we say that the goal of the secular project was the establishment of a complex modern society as against the counter project of a single religious community, we reiterate the difference between heterogeneity and homogeneity. The identification and occupation of places of memory and its monopolisation destroys the complexity of the palimpsest. The destruction of the mosque was in fact the drive to create a blank *Urtext* as *tabula rasa*. Places of memory become contested sites for violent appropriations of the past. The destruction of the mosque by Hindu fundamentalists in December 1992 led to widespread communal violence between Hindus and Muslims in India. Inventing the myth of origins seeks to destroy the palimpsest of culture and to replace the multi-layered nature of monuments and sites of memory in a city with uni-dimensional points of reference to a *single* past, to a single fundamentalist urban space.

The following illustrations remind us in their stark unambiguity of this turning point in India's contemporary history:

Figure 1: The Babri Masjid as it was before December 1992
(Photo: © Shaid Khan http://en.wikipedia.org/wiki/Babri_Mosque,

Figure 2: Storming the mosque
(Photo: © http://www.islam-online.net, http://en.wikipedia.org/wiki/Babri_Mosque)

Figure 3: The result of destruction
(Photo: © http://www.islam-online.net, http://en.wikipedia.org/wiki/Babri_Mosque)

What remains after stone and rubble? A reference to another work of art may serve as a tentative conclusion. In *Speaking Stones*, an installation by the artist N. M. Rimzon,

Figure 4: Speaking Stones; N. M. Rimzon (Photo: © N.M. Rimzon)

we see the figure of a mourner crouching within a circle of stone fragments that hold down photographs of India's history of communal violence, which, invoked in this manner, become testimony to the history of violence and our "responsibility to grieve" (Kapur 2003: 59).

We have here an instance of how the labour and work of mourning and grieving (*Trauerarbeit*) lead to what one may, following Peter Weiss, call the *Aesthetics of Resistance* (Weiss 1975-81), which has emerged out of India's troubled trajectory from secular visions to violent struggles over the control of the memory of the past. Combined with mass movements for the renewal of secular politics, this has the potential to restate the projects in favour of cultural complexity in contemporary India and its beleaguered cities.

References

Acharya, Swati (2002) *Mapping of M(B)umbai: Metamorphosis of a Metropolis – Urbanisation and Indian Popular Cinema*, Unpublished Manuscript.

Bayly, Christopher Allan (1996) *Empire and Information. Intelligence gathering and social communication in India, 1780-1870*, Cambridge: Cambridge University Press

Bhargava, Rajeev (ed., 1998) *Secularism and its Critics*, New Delhi: Oxford University Press.

Bhatti, Anil (2005) "Der koloniale Diskurs und Orte des Gedächtnisses." In Moritz Csáky/Monika Sommer (eds.) *Kulturerbe als soziokulturelle Praxis*, Innsbruck.

Bloch, Ernst (1979) *Erbschaft unserer Zeit*, Frankfurt am Main: Suhrkamp.

Chatterjee, Partha (1998) *Wages of Freedom. Fifty Years of the Indian Nation-State*, Delhi: Oxford University Press.

Csáky, Moritz/Kury, Astrid/Tragatschnig, Ulrich (eds., 2004) *Kultur-Identität-Differenz. Wien und Zentraleuropa in der Moderne*, Innsbruck/Wien/München/Bozen: Studien Verlag.

Cohn, Bernhard S. (1985) "The Command of Language and the Language of Command". In Ranajit Guha (ed.) *Subaltern Studies IV*, Delhi: Oxford University Press, pp. 276-329.

Herder, Johann Gottfried (1989) *Ideen zur Philosophie der Geschichte der Menschheit*, Frankfurt a.M.: Deutscher Klassiker Verlag.

Kaarsholm, Preben (ed., 2002) *The Cities of Everyday Life. The Sarai Reader 2*, Delhi: Sarai.

Kaarsholm, Preben (ed., 2004) *City Flicks. Indian Cinema and the Urban Experience*, Calcutta and New Delhi: Seagull Books.

Kapur, Geeta/Rajadhyaksha, Ashish (2001) "Bombay/Mumbai 1992-2001". In Iwon Blazwick (ed.) *Century City,* London: Tate Publications, pp. 16-41.

Kapur, Geeta (2003) "subTerrain: artists dig the contemporary". In *body. city. sitting contemporary culture in India,* Delhi: Tullika, pp. 46-83.

Kaviraj, Sudipto (2004) "Reading a Song of the City – Images of the City in Literature and Films". In Preben Kaarsholm (ed.) *City Flicks. Indian Cinema and the Urban Experience*, Calcutta and New Delhi: Seagull Books, pp. 60-82.

Khilnani, Sunil (1997) *The Idea of India,* London: Hamish Hamilton.

Lützeler, Paul Michael (ed., 1982) *Europa. Analysen und Visionen der Romantiker*, Frankfurt a. M.: Insel Verlag.

Manto, Sa'adat Hasan (1993) "Toba Tek Singh". In Balraj Menra/Sharad Dutt (eds.) *Dastavez*, Delhi: Rajkamal, pp. 192-198.

Manto, Saadat Hasan (2001) *A Wet Afternoon. Stories, Sketches, Reminiscences,* Islamabad: Alhamra.

Müller, Lothar (1988) "Die Großstadt als Ort der Moderne. Über Georg Simmel". In Klaus Scherpe (ed.) *Die Unwirklichkeit der Städte. Großstadtdarstellungen zwischen Moderne und Postmoderne*, Reinbek bei Hamburg: Rowohlt, pp. 14-36.

Mushirul, Hasan (ed., 2000) *Inventing Boundaries*, New Delhi: Oxford University Press.

Nehru, Jawaharlal (1999) *The Discovery of India*, New Delhi: Oxford University Press.
Noorani, A.G. (2003) *The Babri Masjid, 1528-2003. 'A Matter of National Honour'*, 2 Vols., New Delhi: Tullika.
Patel, Sujata/Thorner, Alice (eds., 1996) *Bombay: Metaphor for Modern India*, Bombay: Oxford University Press.
Patnaik, Prabhat (2003) *The Retreat to Unfreedom. Essays on the Emerging World Order*, New Delhi: Tullika.
Pinto, Jerry/Fernandes, Naresh (eds., 2003) *Bombay, meri jaan*, New Delhi: Penguin.
Prakash, Gyan (2002) "The Urban Turn". In Preben Kaarsholm (ed.) *The Cities of Everyday Life. The Sarai Reader 2*, Delhi: Sarai., pp. 2-7.
Rai, Alok (2001) *Hindi Nationalism*, Delhi: Orient Longman.
Ravikant/Saint, Tarun K. (eds., 2001) *Translating Partition*, New Delhi.
Ray, Manas (2004) "Chalo Jahaji. Bollywood in the Tracks of Indenture to Globalization". In Preben Kaarsholm (ed.) *City Flicks. Indian Cinema and the Urban Experience*, Calcutta and New Delhi: Seagull Books, pp. 140-182.
Rushdie, Salman (1996) *The Moor's last Sigh*, London: Vintage.
Schmitt, Carl (1965) *Verfassungslehre*, Berlin: Duncker & Humboldt.
Simmel, Georg (1958) *Philosophie des Geldes*, Berlin: Duncker & Humboldt.
Singh, Khushwant (2003) "Impressions of Bombay". In Jerry Pinto/Naresh Fernandes (eds) *Bombay, meri jaan*, New Delhi: Penguin, pp. 23- 28.
Thapar, Romila (2000) *History and Beyond*, New Delhi: Oxford University Press.
Tönnies, Ferdinand (1991) *Gemeinschaft und Gesellschaft*, Darmstadt: Wissenschaftliche Buchgesellschaft.
Weiss, Peter (1975-1981) *Ästhetik des Widerstands*, Frankfurt am Main: Suhrkamp.

II. Spatializing Identities

The Politics and Poetics of Religion: Hindu Processions and Urban Conflicts

LILY KONG

In this paper, I will explore the ways in which processions, by their very visibility, foreground the relationships between the secular and the sacred, while contributing to a construction of identity and community, and simultaneously surfacing fractures therein. Using the example of multireligious yet secular Singapore, I will examine the state's management of a Hindu procession, Thaipusam; the tactics of adaptation, negotiation, and resistance that participants engage in; and the participants' experience of these processions, including the nature of their "sacred experience."[1]

Introduction

Processions have long been an integral part of religious life. They are among the most visible of religious activities in public spaces, and thus have the greatest opportunity for contact with secular activities and religious practices of other faiths. Because they tend towards the "spectacular," they heighten the potential for conflict. As events that attract crowds, the possibility of violence is real, as the experience in many countries reminds us. The politics of such events must be understood to avoid the troubles in various parts of the world.

---

1 This is an abriged version of a fuller paper titled "Religious processions: urban policites and poetics" that has appeared in *Temenos, the Nordic Journal of Comparative Religion* (2005) Volume 41, No. 2, pp. 225–49.

To understand the politics, it is imperative to understand the meanings and values invested in such events—the poetics—thus enabling policy-makers and enforcement agencies to become aware of what sacred meanings are negotiable and which should remain fixed values.

Much of the geographical literature on processions addresses secular processions, including national parades (Kong and Yeoh 1997) and community parades (Jackson 1988, Lewis/Pile 1996). A parallel literature on religion deals with pilgrimages (cf. Kong 1990; Kong 2001). Indeed, there are many similarities between the nature and experience of processions and pilgrimages, though the latter is at a larger scale, often traversing greater distances, involving greater commitment of time, and possibly enduring more privations. In drawing on insights from existing literatures, I engage with the literatures on both secular processions and religious pilgrimages.

What is the nature of processional experience? In particular, in modern cities where functionalist urban planning may come up against sacred sites, and where Hindu, Jew, Buddhist, Christian, and Muslim may live cheek by jowl, what sorts of conflicts have to be negotiated in the continued performance of such religious practice? I explore this question using the multireligious case of Singapore, an officially secular city-state where all the major world religions are represented. This analysis is a focus on the micro-politics of urban life and its conflicts, pursued on the basis that such micro-politics is constitutive of the macro-politics of religious conflicts, manifested in religiously-based wars and unrest. Such macro-politics has historical roots, but is also daily constituted and reinforced through a micro-politics of friction that often appears less dramatic, less serious, less pressing than the drama and spectacle of religious wars, but which nevertheless is very real and influential in the warp and woof of everyday life.

Processions and pilgrimages: Some approaches

Pilgrimage is a "social construction, and inevitably, a cultural product" (Graham/Murray 1997: 389). The cultural product must, in turn, be understood in relation to its social, political, and historical contexts. The multidisciplinary literatures on pilgrimage recognize this social and cultural constructedness, and acknowledge how social relations are (re)enacted or challenged during pilgrimages, resulting on occasion in conflict, but also in reinforcement of community and identity.

Pilgrimages are thought to temporarily bring together individuals disparate in age, occupation, gender, ethnicity, social class, and power. Pilgrimages bond together, "however transiently, at a certain level of social life, large numbers of men and women who would otherwise never have come into contact" (Turner 1974: 178). Pilgrimages therefore function as occasions during which communitas is experienced, and is a liminal experience, involving abrogation of secular social structure.

In contrast, scholars such as Eade and Sallnow (1991) argue that pilgrimage is a pluralist experience, a realm in which there are competing religious and secular discourses, leading to the reinforcement of social boundaries and distinctions rather than their dissolution. This is illustrated in a range of studies (e.g. Graham/Murray 1997; Murray/Graham 1997) where the multiple meanings of the pilgrimage route and site give rise to tensions and conflicts. Religious processions, at a scale smaller than pilgrimages, nevertheless encapsulate many of the issues confronted in pilgrimage analysis, and, indeed, are not unlike the experience of secular processions, for which analyses exist of pageants, parades, and Carnival.

Parades and processions '[serve] as a means to focus attention of private people on their collective life and the values they [espouse] through it" (Goheen 1993: 128). Not only do they mark out space, such "civic rituals" also represent "time apart," for they are "time separated from the normal activities" (Goheen 1993: 128). They also stress shared values and reinforce group cohesion by emphasising belonging. Further, they may be "characterized as demonstrations of community power and solidarity and serve as complex commentaries on the political economy or urban-industrial social relations" (Marston 1989: 255). On the other hand, these events may also reflect the spatial constitution of symbolic resistance, achieved through the symbolic reversal of social status (Jackson 1988). They offer a temporary respite from normal relations of subordination and domination, and thus offer a potential platform for protest, opposition, and resistance (Jackson 1988: 222). Yet, as Jackson (1988: 216) points out, the symbolic reversal of social status during these events should not be confused with subversion because it only serves to reaffirm the permanence of the social hierarchy. What they offer is a temporary respite from normal relations.

Fieldwork context

Thaipusam is celebrated in many parts of the world by ethnic communities from South India, such as Fiji, Mauritius, Trinidad, Durban, Toronto, Malaysia, and Singapore. It marks the birthday of Lord Subramaniam, one of the sons of Shiva. The spectacle of the event revolves around a device called a kavadi carried by participants along a processional route. Some may even pierce themselves with skewers or attach hooks to their bodies. The processions are generally accompanied by music and chanting. Some participants also enter a religious trance during the procession. Generally, those who take part in the procession do so as a form of thanksgiving for prayers answered.

In Singapore, Thaipusam is an annual event in which the state's management has evolved. Religious processions in Singapore are carefully monitored and managed, a caution rooted in history. On 21 July 1964, during a procession celebrating the Prophet Muhammad's birthday, riots broke out as the Malay-Muslim procession passed through an area predominantly populated by Chinese. Different accounts exist of how the riots started. Regardless of what happened, given this precedent, much care is given to manage public events, including Thaipusam.

Two Hindu community leaders shared with me insights into the organisation of the procession. Annually, two to three months before Thaipusam, an application is made by the Hindu Endowments Board (HEB), on behalf of the two temples involved (marking the start and end point of the procession, respectively) and participating devotees, to the police to obtain a permit to hold the procession. Additionally, along the processional route are tents set up by Hindu devotees, serving water or milk to those participating in the procession. Tent owners also have to apply to the police for permits after seeking endorsement from the HEB. Following these applications, the police convene a meeting with the HEB and representatives from the two temples to discuss the ground rules and problems encountered during the last festival, so as to propose ways of addressing them.

Almost 10,000 participants can be expected annually: more than 8,000 carry milk pots, and more than 1,000 carry kavadis. Additionally, there are many more who set up tentage, and others who help the devotees. The logistical task is huge, given this scale of events. The two temples thus issue "rules, regulations and conditions governing Thaipusam," constructed to observe state rules pertaining to assemblies and processions (encapsulated in the Miscellaneous Offences (Public Order and Nuisance) Act and its related subsidiary legislation), and to manage the event. Individual kavadi carriers have to buy tickets from the temples to participate in the procession and pay a fee to defray the cost of organizing the event and handling the logistics. Big kavadi carriers pay more because they "take up the most space and need the most supervision" (ST 23 Dec 1999). Kavadi carriers have to inform the temples of the size and weight of their kavadis, which should not exceed certain limits (4 m from the ground up and 2.9 m in diameter), so as to ensure that they do not pose safety hazards to traffic or street wires. Devotees carrying milk pots may leave Perumal Temple from 2:00 a.m. onwards on Thaipusam Day, but kavadis and rathams (shrines on wheels) have between 7:00 a.m. and 7:30 p.m. to leave the Perumal temple. At the other end, the doors of the Thendayuthapani Temple will close at 10 p.m. Tickets are issued upon payment, and devotees are given specific times when they should assemble at Sri Perumal, in order that the crowds may be managed. Further, all forms of musical instruments and recorded music are not allowed along the processional route. Only holy music is allowed within the temples' premises. The temples' rules end with a warning that any infringement will result in the prosecution of devotees and/or supporters by the police and the devotees being barred from future festivals.

Religious processions and the making of social relations

Davis' (1986: 6) description of nineteenth-century Philadelphia parades as "public dramas of social relations" provides an apt perspective for examining the Thaipusam procession in Singapore. Just as the nineteenth-century parades "define who can be a social actor," Thaipusam was both an occasion for boundary-making and one for reinforcing social ties, in particular, religious community, family, and friendship ties.

As an occasion for boundary-making, Thaipusam reminds us that a community is not devoid of internal tensions, and is not always characterized by homogeneous, or even consensual, traits and views. Thus, boundaries are internal to the Hindu community, as they are between the Hindu and other communities in multi-religious Singapore. The procession surfaced conflicts and tensions within the community, evident in two main ways. First, the latent discontent with a prominent foreign-worker population in Singapore, and in this particular instance, with an Indian foreign-worker population, is foregrounded in a public performance such as Thaipusam, with crowdedness and disorderliness attributed to them. One interviewee complained that the procession had become very protracted, with many delays, because of the growth in the number of kavadi carriers and the larger crowds. He attributed this to the increase in the number of foreign workers participating. Another intimated that "Thaipusam has been spoilt" because of the intrusion and rowdiness of "foreign elements." Yet others pointed fingers at "the younger generation" instead. One interviewee blamed the "youngsters," criticizing "the way they dance, the way they cheer, the way they change those movie songs to God songs." Boundary-making thus drew on age, class, and nationality as divisive factors.

The consciousness of "self" and "other" was also evident through repeated references to boundaries between the Hindu community and other communities. These references revealed awareness that this public display of Hinduism had the power to shape public perceptions about the Hindu community, and also offered the occasion for the "other" to show sensitivity to the Hindu community. In the former instance, Hindu interviewees referred to the unruly behaviour of some young Hindu boys in the processions, and expressed deep regret that "You have other races watching you, so when all these happen, it gets wrong ideas into people's heads about us." In the latter instance, some interviewees expressed disappointment at the lack of understanding and respect by other communities of the sacredness of the event:

> Frankly speaking, it is okay for them to watch, but I think there are members of the public who are not dressed properly and who don't behave well. [...] We feel very offended when we are participating. [...] We like people to be more properly attired rather than coming as though you are going for a show, a disco (Shamala, late 30s).

Simultaneously, the procession did not just serve as occasions of internal and external boundary-making. It was also an opportunity for the reinforcement of family and friendship ties, and the reaffirmation of community identity. At the most fundamental, the commitment to Thaipusam was viewed as a total family obligation. Mano, who has participated annually in Thaipusam for 27 years, says:

> I have seen cases where people take it just for granted. Everybody carry, I also can carry. After they start walking, they just collapse. Just cannot fulfill the route. And some of them, when you're piercing, you can see them pinching because it's painful. It's hurting them. I wouldn't really say whether they did fast properly or not, but I know there's something wrong. Something is not right in the family. Maybe they did not fast. Maybe in the house, in the family, something is wrong. When I want to carry the kavadi, the whole family joins in. We all fast together.

This family involvement has the effect of bringing the family together. Such family participation extends to the day of the procession itself, during which family and friends provide both practical and moral support. Mohan says:

> Just say for example, this big chariot which I carry. For some reason, if I can't pull it, somebody can help me to push. And if this big kavadi I'm carrying, for some reason I cannot carry, balance myself, the people all round, four of them, could hold me and ... [help to] adjust it. And in the worst case, if you really cannot walk, they can dismantle it and bring you to the temple in whatever way they could help. Yes you need them to help because you will never know...That's why it's not just you yourself. I may be in the procession, but everybody is helping, also participating in this holy festival.

Spiritually and emotionally, Rama acknowledges the need for support, when the journey gets long and delayed:

> The procession is about four km, and at some point of time, there would be a jam, and we have to wait for 2½, three hours. During that period, family is there or friends or relations to give you the moral boost.

But the strengthening of social relations is not confined to pre-existing ties. The sense of community among participants and well-wishers is enhanced through the support given to those completing the thanksgiving journey, even among strangers. As Vani shared:

> Usually what happens is that after you are done with your procession, that means you have finished your task already, right. So then, it doesn't have to be someone that you know. You can also carry on and cheer along with everybody else, even if it is strangers. It does not have to be someone you know. We cheer other participants along to encourage them to the finish.

When probed, Vani and others were clearly aware of the boisterous youths and burgeoning foreign workers, and indeed expressed their annoyance and disapproval. Yet, their enthusiasm and support for participants, particularly when nearing the destination, were co-existent with their awareness of social difference. They did not feel a sense of egalitarian association, after the manner of Turner's (1974) communitas. Rather, it was a sense of support for those who have made sacrifices and bore the privations of the journey, not unlike support for athletes on the track. This did not amount to a numbing heap of emotions "where the lofty is combined with the low, the great with the insignificant, the wise with the stupid" (Folch-Serra 1990: 265). The experience of communitas, long accepted in many anthropological writings about pilgrimage, did not replicate itself in the context of the Thaipusam procession in Singapore. This may suggest that pilgrimages and processions are not directly comparable, but it may also suggest that the sense of sameness and egalitarian association may be a somewhat romanticized interpretation of the pilgrim experience.

Religious processions and the negotiation of poetics and politics

Religious processions also exist at the nexus of "poetic" performance and public politics, the negotiation of which forms the analysis in this section. Conceptually, I have framed the material in terms of the negotiation of soundscapes, timescapes, and sacred pathways, reflecting the multiple dimensions of the processional phenomena.

Negotiating aural space

That Thaipusam occupies aural space, and derives significant meaning from the manufacture and consumption of sound, may not have been so apparent if music did not become subject to policy and policing. No interviewee failed to discuss the significance of music to the creation of an appropriate atmosphere, and as an integral part of the ceremony. Many took pains to explain the place of music in religion and in this particular public performance. Pany shared this perspective:

> Music is part of religion. If you notice, the drums, the long pipes played during prayers ... traditionally, music, dances, language were performed in the temples, where culture was propagated. For the kavadi carriers, the music is to let them forget the pain and let them concentrate and to fulfill their mission.

However, over the years, restrictions have come to be placed on the noise level generated at public events. Music is disallowed along the processional route. This reflects a larger policy in Singapore, applicable in a variety of contexts. For example, the traditional Islamic call to prayer used to be made on a loudspeaker, outward from a mosque. It became regulated because, with population growth and urbanization, such sound production risked being regarded as intrusive by those not involved in that religion (Lee 1999). State regulations on "noise pollution" were therefore introduced, including turning the loudspeakers inwards towards the mosque, specifying acceptable noise levels for events such as Chinese operas, funeral processions, church bells, record shops, and places of entertainment. Even state-endorsed nation-building activities, such as pledge recitation in schools, are subject to these rules.

As a consequence, the desired "poetic" value of music is lost, and the continuing quest has become one for aural, not physical, space for religious activity. This politics of sound and space is expressed in a variety of ways, from the most supportive to actions that attempt to circumvent the intent of the law. At one end of the spectrum, Vani expresses full support for the regulations:

> I fully support the government doing this ... because teenagers especially tend to take advantage if there are no rules, so they made the whole procession look like a hooligan get-together because they would dress in black and they end up taking garbage cans and turning them upside down like playing drums. So what happens was that it led to unnecessary fights because you have a lot of gangs there and compete who can make louder noise and stuff like that. ... So after the restrictions were imposed, you can't find things like that now and it looks more festive.

Others accept, but without the same sense of support, such as Rama, who points to Singapore's perceived political culture of compliance:

> I think we just learn ... you know we Singaporeans are so obedient. As long as the government says, we obey, you know. We may complain, but ultimately we still follow the rules.

In contrast, others are quite vituperative. Mano offers a pointed critique, and reveals that appeals have been made to no effect:

> We asked the temple and everything. They said no, they said it's against the law. Most of them, some of them, even myself, sometimes, I say walking like that, it's just like attending a funeral with no music and all. ... Sometimes, with so many regulations, after a while, you're fulfilling the vows and everything, you should do it happily. Wholeheartedly. Not while cursing somebody.

For some, the appeal is built on the logic that if there are those misbehaving, action should be taken against them rather than to have a blanket ban on music, thus calling on the authorities to be more discriminatory in their strategies of management.

Finally, in a circuitous way, some interviewees point out that it is because musical instruments are banned that there are those who use empty tin cans and dustbins for improvisation, thus resisting sanctions in symbolic ways:

> These guys use dustbins. So when they see the police officer, they just put it down. After that they just pick it up again (Shamala).

Thus, the ban on music led to the creation of improvised sound, which in turn led to the perception amongst other participants and observers of a lack of respect and religious value, thereby ironically prompting their support of a ban.

Negotiating sacred time

Just as the poetics and politics of soundscapes are negotiated in aurally defined sacred space, so too has the bracketing of time come to shape the practice of religion. In the history of religion, particular days and specific times of the day have traditionally been set aside for religious practice, what Eliade (1959) has referred to as "sacred time," set apart from secular time. In contemporary society, what time is marked out as sacred is again a negotiated outcome between secular and religious agents. This is evident at two levels in the context of Thaipusam in Singapore: in the official appointment of public holidays tied to religious festivals, and in the allocation of time for religious activity in the public sphere. Indeed, apart from the choice of the day, other aspects of managing that time are much more guided by pragmatic secular considerations than religious ones.

In the official Singapore calendar, a series of public holidays are identified, corresponding to religious festivals for Buddhists, Muslims, Hindus, and Christians. There are also the culturally defined ones: New Year's Day and Chinese New Year, and secular public holidays: Labour Day and National Day. The choice of religious festivals that deserve public holiday status in many ways defines the extent of religious activity and participation that is facilitated for particular religious groups. Thus, several interviewees lamented the lack of a public holiday for Thaipusam and attendant difficulties. Shamala explained that, as she was not able to take time off work, she had to participate in the procession very early in the morning or late in the evening. This posed other problems—the extra cost of transportation in the early hours of the morning, recalling that milk pot bearers start at 2:00 a.m. ("you have to pay double charges for taxis"), and the congestion in the post-work rush hour ("tempers flare for those in the traffic jam held up by us").

And what of the bracketing of time within the day itself? This is guided by temple regulations based on pragmatic considerations of crowd control and safety, as well as by self "regulation," based on the pragmatics of tropical, urban living. Temple regulations stipulate that those carrying milk pots may start at 2:00 a.m., though kavadis and rathams may only begin at 7:00 a.m., with the last participant beginning at 7:30 p.m. This bracketing of time is based essentially on pragmatic considerations to spread out the activities over as many hours as possible to avoid congestion, and to have those with the bigger paraphernalia (kavadis and rathams) on the streets only after the break of light. Additionally, participants further bracket the time in view of the hot afternoon sun in Singapore, so that few take to the streets during the afternoon hours. Whereas scholars of religion have written about sacred time as set apart from ordinary time, during which religious activities are propitious, in the context of Thaipusam processions, apart from the identification of a sacred day, which hours of the day particularly attract religious activity and which do not are guided more by pragmatic considerations than religious ones.

Negotiating sacred pathways

The processional route begins from Sri Srinivasa Perumal in Serangoon Road and ends in Sri Thendayuthapani in Tank Road, a journey of some 4 km. The former is in the heart of Singapore's Little India district, and the journey brings participants past a number of temples in that district. Previously, the route was symbolically significant because participants would wind past the Kaliaman[2] Temple (known as the "mother's temple"), and the Sivan Temple (known as the "father's temple") in Dhoby Ghaut. Devotees passing these temples would therefore pay homage to the "mother" and "father." However, the Sivan temple was relocated from the Dhoby Ghaut area to a temporary site next to Sri Perumal in 1984, and then to a permanent site in Geylang East in 1993. This move occurred because of the construction of a mass rapid transit station where it stood, and, despite appeals to the contrary, it was relocated.

Since 1993, the deity Siva has been brought annually to Sri Perumal on the eve of Thaipusam, staying there until the next night. This allows devotees to pay homage to the "father" from the start of the procession, before passing by the "mother" en route to Sri Thendayuthapani. In short, despite the community's investment of symbolic meaning in the Sivan temple and its location, secular priorities prevailed, and ritual adjustments were introduced to manage secular changes that impact on religious practice.

---

2   Kaliaman is the consort of Siva.

Conclusions

Since 1964, when the Mohammedan procession erupted into riot, Singapore has been carefully managing the public expression of religion, and indeed, other processions involving assemblies of people and public displays of spectacle. This is understandable, particularly given how the preceding analysis endorses the view that processions are arenas for competing religious and secular discourses, and are multivocal, of social and political significance.

In focusing on the social and political dimensions of procession, I have illustrated how social relations (including family, friendship, and inter- and intra-community ties) are reinforced or challenged through the event. I have also demonstrated how belief in egalitarian association on account of common participation and mutual support among participants is misplaced. I conclude therefore that the traditional concept of communitas associated with pilgrimages and the notion of solidarity, belonging, and group cohesion in processions perhaps remain relevant in some ways, but may have been over-extended in a somewhat romanticized notion of egalitarianism and bounded community.

Politically, the processions are occasions when meanings are balanced and negotiated by state, temple, and religious individual. These may revolve around the significance of sound in religious experience and the associated symbolic resistance to state prohibitions and temple regulations. They may be about the secular acknowledgement of religious time through suitable bracketing out of that time in the secular calendar. They may involve the ritual adjustments made to accommodate state modifications of sacred pathways. In all of these, the politics at work is not that of overt confrontation or party politics or grand strategy, but one of everyday negotiations and local-level "tactics" (de Certeau 1984). Given Singapore's freedom of worship policy, time and space have been available for adherents to participate in the procession (despite some inconvenience). Participants have also been able to renegotiate meanings and values, finding ways to make music and pay homage to the "father" god. As a consequence, one of the conditions for the negative violence and aggression sometimes associated with religion in general, and such events in particular, is removed, that is, extreme feelings of deprivation in relation to the practice of one's faith. However, the seeds of some dispirited, and sometimes exasperated, disappointment are present, directed at the constraints on religious music-making, the perverse and unintended encouragement it gives to rowdy noise-makers on the pretext of creating an aurally-defined sacred atmosphere for participants, the crowdedness of the event, which lends itself to a channeling of frustrations towards "foreigners" and "youngsters," and the absence of an acknowledgement of this religious event via marking on the secular calendar, which is deemed to further contribute to early morning pre-workday crowdedness. Together, they have not seemed sufficient to constitute severe discontent. Nevertheless, it is imperative that these sources of irritation and discontent are recognized, with potential adjustments made to policy as circumstances change, for example, when the number of participants and observers grow, or when the profile of participants changes.

Finally, that religious experience is a multifaceted one bears emphasis here. Sacred space is defined visually and materially through landscapes, but it is also constituted of soundscapes and timescapes. Religion, to that extent, is an integrative institution, and religious experience may be best understood as a wholly integrated one, of sight, sound, emotion, time. It is only with this understanding that secular rules and regulations may be crafted to achieve pragmatic secular ends, particularly in multireligious urban contexts, while respecting religious imperatives.

References

Davis, Susan G. (1986) *Parades and Power: Street Theatre in Nineteenth Century Philadelphia*, Philadelphia: Temple University Press.

De Certeau, Michel (1984) *The Practice of Everyday Life*, Trans. Steven F. Rendail, Berkeley: University of California Press.

Eade, John/Sallnow, Michael J. (eds.) (1991) *Contesting the Sacred: The Anthropology of Christian Pilgrimage*, New York: Routledge, Chapman and Hall.

Eliade, Mircea (1959) *The Sacred And The Profane: The Nature Of Religion*, Translated from French by Willard R. Trask, San Diego: Harcourt Brace Jovanovich.

Folch-Serra, Mireya (1990) "Place, voice, space: Mikhail Bakhtin's dialogical-landscape". Environment and Planning D: Society and Space 8, pp. 255–74.

Goheen, Peter G. (1993) "The ritual of the streets in mid-19th-century Toronto". Environment and Planning D: Society and Space 11, pp. 127–45.

Graham, Brian/Murray, Michael (1997) "The spiritual and the profane: the pilgrimage to Santiago de Compostela". Ecumene 4/4, pp. 389–409

Jackson, Peter (1988) "Street life: the politics of Carnival". Environment and Planning D: Society and Space 6, pp. 213–27.

Kong, Lily (1990) "Geography and religion: trends and prospects". Progress in Human Geography 14/3, pp. 355–71.

Kong, Lily (2001) "Mapping 'new' geographies of religion: politics and poetics of modernity". Progress in Human Geography 25/2, pp. 211–33.

Kong, Lily/Yeoh, Brenda S.A. (1997) "The construction of national identity through the production of ritual and spectacle: an analysis of National Day Parades in Singapore". Political Geography 16/3, pp. 213–39.

Lee, Tong Soon 1999, "Technology and the production of Islamic space: the call to prayer in Singapore". Ethnomusicology 43, pp. 86–100.

Lewis, Clare/Pile, Steve (1996) "Woman, body, space: Rio Carnival and the politics of performance". Gender, Place and Culture 3/1, pp. 23–42.

Marston, Sallie A. (1989) "Public rituals and community power: St. Patrick's Day parades in Lowell, Massachusetts, 1841–1874". Political Geography Quarterly 8, pp. 255–69.

Murray, Michael/Graham, Brian (1997) "Exploring the dialectics of route-based tourism: the Camino de Santiago". Tourism Management 18/8, pp. 513–24.

Straits Times, Singapore.

Turner, Victor (1974) *Dramas, Fields and Metaphors*, Ithaca: Cornell University Press.

Negotiating the City—Everyday Forms of Segregation in Middle Class Cairo

ANOUK DE KONING

As a consequence of economic restructuring, Cairo's urban landscape has seen increased social polarization and segregation. In order to explore these changes, I examine the urban trajectories of young upper-middle class women. Their trajectories highlight the ways in which social distance and segregation are embedded in the minutiae of the urban landscape and the fabric of city life. Their privileged lifestyles and routines hinge on combinations of class privilege, social avoidance, and segregation.[1]

This paper attempts to read the urban landscape by exploring the ways specific people move through it. These specific people are young female upper-middle class professionals in Cairo. To walk the city with these urbanites allows me to bring out some of the logics implicit in urban life, to map the knowledge and the specific cartographies movement through the city presupposes. Their urban trajectories, moreover, offer a complex picture of Cairo's public spaces and allow a glimpse of the everyday life of segregation in what has been called "Egypt's new liberal age" (Denis 1997).

My ethnographic observations speak to a larger story of a shift from a developmental to a more neoliberal state, and the effects of this shift on Cairo's professional middle class. While the mid-1970s saw a move away from the

---

1 This contribution is an abridged version of a longer chapter of my dissertation on the changing sociocultural landscape of middle-class Cairo under conditions of neoliberal policies and a search for global inclusion (cf. de Koning 2005). This article has profited much from a follow-up research trip in 2004 that was financially supported by the Netherlands Organization for Scientific Research (NWO).

earlier national development path with Sadat's infitaah (open-door) policies, attempts to transform Egypt into a more liberal market economy integrated into the global market sped up significantly in the 1990s with Egypt's adoption of structural adjustment policies.

In Egypt's new liberal age, new lines of segmentation in schooling, the labor market, and consumption are giving rise to new divisions and distinctions within Cairo's professional middle class. These divisions and distinctions rely importantly on cosmopolitan capital: familiarity with Western repertoires and standards—for example, fluency in English—as well as the ability to participate in distinctive cosmopolitan lifestyles (de Koning 2005). There is a still tentative formation of a distinct professional upper-middle class, which is employed in the more internationally oriented up-market segment of the urban economy and inhabits Cairo's up-market spaces. This up-market segment of the urban economy offers relatively good wages and careers when compared to the meager pay of the generally highly insecure private sector employment or the low-level government jobs on which less privileged middle-class strata are forced to rely. While the latter often range from 150 to 1000 LE, wages in the up-market sector might start at 1000 LE, but can reach 10,000 LE.

The upper-middle class professionals employed in this up-market segment can be seen as the protagonists of new state narratives and projects. They are the ones who can match global standards and staff transnational workspaces, not unlike India's "new middle class," which, as Leela Fernandes argues, is constructed as "the social group which is able to negotiate India's new relationship with the global economy in both cultural and economic terms" (2000: 91). These divisions have their counterpart in the urban landscape, most notably in the form of the upscale coffee shops that have carved out a specifically young, upper-middle class presence in Cairo's landscape.

By examining the urban trajectories of some female upper-middle class professionals in their mid-twenties to mid-thirties, I explore the way these changing class configurations are expressed in, and constituted through, the urban landscape. I first explore the ways in which gender, class, and space combine in the constitution of the coffee shop as a "safe space." I then turn to the more ambivalent spaces of the street and explore the ways these women navigate these "unsafe spaces." I finally come back to the insights that can be drawn with respect to the changing features of Cairo's urban landscape.

The "safe" space of the coffee shop

Cairo's up-market districts are dotted with coffee shops and restaurants that serve a mixed-gender clientele. Up-market coffee shops, modelled after American examples like Starbucks, have become an essential part of the daily routines of many young and relatively affluent Cairenes. These coffee shops, always referred to in English, are never to be confused with 'ahawi baladi, the male-dominated sidewalk cafés for which Cairo is famous. Different coffee shops have become spatial orientation points, as well as markers of social belonging. A new and distinctive leisure culture has emerged in and around these coffee shops, centered on, but not exclusive to, young single affluent professionals. Yet coffee shops are a relatively recent phenomenon. Coffee shops started appearing in the mid-1990s in central affluent districts like Zamalek and Mohandisseen, as well as in outlying Heliopolis and Maadi. New coffee shops open regularly, crowding certain streets and turning formerly residential areas into lively Downtown hotspots.

Figure 1: Coffee shop Becno's in Zamalek, an upscale neighbourhood in Cairo (Photo: © Anouk de Koning)

An elderly middle-class lady shook her head when I told her about the significant female public presence in such coffee shops. Those frequenting coffee shops must be impolite girls or women, hiding their outings from their parents. No respectable woman would sit in a public place without the company, protection, and control of her relatives. Her comments resonated with widely shared ideas regarding female propriety and mixed-gender socializing outside the purview of the family (see MacLeod 1991; Ghannam 2002).

Yet many young upper-middle class women live highly mobile and public lifestyles, outside the purview of the family. The presence of these young women in both professional and social public life has become normalized, even critical, to upper-middle class lifestyles, which are marked by the mixed-gender character of contacts and places. Their presence, however, is a fragile one, lived out in closed, class-homogeneous spaces, with respectability and protection being the sine qua non of their ventures into public space. The emergence of spaces like the coffee shop that are deemed acceptable and respectable for single, marriageable women is crucial to these new routines. But what creates these coffee shops as safe spaces, and how are their borders guarded?

Up-market coffee shops are generally seen as safe and respectable places where upper-middle class Cairenes can engage in mixed-gender socializing. These coffee shops have created a protected niche for non-familial mixed-gender sociabilities in the more contentious public geographies of leisure. They have been able to wrest such mixed-gender sociabilities away from associations with immorality and loose sexual behavior that cling to less exclusive mixed-gender spaces outside of the redemptive familial sphere.

Comparatively high prices and a minimum charge regulate access to upscale coffee shops. These economic controls are often augmented by an entry policy, which bars those who seem not to belong. The constant fear of attracting those of a lower "social level" is not only based on the importance of guarding the class markers of a place, but is also stirred by the conviction that they might not abide by the implicit rules of gendered sociability. Young men might flirt or harass, overwhelmed by the availability of young women, and some young women might come to pick up wealthy regulars. These fears echo assumptions about other, less elitist leisure spaces with a mixed-gender public, which are thought to be market places for easy relationships that involve some kind of exchange of money.

Venues were primarily judged on the "level" of their public and the extent to which the mixed-gender interactions were assumed to be respectable. Tamer, a middle class professional in his late twenties, said that he would never take his fiancée to, for example, the coffee shops located on Gamaaᶜit id-Duwal Street, a major shopping street and thoroughfare in upscale Mohandisseen. He argued, "In these coffee shops, most of the girls are prostitutes. I can't go there with my fiancée. Others will think that she is not my fiancée, but my girlfriend. She will be seen as one of those girls."

Nihal, an upper-middle class professional in her early thirties, emphasized the issue of being looked at and the "social level" of those who look. She summarized the logics of the coffee shop as a safe space as follows: "A place has to have a certain standard, it shouldn't be cheap. This guarantees your safety. It guarantees that our kind of people go. This is crucial with respect to the image of women in a certain place. If people look at me in a certain place, it is enough to make me wonder what they say about me. It makes me insecure." Karim, also in his early thirties, had similarly given the logics of the coffee shop a lot of thought. "The 'ahwa [sidewalk café] does not have a door," he said. "Coffee shops, in contrast, are closed. Not every passerby will see you when you sit there; you do not get influenced by other people. My girlfriend would not like to sit in a place where she would be seen and would have to hear comments. She would refuse to sit in the street. She prefers a safely closed place."

Figure 2: Trianon, coffee shop on Gamaacit id-Duwal Street, Mohardisseen (Photo: © Anouk de Koning)

The look or gaze is central to comments and stories about coffee shops. It is a specific gaze that is viewed as problematic and even harmful: the invasive look of undeserving men directed at respectable and classy women. Public visibility is a central, yet highly ambiguous trope (cf. Ossman 1994). The essential question was who could be seen by whom. The recurrent references to "a certain standard of people" and "our kind of people," as well as the frequent negative mention of less classy others, indicate the importance of "social level" with respect to mixed-gender spaces. "Social level," which combines notions of class and culture, determined the interpretation of specific looks. A look might be part of an appropriate and desired visibility, or might be harmful and defiling, depending on "social level." Not being looked at by certain people was central to all discussions of coffee shops, and, more generally, movement through public space.

Besides the gaze, the specter of prostitution is a central theme in these stories. They reflect a constant concern about the "level" of the female patrons and the nature of the relationship between men and women in upscale venues. The specter of prostitution is indicative of the symbolic minefield that these young women negotiate in Cairo's public spaces. The core of this ambiguity consists of the contrastive possible interpretations of a young woman's presence in public. Does her presence indicate a disreputable openness to sexuality, or is it part of a more respectable lifestyle and everyday routine?[2]

Wealth, social origin, and class position guarantee certain interpretations of a woman's presence in public. "Social level" was seen as central to a person's ability to indulge in casual, mixed-gender contact and play with features that otherwise suggest a lack of respectability. It frames such behaviour as part of a class-specific respectable normalcy. Similarly, wearing revealing ['iryaan] clothes need not indicate a lack of respectability, as long as the good origins of the wearer are beyond doubt. These clothes are then framed as part of respectable class-specific norms and lifestyles, as much as the stylish clothing of upper-middle class muhagabbaat [veiled women]. Though class markers are a crucial part of a person's embodied performance, the surest way to avoid confusion and contestation of this sexy-but-respectable self-presentation is to move in classy places, by way of classy means of transport. Such class framing defines these women's public lifestyles and sexy appearances as normal and respectable.

The gendering of public (and private) spaces and the spatial inflection of gendered conceptions of propriety present old, yet recurring themes in urban landscapes (Bondi/Domosh 1998). Coffee shops frame the public presence of upper-middle class women as appropriate and respectable. By way of their prices and their explicitly cosmopolitan connections, which signal distance from

---

2   Elizabeth Wilson's sketch of the dilemma of the "public woman" in the nineteenth-century city highlights some of the central features of this ambiguity. As Wilson argues, "the prostitute was a 'public woman,' but the problem in the nineteenth-century urban life was whether every woman in the new, disordered world of the city, the public sphere of pavements, cafes and theatres, was not a public woman and thus a prostitute. The very presence of unattended-unowned women constituted a threat both to male power and a temptation to male 'frailty'" (Wilson 2001: 74). This ambiguity remains a central theme in numerous settings, among others in contemporary Cairo. It pervades the ambiguous views of young middle class women who—apparently unowned—move on their own through public space.

surrounding places and their gender norms, coffee shops institute a normalcy of women's presence and mixed-gender socializing. The anxiously guarded mixed-gender nature of the coffee shop allows for the performance of upper-middle class gendered identities: the leisurely socializing of mixed-gender groups and the public lifestyles of young career women.

In the streets, where up-market norms are not hegemonic, and a clear class framing is absent, such self-representations may well be overturned. The same fashionable cut [sleeveless top] becomes minimally something out of place, but may also be seen as disreputable and taken to indicate easy morals, an open invitation to comments and even harassment. A young professional who was also a frequent visitor of the coffee shop scene told me of his annoyance with some of his friends. They insisted on harassing women they perceived to be less-than-respectable. A girl smoking or wearing tight clothes in the streets would qualify as such in their eyes. "Shame on you!" he reported telling them, "doesn't your sister dress just like her?" Such inversions indicate the extent to which impromptu identifications are framed, and to a large extent determined, by specific spatial contexts.

Crossing the city

In contrast to the closed coffee shops, the streets are largely characterized by male entitlement, even if male prerogatives to look at and judge women in public space can be partially mitigated by recourse to class hierarchies.[3] Women, particularly young women who are not accompanied by men, have a liminal and ambiguous status. They are supposed to be on their way somewhere, have a clear destination, and not linger for too long. Hanging around in the streets, especially on their own, is taken as an open invitation for men to make contact. As a consequence, most of my female acquaintances carefully planned their schedules and meetings to avoid time gaps during which they would have to spend time waiting in an open public space.

A young woman's presence in the street is subjected to constant observation and judgments. Such judgments are based on looks, class markers, and signs of modesty, such as the higaab [veil] or loose fitting clothing. These markers are evaluated with respect to possible definitions of a woman's pres-

---

3   Streets in up-market areas like Zamalek and Maadi differ significantly from their lower-class counterparts, as do shopping streets from big thoroughfares and more residential streets. Despite such significant differences, a dominant male presence and women's liminality are shared features of Cairo's street life. Streets, moreover, share a certain indeterminacy with respect to class. Some residential areas constitute marked exceptions to these gendered definitions of the street, while women peddlers who occupy sidewalks in central streets defy notions of women's liminality.

ence in a specific place at a specific time. Different styles of women's dress have become central to, and iconic of, different styles of femininity. As Secor (2002) argues with respect to regimes of veiling in Istanbul, specific attires allow for certain interpretations and interventions in public space and are therefore crucial with respect to the micro-politics of interaction in public spaces.

"Before going out I look ten times in the mirror to check my appearance. Will this do? Will I be left alone this time?" Nihal told me she would invariably ask herself these questions before leaving the house in the morning. Many women told me they ask themselves similar questions, going over the different places they would visit and the kind of self-presentation required in them. Women's strategies in crossing the city depend on social maps of Cairo that indicate what to expect in certain places, and mark these places with a sense of ease and tension, safety and danger.

Figure 3: Two women on Gamaacit id-Duwal Street (Photo: © Anouk de Koning)

Nihal told me of her one-time venture out to a disco that was not clearly marked as upper-middle class. She felt embarrassed as soon as she entered. She estimated many of the women present to be easy with regard to sexual morals and suspected that some might be prostitutes. Despite her self-identification as a proper upper-middle class woman, she felt she was included in this group of loose women as a result of her mere presence, and felt tainted by the experience. A number of women told me similar stories, imbued with similar feelings. Some stressed the social repercussions of being seen in a certain place, whereas others emphasized their sense of embarrassment or even defilement by being identified as less than respectable. This sense of embarrassment can be elicited by anything from personal misgivings to subtle signs of others present, from benevolent teasing and flirting to concrete interventions. A woman may feel the presence of such interpretations because of the concrete actions of others around her. Such interpretations may, however, also be attributed to an abstract, imagined public. Regardless, the women to whom I spoke were all sensitive to such interpretations.

Navigating the city thus requires extensive knowledge of the urban landscape. But no such mental map is perfect; one cannot rule out mismatches and embarrassment by mistaken identifications. Urban life is a process of negotiation and contestation, of indeterminate social interactions with unpredictable outcomes. Of course, one can try to rule out such mishaps through diverse preventive measures going out by car, visiting only those places that are unmistakably classy. Such routines depend on the financial means to do so (cf. Armbrust 1998). For others, "It is a matter of fitting in, of being invisible," as Marwa, a middle-class professional in her early thirties, explained. For many of these women, visibility, or rather invisibility, is a central issue, a feat that relies on a presentation of the embodied self as respectable and in place. Since she lived in a working-class area, Marwa had comparatively extensive experience with a range of urban neighbourhoods. She said that as a muhagabba [veiled woman] she is able to blend in more easily. However, her veil does not protect her from flirts and harassment in the streets. "You don't do anything to look like somebody who can be picked up from the street. How can you feel safe like that," she wondered. Many women similarly complained that there is nothing that will stop men from harassing women in the streets.

Mu^{c}aksa [pl. mu^{c}aksaat], from "to bother, hassle, annoy," is mostly used for encounters with a sexual overtone, and ambiguously denotes anything between flirt and harassment. The term carries an inbuilt tension: whereas a 'ya ^{c}asal' [hey, honey] in the street can push a woman to step up her pace, a "charming" compliment in a closed-off, classy place will likely be perceived quite differently.

Mu^{c}aksa is a topic of society-wide debate and is experienced as a major nuisance and deterrent to women's ventures into public space (cf. Ghannam 2002: 100; MacLeod 1991: 63). For those living in the closed-off places of up-market districts, mu^{c}aksa comes to symbolize the streets tout court. They have never learned, have forgotten, or are no longer willing to adapt to the Cairene streets, or to try to be invisible. As Marwa commented, "You get used to your privacy, comfort and being free from harassment. You then find it difficult to adapt once more to a certain attitude, to step down." Many of those not willing or able to be invisible avoid the streets if they can. The question is: Who can afford to do so?

Transport and the mobile framing of class

Purity and defilement are central issues with respect to women's movement in public space. An improper gaze can constitute injury to the upper-middle class female body. The avoidance and barring of unwanted gazes are crucial upper-middle class strategies in moving through public space. A woman should not get tired, should be at ease and free of the unwanted touches of other bodies.

Two common means of transport have come to symbolize the two extremes of experiences in public space: while the car represents control, protection, and absolute freedom, the public bus has come to stand for forced proximity and possible harassment. Whereas a man might brave these nuisances, a woman should never be forced to undergo the horrors of crowdedness in an open yet closed space like the public bus, where one is condemned to the proximity of others and their unclean bodies, and, worst of all, physical harassment.

Cairo is generally seen as relatively safe, yet fears of sexual violence, especially rape, were commonplace. Stories of harassment in public transport abounded. When the subject of public transport came up, so did stories of the dangers of the mini- or microbus, which invariably featured men waiting to harass women moving on their own. Concerns about women's movement centrally focus on their unscathed passage through public space. Whereas rape is the ultimate desecration, even a look can harm and defile the pure, unsullied, and properly sexualized female body.

The need to take public transport or move by foot in the streets exposes upper-middle class women to infringements on their established routines and preferred lifestyles. Hoda commented that she had to change her way of dressing when she moved house after her marriage. Now that she is taking a taxi from home to the metro station located in a popular neighborhood, she has stopped wearing tight clothes and obvious make-up to avoid being too visible and thus warranting comments. "You cannot wear professional clothes, such as a skirt, unless you have a car," she said. She complained that she is therefore no longer able to live up to the image of the professional career woman she would like to present. For many middle-class women who can, and even those who cannot afford it, the car has become an indispensable item. The car allows them to dress the way they like and protects them from unwanted encounters. It allows them to be bi-rahithum, at ease. The next best thing is the taxi, a favourite, but expensive option for many non-car owners.

In contrast to the stories of danger and defilement that surround public transport, the car thus becomes the symbol for and guarantor of a perfect world of professional life, self-representation, and respectable socializing. It provides a mobile framing of the self that confirms a certain class standing, akin to the fixed spatial framing of the up-market coffee shop. As a man in his early thirties remarked, "A woman who takes a taxi still has a relation to the street. She will eventually return to the street and can therefore be flirted with. A woman with her own car can dress in whatever way she likes. Nobody will harass her." The public lifestyles of young upper-middle class women depend on the financial means to sit in certain places and to take certain modes of transport—in short, to move exclusively in up-market Cairo. The car crowns attempts to create a controlled environment. It transports women unscathed and free of unwanted interventions from one safe space to the next.

Nihal sketched her paramount image of the young upper class woman: driving a Cherokee with closed, tinted windows, air-conditioning on, moving between different places dominated by her own norms of respectability and sociability. This image rings quite true. The ability of many upper-middle class women to engage in their preferred lifestyle and specific modes of sociability and self-presentation depends on such class closure and control over their environment.

Moving around with these female professionals, the map of Cairo seems to shrink to include only those areas where their distinctive lifestyles are the norm: the up-market districts of Mohandisseen, Zamalek, Maadi, and Heliopolis. For some, spaces outside of this class-specific economy seem a vague and distant reality. These other spaces are marked as dirty, full of bacteria and health hazards, uncouth people, and mu^{c}aksaat. Some of these spaces outside up-market Cairo, like the "popular" or "informal" housing sectors (^{c}ashwaa'iyyaat) (cf. Bayat/Denis 2000), are places never to be visited, unless by accident when one gets lost and is stranded in a popular area like Dar es-Salaam, full of unknown but lurking dangers.

Performing fragile identities

[The daughters of the high aristocracy] dreamt solely of a regular sojourn abroad, lived surrounded by electronic gadgets and refused to go out into the streets, afraid that the contact with all those poor drifting about the sidewalks would defile them. They would only go out by car, and then exclusively to closed establishments: restaurants, cinemas or beaches where they could be sure they wouldn't encounter any plebs.
They were right. Wherever they went, the atmosphere grew tense. Their beauty was almost impermissible. Even if the girls laughed very modestly, it looked like a provocation When they pushed up their hair, the gesture would become erotically charged The pointed breasts under their shirts inflicted more chaos than a machine gun. Their transparent cheeks seemed made to be kissed.   Rachid Mimouni (1991: 88; my translation)

This passage is taken from *Une peine à vivre*, a novel about the life of a dictator in an unnamed country by the Algerian writer Rachid Mimouni. It describes the lives of women in a far more privileged position than the women whose trajectories have informed this paper. Yet it sketches a similar ironic situation in which elite fears and anxieties that surround less exclusive places and their inhabitants combine with the segmented everyday realities of a divided city. Elite norms increasingly clash with those of other city dwellers, thereby confirming the impossibility of "going out in the streets." As Mimouni writes, they were right not to go out into the streets. Even the simplest gesture could be "misread," creating confusion, inciting harassment and the defilement of otherwise pure and respectable embodiments of upper-middle class femininity.

Social avoidance and segregation are widespread phenomena in Cairo's socio-cultural landscape. The itineraries of these women highlight the everyday existence of social distance and segregation within the urban landscape and the fabric of city life. These are the footsteps of social segregation that play out against the more obvious maps of privilege and affluence and exclusion and poverty inscribed in the built environment, most markedly in the form of the gated communities that now surround Cairo. Their urban trajectories show the existence of specific upper-middle class norms of gendered propriety in public space, which are secured through the social closure of up-market spaces.

While their class status gives them a certain leverage vis-à-vis the male entitlement in the streets, most upper-middle class women I knew preferred to resort to the more reliable strategies of class closure to secure their unscathed passage through such open public spaces. Their trajectories were invariably based on class maps. It is only in exclusive up-market places that they can be at ease and dress and socialize as they see fit without being annoyed or being seen as disreputable. This points to what seems to me to be a crucial contradiction at the core of these high-mobility and rather public routines: their condition of possibility is social closure, the avoidance of any disturbance and the ability to avoid any unwanted contacts.

In the context of her discussion of exclusive urban developments in Sao Paulo, Teresa Caldeira argues that the tendency to spatialize social distance is connected to "the inability [of more privileged inhabitants] to impose their own code of behaviour – including rules of deference – onto the city" (2000: 319). Gender is an integral part of the drawing of class boundaries and justifications of social segregation in Cairo. These women's everyday routines and lifestyles are predicated on class closure, which keeps other codes and norms regarding public sociability and propriety at bay. Arguments about gendered behavior, and the need for the protection of "classy" women in turn, come to legitimize such social segregation. Many of the women featured in this paper were concerned about harassment and those even worse things that might happen in public spaces that were not explicitly marked as upper-middle class and appropriate or safe for women. These fears concern non-upper-middle class public spaces and tend to have strong implicit or explicit classist undertones. They concern upper-middle class women and the mass of lower class men of whom they must be aware.

The diverse attempts at closure discussed here must be located against the background of growing class differences and a larger trend towards social segregation in Cairo's urban landscape (cf. de Koning 2005). In Egypt's new liberal age, the city is being transformed through seemingly unbound private-sector initiative in combination with government attempts to bring the country up to speed with the global. New forms of class closure are a main component of these new urban developments. Parallel to developments in other major cities around the world, Cairo has witnessed a flurry in the building of gated communities (in local terms: compounds) in the desert, providing members of the upper (middle) class with pollution-free, exclusive, and prestigious housing. Next to these compounds, private hospitals, language schools, and universities have sprung up, which advertise American or British standards, teaching methods and curricula, and grant degrees that are only partly valid in the Egyptian context. The recently completed network of fly-over bridges, tunnels, and highways that connects different up-market areas of Cairo allows one to move from one part of this "other Egypt" to the next, without having to descend into some of Cairo's less palatable realities.

References

Armbrust, Walter (1998) "When the Lights go down in Cairo: Cinema as Secular Ritual". Visual Anthropology 10/2-4, pp. 413–442.
Bayat, Asef/Denis, Eric (2000) "Who is afraid of *ashwaiyyat*". Environment & Urbanization 12/2, pp. 185–199.
Bondi, Liz/Domosh, Mona (1998) "On the contours of public space: A tale of three women". Antipode 30/3, pp. 270–289.
Caldeira, Teresa P.R. (2000) *City of Walls: Crime, Segregation, and Citizenship in Sao Paulo*, Berkeley and Los Angeles: University of California Press.
Denis, Eric (1997) "Urban Planning and Growth in Cairo". Middle East Report, Winter 1997, pp. 7–12.
Fernandes, Leela (2000) "Restructuring the new middle class in liberalizing India". Comparative Studies of South Asia, Africa and the Middle East 20, pp. 88–104.

Ghannam, Farha (2002) *Remaking the Modern in a Global Cairo: Space, Relocation, and the Politics of Identity*, Berkeley: University of California Press.

Koning, Anouk de (2005) *Global Dreams: Space, Class and Gender in Middle Class Cairo*. Ph.D. thesis, University of Amsterdam.

MacLeod, Arlene Elowe (1991) *Accommodating Protest: Working Women, the New Veiling, and Change in Cairo*, New York: Columbia University Press.

Mimouni, Rachid (1992) *Straf voor het leven*, Amsterdam: Maarten Muntinga. Translation of *Une peine à vivre* [1991].

Ossman, Susan (1994) *Picturing Casablanca: Portraits of Power in a Modern City*, Berkeley: University of California Press.

Secor, Anne J. (2002) "The Veil and Urban Space in Istanbul: women's dress, mobility and Islamic knowledge". Gender, Place and Culture 9/1, pp. 5–22.

Wilson, Elizabeth (2001) *The Contradictions of Culture: Cities: Culture: Women*, London: Sage.

Negotiating Public Spaces: The Right to the Gendered City and the Right to Difference

Tovi Fenster

Negotiating public spaces has become part of everyday life in globalized urban spaces where individuals and communities of different ethnicities, races, cultural backgrounds, or religious orientations struggle for territorial control. The paper illustrates a conflict entailing the denial of the right to use of secular women living in Jerusalem of certain public spaces in the city in the name of the right to difference of the ultra-orthodox community living in Mea Shearim neighborhood in Jerusalem.[1]

Negotiating public spaces has become part of the realities of everyday life in globalized urban spaces. It is connected to the politics of identity and consists of the struggles for territorial control between individuals and communities of different ethnicities, races, cultural backgrounds or religious orientations. Conflicts over the use of public spaces also occur between communities and institutions, which for their part sometimes assume the role of "negotiators"—with varying degrees of success. In recent decades, negotiations on the use of urban spaces have become even more discursive with the acknowledgment of the Lefebvrian notion of the right to the city side by side with its daily denial because of security considerations, feelings of fear (especially from what is termed "the other"), religious norms, cultural values, and economic interests. This results in a situation where globalized cities are less accessible to the "public" than they were before, and everyday negotiations on the use of public space are becoming part of the routine life of city inhabitants.

---

1 For an elaborated version of this paper, see Fenster 2005, Fenster (forthcoming).

This paper illustrates one particular case of urban conflict and everyday negotiations over the use of public spaces. In this particular case the urban conflict entails the denial of the right to use of secular women living in Jerusalem of certain public spaces in the city in the name of the right to difference of the ultra-orthodox community living in Mea Shearim neighborhood. Here the conflict focuses on gender and religious identities because the denial of the right to use is practiced against women since it entails codes of modesty and clothing. The conflict also involves the religious identity of the ultra-orthodox community, for whom the practice of the Lefèbvrian right to use of public spaces in their neighborhood contradicts their basic beliefs and norms of women's modesty. This situation illustrates the discourse around Lefèbvre's (1991a; 1991b) terminology of the right to the city and the right to difference and the conflicts between universal citizenship—expressed in the right of the city—and the group's right to difference (Young 1998). In addition, the paper discusses the role of institutionalized forms, in this case, the Jerusalem Municipality, which is the sovereign and has the responsibility for ensuring that the right to use public spaces of its citizens is maintained.

Despite the fact that this is a very unique and specific case, it reflects the nature of women's and men's everyday life realities and experiences in many cities around the globe when they have to negotiate their right in the city, a right which is denied in the name of religious or cultural norms, fear, security, or economic interests.

The individual right to the city

What is the Lefèbvrian notion of the "right to the city?" The right to the city (Lefèbvre 1991a; 1991b) asserts a normative rather than a juridical right based on inhabitance. Those who inhabit the city have a right to the city. It is earned by living in the city and it is shared between the urban dweller and the citizen. This concept of a right to the city evolves within itself two main rights (Purcell 2003): the right to appropriate urban space in the sense of the right to use, the right of inhabitants to "full and complete use" of urban space in their everyday lives. It is the right to live in, play in, work in, represent, characterize, and occupy urban space in a particular city—the right to be an author of urban space. It's a creative product of, and context for, the everyday life of its inhabitants. The second component of the right to the city is the right to participation. The rights of inhabitants to take a central role in decision-making surrounding the production of urban space at any scale, whether it is the state, capital, or any other entity that takes part in the production of urban space.

Many academic works have incorporated the notion of the right to the city in their analysis of urban everyday life (Kofman 1995; Kofman/Labas 1996;

Dikec 2001; Mitchell 2003; Purcell 2003; Yacobi 2003; Cuthbert 1995; Fenster 2004). This analysis is usually integrated in the discussion of new forms of citizenship that challenge the traditional, hegemonic, nation-state forms of this notion. These new forms of citizenship refer not only to the legal status of citizens provided them by the state but also to membership and belonging within a community and the tactics and practices to claim citizen rights. Citizenship is viewed as continuously negotiated through everyday practices (Secor 2004). These new forms of citizenship challenge capitalist power relations and their increased control over social life (Purcell 2003). They also challenge the static "top down" analysis of citizenship and present an approach to citizenship as spatial strategy, which includes certain definitions of belonging, identity, and rights (Secor 2004). As Purcell (2003) indicates, these processes entail rescaling, reterritorializing, and reorienting of both economy and forms of citizenships. In this context of political and economic restructuring, the Lefèbvrian construction and meanings of "the right to the city" can be interpreted as a form of resistance to traditional structures of citizenship. It is a normative phrasing of citizenship and its resisting nature begins with the fact that the right to the city is based on inhabitance, that is, those who inhabit the city have the right to the city as opposed to other forms of membership that are determined by nation-state citizenship. The right to the city or the right to urban life, which is based on inhabitance, entails two main rights: "the right to appropriate" urban space or "the right to use" urban space and "the right to participate" in the production of urban space (Purcell 2003). As already mentioned, these normative rights encompass not only rights to resources but also the right to be the author of urban space, the right to belong in the city and to contribute to its creation.

The denial of the right to use certain urban spaces in Jerusalem and at the same time the spatial expression of the right to difference come from the fact that the ultra-orthodox community has determined or defined different conceptions of the boundaries between the "permitted" and the "forbidden," conceptions which reflect their own religious beliefs. They have established what they term "modesty walls" expressed in large signs hung at the two main entrances to the neighborhood in the Mea Shearim Street and also in entrances to the small alleys and shops located within the neighborhood. These signs pose a clear request in Hebrew and English. Sometimes the message in Hebrew and English is similar, sometimes it is slightly different: Please do not pass our neighborhood in immodest clothes.

The signs also specify the exact meaning of modest clothing: Modest clothes include: closed blouse with long sleeves, long skirt, no trousers, no tight-fitting clothes.

These specifications do not leave any room for individual interpretations as to what the meaning of "modest" is, as it is culturally constructed. And thus, there are very detailed specifications related to the appropriate ways to cover all parts of women's bodies.

Secular women living in Jerusalem find this restriction to be a denial of their right to use urban spaces and as a conduct that forces them to negotiate their use of public spaces with appropriate dress. In a study carried out in Jerusalem (Fenster 2004), women talked about this neighborhood as a public space in which they feel discomfort and where they need to prepare in advance in terms of their clothing when they want to cross this neighborhood. For secular women living in Jerusalem, no matter what their nationality, ethnicity, or religious identity, certain urban spaces represent conflict and thus a cause for discomfort because of their dress. Obviously, tensions within multi-religious communities exist in many other cities (Naylor/Ryan 1998), and sometimes these tensions have effects on women's movement in urban spaces (Secor 2002). However, this discourse represents a more complicated situation, which is becoming more and more significant in multicultural cities around the world, of constant negotiations of using public spaces when sacralization of space, in this case, denies individual rights of secular women to the city, but it reflects the group right to difference claimed by the ultra-orthodox.

The group right to difference

The group right to difference also has its spatial expression, as we have already mentioned, with the signs asking women not to cross the neighborhood with "immodest" clothing. But this expression of the right to difference has a historical background. Mea Shearim was already established in 1874 as a segregated neighborhood for ultra-orthodox people who wished to maintain their religious norms and beliefs—separated from the majority of the population (Ben Arie 1979). In the mid-19th century this neighborhood was indeed very isolated from the city center, which at that period consisted of the old city of Jerusalem, but as the city expanded and grew the neighborhood became part of the city and is now even located near the current city center, a fact that makes "the publicity" of the neighborhood more explicit and the use of its streets more frequent for the general public than before.

This practice of spatial segregation, which reflects their desire for difference, exists in many other ultra-orthodox Jewish neighborhoods in different cities around the world. Even today, ultra-orthodox communities usually choose distant sites as their preferred locations. For example, Kiryat Joel, a

Satmar[2] town in New York State, was established in the 1970s at a distance of 70 km from the city center, to protect the residents from "external influences" and to allow the children to grow up with no drug and crime influence (Mintz 1994).

It can be argued that the right to difference of the Mea Shearim residents is historical and had been a principle of their everyday life from its construction. The roots of this need and claim of sacredness or "difference" of their neighborhood is based on their belief of the sacredness of the Land of Israel as the promised Biblical land. This holiness necessitates practices of modesty and dress not only by ultra-orthodox women but also by secular women as well because women's modesty is a very basic rule in the religious Jewish lifestyle (Shilav 2004). These practices can be seen as symbolic "border guards" that help to identify people as members or non-members of the community. Women's dress is often one of the major signifiers of such border constructions (Yuval-Davis 2000). Women's dress (Muslim or Jewish) indicates the body and its covering as expressions of dominant ideologies and representations either of "Muslim women" (Dwyer 1998) or "Jewish women" and also as sites of contested cultural representations.

Thus one interpretation of these signs is that they demonstrate the gated nature of the neighborhood with "modesty gates," or as its residents phrase it: "modesty walls." These "walls" construct the boundaries of the religious and cultural identities of its residents and transform its main streets into sacred spaces, which in fact exclude secular women who do not follow the strict rules of clothing and mixed-gendered groups who disobey practices of modesty and impurity. However, such signs can also be interpreted as part of the politics of identity of the community, which struggles against "intolerance of difference" in modernity (Kong 2001).In this regard, these signs express the "right to difference" of ultra-orthodox women themselves who feel more comfortable in such a "gated" space in which their own modest dress is a norm rather than an exception, as they feel in other secular public spaces in Jerusalem (Fenster 2004).

From the point of view of the right to difference, these signs serve as a defense against "inappropriate" dress and lifestyle which contradict the group's norms and standards of behavior. Such a construction of public spaces as sacred is contested in any case (Kong 2001), mainly because sacred is a "contested category," as it represents "hierarchical power relations of domination and subordination, inclusion and exclusion, appropriation and dispossession"

---

2 Satmar is one of the ultra-orthodox Hasidic Jewish groups that live in Orange County, near New York. Hasidim are the followers of an 18th-century pietistic movement. The major Hasidic groups include: Belz, Bobov, Ger, Lubavitch, and Satmar. Their names typically derive from their town of origin. Each group is led by a religious leader (a *rebbe*) (cf. Valins 2003; Mintz 1994).

(Chidester/Linenthal 1995: 17; Kong 2001). A sacred place is constructed by appropriation of property, politics of exclusion, maintaining boundaries, and distancing the inside from the outside (Kong 2001). As Sibley (1995; 1999) mentions, forms and norms of exclusion are not only the practices of the majority against the minority but also the practices of the minority against the majority—as the case of Mea Shearim indicates.

Moving the discussion to group identity and rights, can we discuss the right to difference of the ultra orthodox as a group right and the practices of "modesty walls" as its expressions? In other words, is the "group" unit, rather than the individual, a valid component in the discussion of the right to difference? Young (1998) asserts the political importance of the concept "social group" as the unit, which motivates and mobilizes social movements such as the women's movement, the gay movement, or elder's movements more than exclusively class or economic interests. However, she claims that group identity should be understood in relational terms, and, although social processes of affinity and separation define groups, they do not always give groups a substantive identity, because each of the group members possess multiple identities besides the "group identity": "There is no common nature that members of a group have," she argues (1998: 273). However, she argues that the inclusion and participation of everyone in social and political institutions sometimes requires the articulation of "special rights" that meet the needs of a group's difference. Here she mainly refers to "oppressed groups," such as women, gay communities, elderly people, or in general groups who suffer from exploitation, marginalization, powerlessness, cultural imperialism, and violence and harassment. Can such conditions be related to the position of the ultra orthodox in Jerusalem? Perhaps so in their eyes, but some would argue that these terminologies of group oppression better apply to secular women. Kymlicka's (1998) definition of "religious sects" as groups that demand exemption from civil society because its norms contradict some of the groups' religious practices, can be useful in this discussion. Sometimes, he argues, these demands for exemption are indeed a form of withdrawal from the larger society, but some of them show a desire for integration. For example, Kimlicka (1998) says, Orthodox Jews wanted to join the US military, but needed an exemption from the usual regulations so that they could wear their yarmulkes. This practice can be seen as an example of a group right to difference, which expresses a will to integrate in civil life and duties. Following this line of thinking, can we then interpret the "modesty walls" as an expression of the ultra-orthodox's desire to integrate in the sense that these "walls" are more symbolic than physical, or is this a struggle against the intolerance of the modernized secular, with women's modesty practices the price paid for this struggle?

The role of governance in negotiating urban conflicts

What is the role of local governance in negotiating or solving urban conflicts? In other words, how do municipalities act in their policies between the Lefèbvrian standpoint of the right to the city and the group right to difference? In the former case municipalities should prohibit practices such as "modesty walls" in the city as they deny the "right to use" of women in the city. In the latter, municipalities could argue that this practice expresses the group's identity in maintaining privatized public spaces as sacred that should be respected, especially in an era when the Lefèbvrian right to the city is denied in the name of security, for example.

Relating to this discourse between the right to the city and the right to difference, Benvenisti (1998) argues that the claim for religious autonomy or the sacralization of space is justified only if it does not contradict fundamental norms and state legislation. As he argues, the formulation of such a "religious ghetto" is acceptable as long as it is based on cultural and religious preservation principles and heritage necessity. This is the case of the ultra-orthodox, Benvenisti argues, as much as the claims of the Aboriginals in Australia and the First Nations in Canada and the Sami in Scandinavia to maintain their traditional life. The only problem Benvenisti sees is in the fact that such norms, which create exclusion, can harm women's rights. The solution Benvenisti suggests is to allow such principles of autonomy of these communities to take place, but without offending the rights of the majority. Similar debates have been discussed elsewhere (Fenster 1999a; 1999b) regarding planning procedures for ethnic groups such as the Bedouin in the Negev. There the particularistic cultural-religious identity of the male Bedouin perpetuates women's subordination by dictating norms of modesty and seclusion. Modernist-professional planning, which is intolerant to such identity-related issues, actually designs Bedouin towns in such a way that women cannot use public spaces because of the danger that their modesty may be abused in the eyes of the males. These principles enhance the chances of unwanted meetings between women and men of different tribes and threaten women's modesty (Fenster 1999a; 1999b).

In other cities in Israel, such as Tel Aviv, certain neighborhoods are populated by ultra-orthodox communities, but with no explicit exclusionary signs. There are similar signs in the city of Benei Brak for example, a city with mostly religious[3] residents, but these signs are less offensive and perhaps less exclusionary. Shilav (1997) analyzes the management of ultra-orthodox cities

---

3 As mentioned above, the ultra-orthodox, as well as other religious groups in Israel, are not homogeneous, and each represents a different degree of tolerance towards secular groups.

in Israel relating to the extent to which the ultra-orthodox communities themselves are flexible or tolerant to the "other"—mostly secular groups or people with less rigid religious practices living with them.

Practices of sacralization of public spaces are also not known in cities outside Israel where ultra-orthodox communities live, such as in the USA, Canada, and Britain. This is perhaps because they live in isolated areas anyway and do not need to protect themselves from outside "negative" influence (Valins 2003).

In Jerusalem the role of the municipality in negotiating urban conflict is different. In order to understand this, I talked to the Chief of the City Enforcement Department at the Jerusalem Municipality, a department which deals with enforcing municipal bylaws, including those concerning licensing for street signs and businesses. I asked him about the legality of the signs hung up in the streets of Mea Shearim. He stated that in general the municipality is very rigid in enforcing municipal bylaws by imposing licensing for street signs and businesses. But in Mea Shearim, he said, this is different. Although the signs there are illegal, as they were not approved and licensed by the municipality, the municipality's workers cannot enforce the law. The Chief of the City Enforcement Department defined this area as "outside the law and outside enforcing the law" (interview, 20 July 2003). He explains that the difficulty in enforcing this bylaw in Mea Shearim is due to lack of enough labor power. He says: "Even if we take down these signs they will put them up again." This, in fact, reflects the struggle of the ultra-orthodox group to establish its politics of identity and community by challenging the sovereignty of the municipality, and perhaps its "intolerance to difference." It also expresses the fact that the Mea Shearim group does not recognize the sovereignty of the municipality. But this is probably also an expression of the municipality's implicit politics of not interfering with these practices, probably because of local politics and power relations within the municipality's council. The Chief of the City Enforcement Department admits that if such signs restricting movement had appeared in secular neighborhoods, the municipality would have reacted forcefully against this practice. Thus, in spite of their illegitimate status, these signs still hang in public spaces, transforming the neighborhood into a gated one.

Conclusions

This paper illustrates how everyday life in urban spaces today entails negotiations over the use of public space. It also highlights the frequent clashes between different sets of rights: the individual right to the city and the group right to difference in this case. The paper suggests that these apparent clashes between identity rights are becoming part and parcel of everyday realities in globalized urban spaces.

The case of Mea Shearim represents an extreme example of an ultra-orthodox community, which, because of its desire to maintain "pure" and "sacred" ghettoized spaces, acts illegally by constructing symbolic gates at the entrances to the neighborhood, thus denying the right to use of secular women in Jerusalem.

The paper also illustrates the rather sensitive and complicated situations of local governance and municipalities, which sometimes find themselves as "negotiators" or even moderators of urban conflicts. The Jerusalem municipality does not take this standpoint, and its attitude reflects a dilemma between various sets of rights more than reflecting a clear-cut policy.

The paper does not suggest a solution but aims to expose the multiple implications of such situations. A feminist's first reaction to such exclusionary practices in the city might be negative, but discussing such issues in depth reveals the different meanings and implications of such situations that forces one to deal with sometimes contradictory meanings of the right to the city and the contrast inherent between them, a situation which becomes more and more apparent in multi-ethnicized, multi-sacralized and multi-nationalized global urban spaces. Such dilemmas will be part of city governance's daily occupation, as diversity becomes an increasingly important issue in new global spaces. One of the major challenges of city governance is how to respect both individual and group rights while maintaining women's and other groups' rights to freedom of movement in the city.

References

Ben Arie, Yehoshua (1979) *City as a Mirror of a Period – The New Jerusalem at its Beginning*, Jerusalem: Yad Itzhak Ben Zvi Publications (Hebrew).

Benvenisti, Eyal (1998) "'Separate but Equal' in the Allocation of State Land for Housing". *Law Review* 21/3, pp. 769–798 (Hebrew).

Chidester, David/Linenthal, Edward T. (1995) "Introduction". In David Chidester/ Edward T. Linenthal (eds.) *American Sacred Space*, Bloomington, NI: Indiana University Press, pp. 1–42.

Cuthbert, Alexander R. (1995) "The Right to the City: Surveillance, Private Interest and the Public Domain in Hong Kong". *Cities* 12/5, pp. 293–310.

Dikec, Mustafa (2001) "Justice and the Spatial Imagination". *Environment and Planning A* 33, pp. 1785–1805.

Fenster, Tovi (1999a) "Space for Gender: Cultural Roles of the Forbidden and the Permitted". Environment and Planning D: Society and Space 17, pp. 227–246.

Fenster, Tovi (1999b) "Culture, Human Rights and Planning (as Control) for Minority Women in Israel". In Tovi Fenster (ed.) *Gender, Planning and Human Rights*, London: Routledge, pp. 39–54.

Fenster, Tovi (2000) "Ashkenazi Man – Ethiopian Woman: Between Centralistic and Social Planning". Panim – Journal of Culture, Society and Education 13, pp. 54–60 (Hebrew).

Fenster, Tovi (2002) "Planning as Control – Cultural and Gendered Manipulation and Mis-Use of Knowledge". Hagar – International Social Science Review 1, pp.67–84.

Fenster, Tovi (2004) *The Global City and the Holy City – Narratives on Planning, Knowledge and Diversity*, London: Pearson.

Fenster, Tovi (2005) "Identity Issues and Local Governance: Women's Everyday Life in the City". Social Identities 11/1, pp. 23–39.

Fenster, Tovi (forthcoming) "Gender, religion and urban management: Women's Everyday life in Jerusalem". In: Karen M. Morin/Jeanne K. Guelk (eds.) *Women, Religion & Space*, Syracuse: Syracuse University Press.

Kofman, Eleonore (1995) "Citizenship for Some But Not for Others: Spaces of Citizenship in Contemporary Europe". Political Geography 14, pp. 121–137.

Kofman, Eleonore/Labas, E. (1996) *Writings on Cities: Henri Lefèbvre*, Cambridge: Blackwell.

Kong, Lily (2001) "Mapping 'new' Geographies of Religion: Politics and Poetics in Modernity". Progress in Human Geography 25/2, pp. 211–233.

Kymlicka, Will (1998) "Multicultural Citizenship". In G. Shafir (ed.) *The Citizenship Debate*, Minneapolis: University of Minnesota Press, pp. 167–188.

Lefèbvre, Henri (1991a) *Critique of Everyday Life*, London: Verso.

Lefèbvre, Henri (1991b) *The Production of Space*, Oxford: Blackwell.

Mintz, Jerome. R. (1994) *Hasidic People: A Place in the New World*, London: Harvard University Press.

Mitchell, Don (2003) *The Right to the City: Social Justice and The Right for Public Space*, New York: The Guilford Press.

Naylor, S.K./Ryan, J.R. (1998) *Ethnicity and Cultural Landscapes: Mosques, Guradwaras, and Mandirs in England and Wales*. Paper presented at the Religion and Locality Conference, University of Leeds.

Pain, Rachell (1991) "Space, Sexual Violence and Social Control". Progress in Human Geography 15/4, pp. 415–431.

Purcell, Mark (2003) "Citizenship and the Right to the Global City: Reimagining the Capitalist World Order". International Journal of Urban and Regional Studies 27/3, pp. 564–590.

Secor, Anna (2002) "The Veil and Urban Space in Istanbul: Women's Dress, Mobility and Islamic Knowledge". Gender, Place and Culture 9/1, pp. 5–22.

Secor, Anna (2004) "'There Is an Istanbul That Belongs to Me': Citizenship, Space and Identity in the City". Annals of Association of American Geographers 94/2, pp. 352–368.

Shilav, Yosef (1997) *Governance in an Ultra Orthodox City*, Jerusalem: Floresheimer Institute (Hebrew).

Shilav, Yosef (2004), personal communication.

Sibely, David (1995) *Geographies of Exclusion*, London: Routledge.

Sibley, David (1998) "Problemitizing Exclusion: Reflections on Space, Difference and Knowledge". International Planning Studies 3/1, pp. 93–100.

Valins, Oliver (2000) "Institutionalised Religion: Sacred Texts and Jewish Spatial Practice". Geoforum 31, pp. 575–586.

Valins, Oliver (2003) "Stubborn Identities and the Construction of Sociospatial Boundaries: Ultra-orthodox Jews Living in Contemporary Britain". Transactions of the Institute of British Geographers 28, pp. 158–175.

Wekerle, Gerda (2000) "Women's rights to the city". In E. Isin (ed.) *Democracy, Citizenship and the Global City*, London: Routledge, pp. 203–217.

Yacobi, Haim (2003) "Everyday Life in Lod: On Power, Identity and Spatial Protest" Jamaa 10, pp. 69–109 (Hebrew).

Young, Iris Marion (1998) "Polity and Group Difference: A Critique of the Ideal of Universal Citizenship". In G. Shafir (ed.) *The Citizenship Debate*, Minneapolis: University of Minnesota Press, pp. 263–290.

Yuval-Davis, Nira (2000) "Citizenship, territoriality and gendered construction of difference'. In E. Isin (ed.) *Democracy, Citizenship and the Global City*, London: Routledge, pp. 171–187.

On the Road to Being White: The Construction of Whiteness in the Everyday Life of Expatriate German High Flyers in Singapore and London

LARS MEIER

Based on ethnographic field studies of the everyday life of German professionals working in the financial sector in London and Singapore, I describe the construction of whiteness as an everyday process in interaction with the specific city. The article shows that even the everyday life of the so-called global elite is strongly bound to particular structures and to their images of the city and the "other," brought in as part of the expatriates' travel baggage.

Introduction

Ethnicity should not only be seen as a system that socially classifies the non-white and that is in consequence a powerful system of social subordination. It is also, in the case of whiteness, a system which inscribes social privileges, privileges which are constructed and reproduced in the everyday practices of "white people" and in the everyday construction of self and otherness.

The aim of my article is to make visible the continuous construction of whiteness in interaction with each specific city and, subsequently, to oppose naturalization of whiteness as the norm by denying its validity as an attribute of social classification. "As long as race is something only applied to non-white peoples, as long as white people are not racially seen and named, they/we function as a human norm. Other people are raced, we are just people" (Dyer 2001: 1).

Postcolonial studies show that the durable colonial discourse defined the "others'" culture and geography as primitive or as a stereotypical Orient (cf. Said 1978; Fanon 1967). The colonial division of the "West and the Rest" (cf. Hall 1994) neglects internal differences and divides the world into two homogeneous blocks: "The West" is imaged as modern, developed, civilised and central. "The Rest" on the other hand is imaged as a premodern, undeveloped, and uncivilised periphery. In the meaning of "the West and the Rest," the Orient is not just "there," it is part of the "here"; it is part of the European imagination (cf. Said 1978). The imagination of the "other" and the construction of white identity are historically based (cf. Lambert 2005; Bonnett 2000) and continually produced/reproduced in current everyday action. Thus, being white is a result of learning to be white and to image the other (cf. Frankenberg 1993; Thandeka 1999). Part of learning to be white is to learn the specific places of the whites (cf. Frankenberg 1993). The inscription of meaning in places is intertwined with identities: one's own place and own identity or the foreign place and the foreign identity are bounded concepts. Identities and meanings are socially constructed; this applies to social groups just as it does to the inscription of meanings in places and landscapes (cf. Said 1978, Duncan/Duncan 1988).

By conceptualizing the finance milieu as a travelling culture (cf. Clifford 1997), this article will analyse everyday life not only at a fixed, local level. Following the routes, different places and travel between these places come into the focus of the analysis.

The everyday action of expatriates is conceptualised as a wider activity; it is also fed by practices, assumptions, and images that are learned in distant places, such as in Germany. Limiting the analysis of everyday life to the local level loses the importance of images for local everyday action. I argue that German professionals bring their learned images into Singapore and London and reproduce them in their specific everyday action. Images are part of their travel baggage, which has been packed in distant places and times. Part of this baggage is the construction of whiteness.[1]

My paper is based on ethnographic field studies of the everyday life of the so-called global or transnational elite (cf. Sklair 2001, Castells 1996, Beaverstock 2001), taking the example of German employees in the financial sector of two major international financial centres, London and Singapore. By locat-

---

1 In this article I focus on the identity formation of whiteness. Other identities, such as gender (cf. Frankenberg 1993) and class/milieu identities (cf. Roediger 1992), shine through the construction of whiteness; but they will not be explicitly discussed here.

ing the research project in the same milieu in two cities, it is possible to analyse the construction of whiteness in dependence on the structures of the specific city. Following Anthony King (cf. King 1990), I situate the cities in continuity with their past: On the one hand, London as the former core metropolis of the British Empire (or "The Imperial City"), in which whiteness has its origin. On the other hand, Singapore as a former British-colonized city (or "The Colonial City"), in which whiteness is a category connected with the traveller, the businessman, and the colonizer. I will look into the effects of their histories as Colonial or Imperial cities regarding the contemporary everyday behaviour of white finance employees. My focus is mainly on the construction of whiteness in Singapore, but at the end of my paper I will contrast some of the central findings with my findings on the construction of whiteness in London.

By interviewing employees of the financial sector and investigating the places which they use, I had the opportunity to observe the everyday life of white Germans and their interaction with specific places in each specific city. My research project is based on 19 semi-structured, in-depth interviews with German employees working in the financial sector in London, as well as on 19 interviews with the same social group working in Singapore. In addition to the interviews, I was able to make field notes on participant observations by joining my interviewees in restaurants, cafes, or bars, visiting their homes, meeting them in their workplace, or simply joining them in driving or walking around the city. Investigations of the places in which my interviewees live, work, or engage in leisure activities contributed to the empirical basis of my investigation.

I will follow two lines of argument: First, I will argue that the production of whiteness is not a universal experience. Whiteness has to be created in everyday life in dependence on specific structures of the particular city and on specific images brought in from Germany. Second, I will show that the production of whiteness in each city does not take place only in segregated quarters of the city. It is also produced on the everyday level in small spatial interactions between self and others in a seemingly homogenous city quarter.

Becoming White in Singapore

After an interview with a male German banker who has been living in Asia for more than 15 years, I had the opportunity to see where he lives in Singapore. The field notes from our travel through "his" Singapore will illustrate my central line of argument.

By following me and my interviewee travelling around "his" Singapore, it is possible to learn something about the construction of whiteness in Singapore. But the reader should be aware: Actively reading and following his route means following one's own route. Beyond seeing the process of being white for the German finance employee, a white reader will find some of his or her own images. Non-whites considering that "the subaltern cannot speak" (cf. Spivak 1988) are also part and reproducers alike of this powerful discourse.

At several points I will interrupt this example by examining central findings with the help of passages from other interviews. To avoid confusion, these interruptions are marked in front of the sequence by assigned codes for different interviewees (e.g. S 5).

We start at my interviewee's workplace, in an aluminium-faced building. Entering the building one feels the comfortable air-conditioned coolness. Behind the information desk in the entrance hall stands a dark-skinned man (perhaps, according to Singaporean categories, a Malay) with a dark blue suit, who shows me the entrance to the bank institute.

Ethnic division of labour in which the employed whites are always in top positions
There is an omnipresent ethnic division of labour in Singapore. Essentially all employed whites in Singapore always work as "foreign talents" in qualified work in the developed service sector. My interviewees find themselves to be desired and required by Singaporean society as highly qualified personnel. One mentioned that even the president of Singapore remarked that Singaporean society depends on the knowledge of the expatriates. My interviewees explain this by associating whiteness with creativity, informality, and independence, and contrasting this with an ascription of Singaporeans as uncreative and dependent.
S10: "The people here are so obsessed by what they are fed three or four times every day by the newspapers, the government and so on. This makes them mostly dependent. They cannot do anything on their own. Everything is orderly."

After a short wait, my interviewee welcomes me and invites me into his office. He is in his fifties, has a fit figure with short-cut grey hair and is wearing black trousers, a lilac shirt and a lilac tie, but no suit.

Following my former experiences with the well-dressed German finance employees in London, I had prepared myself to enter the world of the finance employees in Singapore by changing my usual clothing style to wearing black shoes, an ironed long-sleeve shirt, and a suit for the interviews. But after entering the field in Singapore I changed this style, because my interviewees, wearing polo-shirts without jacket or tie, were—to my surprise—mostly dressed more casually than I was.

Differentiation and group formation is based on whiteness, not on clothes
Usually, special clothes are a form of everyday differentiation from the other (cf. Bourdieu 1987). For the German finance employees in Singapore there is less need to differentiate by clothes, as the difference through their whiteness is so obvious and equivalent to the distinction by clothes. The two following interview sequences underline this argument:

S6: "I must say that here in Singapore you don't wear a collar, a tie, and a suit every day like in Germany, the demand is not strong like it is in Germany. I wear casual clothes, with the exception of when there is something special like a ceremony then I will wear collar and tie, but there is normally no need for a jacket."

S10: "If I am leaving for home after work, then I take off the tie and put it there into the drawer [he opens the drawer with different ties in it]. I have five others there and tomorrow morning I'll choose one for wearing. In the evening I don't go home with a tie, there is nobody who knows me outside and if there was somebody who knows me, it would be all the same to me (he laughs)."

After the interview we go to the underground car park and get into a large, immaculate, silver-coloured Mercedes Benz. On starting the engine, the air-conditioning and the radio are automatically turned on. While he shows me his Singapore through the car window, we drive through the streets to the sound of pop music.

Figure 1: On the road with a view of the central business district (Photo: © Lars Meier)

Being an observer from a separate viewpoint and being a brave explorer
Detachment from the outside world of the city is a constant experience for the expatriates. Working in an isolated business park or in an office building with controlled access, driving

129

in a car, living in a separated condominium, or spending leisure time in clubs: all these places have formal entrance controls. The smell of the city, its sounds, and its climate are outside the window. From the inside it is possible to discover the outside. The inside is associated with relaxation and socialising with peers.

Being an observer from a distant standpoint is bounded by its converse, being a brave discoverer of the foreign world. Part of constructing whiteness entails having no fear of entering a foreign world, and considering the foreign as a noble challenge that confers prestige. The whites differentiate themselves from the locals by describing them as anxious. The locals do not play the role of observer, the whites describe them as being tied up in their families and disconnected from the outer world. For the whites, exploring the foreign is described as a strenuous activity that must be planned in advance. But it promises fine rewards of honour.

This is shown in the following interview sequence, in which one of my interviewees describes the difference between the white expatriates and the Singaporeans in the case of Little India, a Singapore city-quarter with a large proportion of Indian workers.

S5: "The expats have little fear of contact with Little India. The Singaporeans don't go to Little India. It is different for the expats…"

LM: "They go there?"

S5: "Yes, of course they go there, but the Singaporeans see it as very dangerous."

For another interviewee the Singaporeans have a lack of interest in contacting different cultures. He contrasted this with his self-description of being interested in foreign cultures, e.g. in eating experiences at local food vendors in the so-called hawker stalls.

LM: "How would you describe your contact with the Singaporeans?"

S10: (Laughing) "It is practically non-existent. […] It is complicated. For example, when we are having an annual dinner, there is a raffle after the lunch or some nonsense like that, and after that they are gone. Then there is one table where the expatriates sit."

LM: "Why?"

S10: "It is a typical Chinese thing: they sit the whole evening and eat. The food is already three days old, but they continue eating it and drinking tea. And if they don't, they want to be amongst themselves, they don't feel comfortable. I feel comfortable when I am going to a restaurant or sometimes to a hawker stall."

Returning now to our car drive around Singapore, we arrive after 15 minutes of driving down a road near Holland Village. The interviewee shows me his former home, where he lived with his children and his former wife some years ago.

Durability of colonial city structures constructs whiteness

Holland Village is a green residential district and a traditional expatriate area. Since it was established in the late 1930s as a British military village, it has been defined as a classical city quarter for Europeans. At that time special shops were installed to serve the needs of the British military personnel (cf. Chuang 1995). The contemporary expatriates' decision to live in Holland Village underlines the durability of colonial structures and their importance for contemporary everyday life in Singapore.

This durability is grounded on inscribed images of Holland Village as an expatriate quarter in the context of the concentration of special places that are seen as specifically expatriate, such as restaurants, boutiques, and particular shops. These images are spread by expatriate social networks. The social networks of colleagues and employers are quite important for gathering initial information about Singapore shortly after or even before arrival in the city. Expatriates' use of these places in their everyday life is inscribed as the norm. The use of other places that do not have the inscription of being expatriate is described as something special, which is sometimes possible, but is necessarily bound to an active decision to avoid the usual expatriate places.

Figure 2: Villa in a preferred expatriate residential district (Photo: © Lars Meier)

He shows me the sign of his former street and says that he is responsible for it. He sent a letter of complaint to the minister because nobody could find the small street since it had the same name as the main road. After that the minister changed the street sign.

Making geography and bringing order to a previously disordered area
Like the structuring of the city into ethnic clusters by the British colonizer Sir Stamford Raffles (cf. Perry/Kong/Yeoh 1997: 25–30), creating order is still part of whiteness.
We continue the ride to the German supermarket and he tells me that he will visit his girlfriend in another Asian country and has to bring some German groceries, like "Prinzenrolle" and "Schwarzbrot." In the small market there are five other white customers and a Chinese saleswoman. After carrying the shopping items to the car, we drive to the Swiss butcher, "a gold mine," says the banker. After entering the butchers, he greets the butcher in German and speaks to a Chinese customer in Mandarin. He tells me that this woman calls herself a banana because she has lived in the USA for a couple of years: yellow on the outside and inside she is white. He claims that he is an egg, the outside is white and the inside is yellow.

The mark of whiteness is seen as durable. Whites have a consciousness of their whiteness and construct this as solid and unchangeable
The following interview sequence with a white woman, talking to me about a weekend trip with friends, underlines this claim.
S5: "A short time ago, when I was trekking on Lombok, there was also an expat there, whom I didn't know, but the others were all South-Koreans. In this context I was not conscious of being an expatriate or that I am a Westerner, that I am not an Asian. I have been living here too long for that and I have too much contact with locals. In that moment I was not thinking that I was different in some way."
LM: "Okay."
S5: "Maybe later on, just on the photographs or so […]. You always play a different role, I think, you can't escape it."

Figure 3: The German supermarket (Photo: © Lars Meier)

Continuing the drive through Singapore, he tells me that the wives of the male expatriates will not leave Singapore, because for them it is such an easy and pleasant life here. Singapore is a golden cage for expatriate women and they become little princesses, according to my interviewee.

There is a special gendered division of labour for the white expatriate couples, which is different from their German home
The white women mostly do not do household work in Singapore. They more often take the role of an employer instructing the maid. Most of the expatriate families have a maid (a woman from Southeast Asia), who organizes the household and looks after the children. The expatriate women organize the cultural affairs and social contacts of the expatriate family in Singapore and with friends and family in Germany. The women are also committed to welfare organizations and to the German school in Singapore.

Continuing on in the car, we pass an Asian woman wearing short trousers. He points at her through the car window and says: "Look, that's the style here and nobody thinks anything of it, they are so naïve here. In Europe everybody would think: 'Oh, hot pants!' But here they don't think about it and simply wear it, because it is comfortable." He said that many expatriates think that they can take them and go to bed with them, but that is not always the case.

The whites contrast the other, the Asian women, as naïve and incapable of judging the effect of their body presentation

He stops at a gate, which is controlled by a Malay guard. The guard opens the gate by remote control. The living area of my interviewee is surrounded by a wall and a metal gate. He lives in a so-called condominium near the central shopping street in Singapore. A condominium is an area with several high rise flats, often with other white expatriate people living there. It usually has a swimming pool, a gym, a barbeque area, sometimes tennis courts, and a small supermarket, which are used communally by the residents of the condominium.

Separation is ubiquitous: The whites live, work, and spend their leisure time in separated and guarded areas (bank buildings, condominiums, and clubs)
Living in clearly separated places is part of the everyday experience of the white expats. The following interview sequence confirms that whiteness is often an entrance ticket to these separated areas.
S2: "It is guarded by official security, there are guards walking around and there is a fence in front. But if you want to enter the area—if you have white skin and if you are a European—the guard will let you in. Then you can drive in, that is not a problem."

Figure 4: Gate of a condominium (Photo: © Lars Meier)

After parking his car in the condominium, we take the escalator to the 6th floor and enter his apartment. In his apartment there are many articles of antique Asian and German furniture and sculptures, which he brought from his previous stays abroad. Hanging on the apartment wall is a picture of his grandfather and a family tree.

The antiques recall the history of the whites. The whites have their own history, which is cultivated by gathering antiques and history-related artefacts such as books on German history.

After entering the main living room he calls for the maid: "Hello, hello!" The maid lives behind the kitchen in a so-called maid quarter, which contains a small sleeping room, a corridor, and a bathroom. While showing me this he mentions the air-conditioning in the maid quarter and tells me that he installed it just for his maid and that this is an unusual service for maids here in Singapore. By this he indicates that the Chinese normally treat their maids less well than the Europeans do.

Being a benefactor is part of whiteness
The other, the Chinese upper class, is ascribed as being less cultivated and consequently not treating their maids with the respect that the Whites do.

He tells me that his maid is from the Philippines and explains that the maids from the Philippines are the most expensive, because they can speak English and they are relatively the most easy-going. He has his maid from an agency, they have pictures and biometrical data of the potential maids, and you choose between them. He says that it is a sort of meat market.

While showing me the apartment, he complains about the absence of the maid. He writes her a note and tells me that it's good when she knows that he has been here and she has not. He says that his maid is certainly at her boyfriend's and is sleeping there. To underline this he says that there is a box of contraceptive pills on the table in the maid's quarter.

The white man has to control the wild and naïve maid. His control impinges on her time and intimate life.
Living in the same apartment with a maid is not a problem of privacy for the white man. The small-scale separation is regulated by the reserved behaviour of the maid, up to being invisible, and by strict time regulation of the maid's presence in the main apartment.

We take the escalator down to the entrance of the condominium and leave by car. My interviewee drives back to his office and I take the bus back home. The ride is over.

Contrasting becoming White in London with becoming White in Singapore

To summarize my findings: Being white and producing whiteness in everyday practice is part of everyday segregation, which is, as I show for the Colonial City Singapore, produced in the direct interaction with the other, the non-White. Whiteness in Singapore is produced by inscribing it with creativity, being experienced, being brave as an observer, having a cultural history, bringing order, and being a benefactor. Of course the other is described as having the opposite attributes.

Understanding the construction of whiteness as a permanent everyday process, I argue that there is a different significance to whiteness in London and in Singapore, mediated by different everyday activities and constructions of whiteness by the German professionals.

German expatriates come to Singapore and London with specific images of the city and the other in their baggage. These images are translated and reproduced in their everyday life. Place also matters for the mobile professionals, it matters in their actions and in their imaginations of the self and the other.

Following a white professional in the developed, modern urban centre of Singapore, I could demonstrate the durability of colonial images and their significance for contemporary everyday life. Everyday life in the international finance centre is strongly dependent on the historical routes which can now be experienced in specific structures and also in specific images of the city. These images are brought to the city, they are learned elsewhere in Germany, and they become lived reality in Singapore. Therefore, from this point of view, Singapore is still the colonial city.

In the case of Singapore, the ethnographic study could show that the other is often not clearly separated in apparently homogenous city quarters. In fact, segregation is produced also on a smaller scale inside the quarters: in the villa or apartment, in interactions with the other in the form of a maid, living door to door. In interactions in the workplace through contact with the other, as a consequence of the ethnic division of labour, with the Asian secretary, the Malay cleaner, and the highly qualified White. Or at places of leisure in contacts between the Indian or Bangladeshi waiter and the white customer.

In the Imperial City London, segregation on the small scale level is not as important as in Singapore; the white bank employees usually do not have maids living in their home. Whiteness in London is not synonymous with being rich and being part of the elite. The other in London is also the white worker or the white pauper. Segregation in London in the everyday life of the bank employees is more important on the scale of city quarters.

For that reason it is not surprising that in London it is far more important for the elite to differ by wearing fine clothes and carrying their entrance tickets to elite places directly on the body: the bank employees in London all wear formal black suits and ties. Achieving entrance to a golf club requires a specific dress code. In contrast to those in London, the white finance employees in Singapore wear less formal clothes, sometimes polo-shirts or short-sleeve shirts, and often no suits or ties. In Singapore being white, a synonym for being elite, is enough to obtain entrance to special places.

With my study I have pointed out that the global elite are not locating their everyday life in a uniform global space. Everyday life is strongly bounded by the specific city. Its history as a Colonial or an Imperial city can be found in images transmitted to the present day, with enduring consequences for contemporary constructions of identity and for everyday action, as demonstrated in the case of the experience of whiteness in Singapore.

References

Beaverstock, Jonathan V. (2002) "Transnational elites in global cities – British expatriates in Singapore's financial district". Geoforum, 33, pp. 528–538.

Bonnett, Alastair (2000) *White identities: Historical and International Perspectives*, Harlow: Prentice Hall.

Bourdieu, Pierre (1987) *Die feinen Unterschiede – Kritik der gesellschaftlichen Urteilskraft*, Frankfurt am Main: Suhrkamp Verlag.

Castells, Manuel (1996) *The Rise of the Network Society*, Oxford (UK)/Malden (USA): Blackwell Publishers.

Chuang, Chang Tou (1995) "The 'Expatriatisation' of Holland Village" In Brenda S.A. Yeoh/Lily Kong (eds.) *Portraits of Places – History, Community and Identity in Singapore*, Singapore: TIMES Editions, pp.140–157.

Clifford, James (1997) *Routes: Travel and Translation in the Late Twentieth Century*, Cambridge (MA)/London: Harvard University Press.

Duncan, John/Duncan, Nancy (1988) "(Re)reading the landscape". Environment and Planning D: Society and Space 6, pp. 117–126.

Dyer, Richard (1997) *White*, London/New York: Routledge.

Fanon, Franz (1967) *Black Skins, White Masks*, London: Pluto.

Frankenberg, Ruth (1993) *White Women Race Matters – The Social Construction of Whiteness*, Minneapolis: University of Minneapolis Press.

Hall, Stuart (1994) "Der Westen und der Rest. Diskurs und Macht". In: Stuart Hall (ed.) *Ausgewählte Schriften*, 2, Hamburg: Argument Verlag, pp. 137–179.

King, Anthony D. (1990) *Urbanism, Colonialism, and the World-Economy – Cultural and Spatial Foundations of the World Urban System*, London/New York: Routledge.

Lambert, David (2005) "Producing/contesting whiteness: rebellion, anti-slavery and enslavement in Barbados 1816". Geoforum 36, pp. 29–43.

Perry, Martin/Kong, Lily/Yeoh, Brenda (1997) *Singapore – A Developmental City State*, Chichester (UK) et al.: John Wiley & Sons.

Roediger, David (1992) *The Wages of Whiteness: Race and the Making of the American Working Class*, London: Verso.

Said, Edward (1978) *Orientalism: Western Conceptions of the Orient*, Harmondsworth: Penguin.

Sklair, Leslie (2001) *The Transnational Capitalist Class*, Oxford (UK)/Malden (MA): Blackwell Publishers.

Spivak, Gayatri Chakravorty (1988) "Can the Subaltern Speak?". In Cary Nelson/Lawrence Grossberg (eds.) Marxism and the Interpretation of Culture, Basingstoke: Macmillan Education, pp. 271–313.

Thandeka (1999) *Learning to Be White: Money, Race and God in America*, New York: Continuum.

Prostitution—
Power Relations between Space and Gender

MARTINA LÖW/RENATE RUHNE

The paper takes a sociological look at the social construction of red-light districts and sex work in Vienna (Austria) and Frankfurt (Germany). By analyzing the organization of perceptions, glances, and corresponding body technologies on the one hand and common strategies of spatio-social control on the other hand, we reconstruct the production of the field as materially and symbolically separated from "normal" everyday life. As a devaluated "space of the other," it is intertwined with the (re)production of gender orders.

By turns glittering and erotic, tragic and destructive, sexwork is rooted in large-scale industry and small-scale trade. As in many other women's professions, including e.g. speech therapy, homeopathy, beauty culture, training is not government-regulated and women themselves usually have to foot the bill. Another aspect that links prostitutes with hairdressers, nurses, and salesgirls is body-related activity and emotional work. Sexwork is surrounded by a world of images—and largely unexplored. There is no classic technical narrative on prostitution that could serve as orientation for practitioners or a subject of study for scholars. What we find instead are endless mythological depictions ranging from the supposed glamour of the red-light milieu to the plight of wretchedly exploited women; on the one hand these depictions provide no orientational knowledge of the field, and on the other hand they present highly disparate technical findings that resist any attempts to weave them into a coherent body of expert knowledge. While sexworkers, pimps, social workers, and police officers are very knowledgeable in the field of prostitution, this knowledge is contradictory and broken up into different strands of the narrative. With the same self-assurance, some sexworkers speak of sexuality fulfilled in the course of work (e.g. Domentat 2003), while others, on talk shows, note that things are getting bad "when you start to feel anything." While police officers in one department underline the important role played in prostitution by the traffic in human beings, a different department, or a street worker, may report on biographies marked by voluntary migration. Sometimes prostitution is described as a filthy, degrading, dangerous trade, sometimes it is depicted as self-determined work pursued to gain a living.

There appears to be no agreement in society—in the sense of scholarly findings—on the world of prostitution. If there is in most social fields a dominant narrative that serves, among other things, to guide the perceptions of the persons involved, what we can observe in the red-light milieu breaks down into numberless truths that exist, unmediated, side by side.

In the midst of this complex of contradictory and yet well-documented expert opinions and evidence, we will, in what follows, attempt a change of perspective, not focusing on sociopolitical, criminological, or legal issues of the kind typical of today's research narratives on sexwork but analyzing, ethnographically, the spaces and places of prostitution. These will serve as the empirical base for a reconstruction of the gender-specific arrangements typical of sexwork. The present paper centers on the findings of three months of research conducted at the International Research Center for Cultural Studies (IFK) in Vienna. The paper is furthermore based on a research project (DFG) on "The Effective Structure of Space and Gender: the Example of Prostitution in Frankfurt on the Main." Apart from evaluations of observations and documents, both projects are based on expert interviews with prostitutes, social workers and police officers, affected neighbors, and legal practitioners. We will concentrate on space-related strategies that use regimes of gazing and social control to create identity and to produce spaces of the Other.

The organization of gazing in Vienna

Flying into Vienna, posters announce to the new arrival what the town has in store for her. The first picture: Welcome in Schönbrunn. Vienna is known for its emperors and kings, famed for its empresses Sisi and Maria Theresia. It was the latter who had prostitution banned throughout Austria. The poster likewise makes reference to the zoo as an idyllic setting for children and as a trove of nature imagines. The second poster is devoted to art. Vienna successfully markets itself as a stronghold of the arts. Now it must be music's turn, we think. "Wine, woman, and song," as the guidebook puts it. But "woman" comes only after Schönbrunn and Giorgione.

When you leave the arrivals section, you can't miss the "Babylon's" attempts to woo customers, old and new. Babylon, symbolic of mankind's attempt to approach God, and its failure, stands for the birth of diversity no less than for the lack of ability to understand it. Women on the poster welcome us, all of them white-skinned, and all of them clad in innocently white undergarments. Angels, creatures without gender and sexuality! And yet—the lascivious posture of the ladies seated on red satin seem suggestive of something. But of what? We think of a musical theater, of a movie poster. Who would have thought that Vienna's noble brothel would advertise here at the airport? Only those in the know. The poster must be meant as a welcome to the regular customer. And be geared to inducing a certain recognition effect in the newcomer: Even at the airport there can be no doubt: in Vienna prostitution is everywhere, but it's decent, not at all conspicuous. The game of hide-and-seek is taken to perfection in Vienna.

In Vienna there is no world-famous red-light district like that in St. Pauli in Hamburg, and Vienna does not welcome its visitors with a sea of whorehouses like Frankfurt on the Main. True, in Vienna, too, there are the bars along the Gürtel, the "Belt." Vienna's main drag, close to the Westbahnhof and the streetwalker district just behind it, but these two sex-miles are more or less inconspicuous, at least compared with the massive presence of an official red-light district. In Vienna the visitor will not find a red-light district.

On the ground: exploring the Belt

We start out with the brothels along the Belt. Today, the spatial arrangement is heterogeneous. The buildings around the subway station house are scene bars, small booths where kebab is sold; and the alleyways are punctuated, at more or less regular intervals, by bars illuminated in red. Both the façades and the advertising are designed to give off stereotyped signals. The lips, the champagne glass, the high-heeled shoe. Again and again! There is music in the air. And there are women standing in front of some of the bars. All with white skin, black getup, and red lips. Somehow they have all managed to be blond on this evening. Sometimes you see women sitting in shop windows.

They don't move. Their legs are stretched upward, their heads tossed back. They seem relaxed, and very attractive. It's still early in the evening. There are hardly any male customers to be seen. Coming in from the dusky light outside, we are overwhelmed by the darkness inside. We can hardly make out the arrangements. Visibility is reduced to a minimum. But there is an odor of sweetish perfume in the air. We were told by the feminist counseling centers that you have to ask the owner or the barmaid whether you can speak to the women there. One of us walks up to a woman. For her, deciding which one to speak to is just as intuitive as the conduct of customers is always reported to be. Customers approach these women, and they in turn signal their readiness to respond openly. The women are not simply passively chosen. They use glances, poises to express sympathy or rejection. Many customers are—like us in this situation—very insecure. We are glad for the signals given by the women. Street workers tell stories about the concerns of a good number of sexworkers who are not often approached by men. For the most part—social workers report—women who despise their own activity have more trouble acquiring customers than women who think highly of, or are at least tolerant of, sexuality, their trade, or their own body. So we approach the women whose gaze we interpret as curiosity and frankness.

What we are in here is an arrangement deliberately staged as "another, a different world." It's oppressively hot. Otherwise the women would be cold, lightly dressed as they are. The dominant colors are red and black. We speak with the sexworker about a concern allegedly often addressed by women, namely about men. She tells us that men—at least those who are not regulars—always first sit down at the bar—and seek to survey the room. They often prefer to remain on their safe seat at the bar and have the women shown to them there—without having to walk through the room, exposing themselves to the gaze of the others. They prefer to gaze themselves. The barmaid helps out. "Come on, show yourselves!" is a call frequently to be heard. This allows the man to gaze and chose.

Change of focus

Men don't want to be seen. Christine Howe, who worked for many years with the now-defunct prostitute project Agisra e.V., reports: "We also do street work, and when you see how men start out by looking around before entering a brothel, you get the impression that their space-related threshold fear is also an endopsychic fear. When, on the other hand, you observe them leaving the brothel, sometimes even falling out the door and having to seek orientation, sometimes even walking off in the wrong direction, then it almost seems as though they had just stepped over the threshold between two completely different worlds" (Howe, quoted after Domentat 2003: 93f.). As one social worker reports, taking a photo in the red-light district is like switching on the light. We have often heard—slightly amused—insiders report that men tend to look around before entering such a bar to make sure nobody is watching them. A brothel operator reports that many men hardly even have the courage to look these women straight in the eye.

As with any social encounter, the culture of the gaze is the essential element here that defines the opening of the encounter. The basic rule is that it is the women—not the men—who have to show themselves. That is, they stage a showing that veils their own gaze, giving the men a greater sense of security. One essential component of this enactment is to seem to cede the voyeuristic gaze to the man.

Studies on film theory and picture interpretation (for a summary, cf. Mathes 2001: 105; Hentschel 2001) suggest that practicing a scientifically detached viewing e.g. of paintings is an approach used to produce and reproduce the cultural construction of heterosexuality. The picture based on perspective creates the impression of depth and thus of spatiality before the eyes of the beholder, a spatiality which is further reinforced by the moving pictures served up in the cinema. "The commercial film aims, by employing inconspicuous cutting and camera techniques, to create the impression of a continuous, homogenous picture space and to place the observer in a panoramic position" (Hentschel 2001: 153). The fact that spaces have traditionally been imagined as women (resp. women's bodies) (cf. Löw 2001: 115ff. for more information) gives rise to a cultural association between spaces viewed and female bodies. As literary criticism has frequently noted, this overlapping of spatial fantasies and female bodies (cf. Weigel 1990; Kubitz-Kramer 1995) ties the perspective-minded voyeuristic gaze, which dissects without being seen, into a genderized and genderizing context. In the absolutist notion of space, the open picture space is experienced as something like the promise of a tendered and open female body, and at the same time described as the womb with its promise of security (Colomina 1997) and of lust (Weigel 1990; Hentschel 2001). Against the background of a dual-gender, heterosexual matrix, two potentially contrary positions become manifest: that of the male gaze and that of the female as the object gazed upon.

Some brothel/bar operators manage to make optimal use of the potentials of the world of the picture and the film. The social constellation inside a bar, devised as it is to having women show themselves, places the man in a panoramic position. The women before his eyes move as if they were in a film—and these are women who are willing to keep the promise of the open female body, and who, using, say, makeup and wigs, shape their body in conformity with stereotyped images of femininity. The picture space is also reenacted through the arrangement of the show windows. Women place themselves in the window frame in such a way as to blur the difference between endless pictures of iniquitous women and a concrete bodily presence. The women become the picture. One thing that is typical here is that establishments that do not advertise by placing women in their windows often replace them with a picture. In astonishing monotony, the typical Viennese façade will feature a champagne glass and a high-heeled shoe as symbols of prostitution. While the high-heeled shoe may be read as a fetish, the champagne glass suggests, to the pornographic gaze, the male organism. The popping cork, the spurting champagne are commonly staged as a symbol for male ejaculation and orgasm. The glass, with its triangular form resting on the stem, is designed to receive the champagne, with its associations of ejaculate. This sets the stage for the inoffensive champagne glass on the façade to tell its tale of promise and well-being.

The organization of social control in Frankfurt

For tourists coming to Frankfurt on the Main (especially lonely business travelers looking for a little relaxation), the "Essential City Guide," available in hotels, recommends a visit to various prostitution areas. Under the headline "Adult Entertainment" there are two pages describing brothels, Eros centers, strip clubs, and sex shops (Essential City Guide Frankfurt, Jan./Feb. 2005: 28–29). Nearly all of them can be found in a very small area of the town, located near the main railway station, named the "Frankfurter Bahnhofsviertel." The area is described as "one of the largest red light districts in the world" and visitors to Frankfurt are informed that they need not worry, since as prostitution is "completely legal" and quite common in Germany.

But at the same time, prostitution is a controversial topic in Germany. As well as being seen as "abnormal" and "immoral," it also still carries the stigma of a sexual taboo (cf. e.g. Laskowski 1997: 80). Although the reality of prostitution is an open secret, it is deliberately kept under cover in the grey area on the social fringe of urban life. Despite being legal—in principle—the need for specific controls is expressed again and again. This is especially so in Frankfurt: according to encyclopedias on the subject, there is hardly another German city as restrictive in its attitude toward prostitution (Feige 2003: 240). And this is confirmed in interviews with brothel owners, for example, who have the impression of being "overwhelmed by a stream of never-ending rules and regulations."

The main political steering mechanism is the so called "Sperrgebietsverordnung" (which roughly translates as: Restricted Area Decree or Law). There are such regulations in many German cities; they serve to restrict and concentrate prostitution to certain areas, and especially to keep it away from family neighborhoods and places of worship. In this way "Sperrgebietsverordnungen," or "restricted area decrees," are officially intended to protect young people and maintain public decency.

But restricted area decrees, which have been introduced by local authorities as a reaction to a phenomenon that is seen as problematic, also play an active part in producing it. The way they do this is by producing spatial patterns of social structure, which—in particular—stabilize gender relations[1]. This will be explained in what follows.

"Restricted area decrees" define those parts of the cities where either special or all forms of prostitution are allowed or forbidden. Absolutely restricted areas in Frankfurt—where prostitution is completely banned—are the districts of "Sachsenhausen" and the "Bahnhofsviertel." However, in this "Bahnhofsviertel" there is a small area with numerous buildings, separate though close to each other, which are permitted to operate as brothels. The Bahnhofsviertel therefore is in a paradoxical situation—produced by the "Sperrgebietsverordnung" itself. On the one hand it is an absolutely restricted area where no prostitution is allowed at all. On the other it is a clearly visible and well established red-light district. Apart from some rather unattractive—and for this reason hardly used—areas, brothel prostitution is also tolerated in two very small districts. In nearly all other parts of the city it is forbidden to practice prostitution on public streets, paths, in squares and public parks, in prostitute accommodations, or in similar facilities. However, one thing that is tolerated is discreet apartment or flat prostitution.

In the following, the specific effects of the "Sperrgebietsverordnung" in the urban structure will be illustrated by two examples: First, there is brothel prostitution in the few tolerance zones, and especially in the "Bahnhofsviertel." With 1200–1500 women working in this sector, this is—even if only by number—by far the most important type of prostitution in Frankfurt. Second, we have flat or apartment prostitution, which is the other main form of prostitution in Frankfurt with about 500 to 700 working women, spread all over the town.

Brothel prostitution in the "Bahnhofsviertel"— a red-light district in the centre of the restricted area for prostitution

Despite being—in principle—defined as a restricted area, the "Bahnhofsviertel" is the center of brothel prostitution in Frankfurt (Molloy 1992: 55)[2] because it includes numerous brothel-oriented exceptions. The term "brothel" is used here to indicate "Laufhäuser," which may be roughly translated as "running-through-" or "drop-in-houses" where the "working girls rent small rooms for the day or just for a few hours" (Essential City Guide) Potential male cli-

---

1   For the basic analytical model see Ruhne 2003.
2   You will find brothel or "running-through-house" prostitution in Frankfurt/M. mainly in the Bahnhofsviertel with a capacity of 650 rooms/ beds in total. On average a house has between 30 to 60 rooms, but the capacity can rise to 180 rooms per brothel.

ents walk in without any restriction and can wander through the halls and corridors of the building, passing closed or open doors, where the female tenants of the rooms present themselves and their services to the customers in the apartment doorways.

As one prostitute explained in an interview, the reputation of a brothel is mainly spread by word of mouth and "fuelled" by its popularity. In this sense an effective public presentation of the business is very important for its profitability. So, in addition to ads in city guides or on the Internet, the house façades are covered with attention-grabbing advertisements. Façades with red hearts, symbolized women's bodies, or huge painted notice boards with "Eros Centre," "Sexy Land," "Erotic Shop," or "Erotic Bar" attract the attention of potential customers, while doormen and styled women in the entrance hall try to entice them in. Buildings "work" with artful stagings, with show-window dummies, day and night, conveying to the outside, in various poses, what must be supposed to be happening inside.

In addition to the public visibility of every single "running-through-house," the brothels are concentrated within the tolerance zone in a relatively small area mainly around the Mosel-, Taunus-, and Elbestrasse. These three streets are where the big brothels are located and where most of the sex industry is to be found in Frankfurt. Even during the day you can't overlook this, despite the fact that the area is broken up by shops, cafés, and fast-food outlets. Paraphrases like "shining red heart district," which were used again and again in interviews, point to the "Bahnhofsviertel" as an area in the city where the sex trade is concentrated and—as a result of this concentration—is highly visible.

And the eye-catching properties of prostitution in the Bahnhofsviertel are intensified especially at night, when the "red hearts" really shine: Light chains, flashing illuminations, pink neon signs in windows, and so on leave one in no doubt about the kind and extent of business on offer there.

Apartment prostitution in Frankfurt—a discreet form of prostitution

In Frankfurt the prostitute working in an individual flat or apartment is another important but less high-profile form of the sex trade. Its discreet and nearly private character is explicitly required by the local authority: "Apartment prostitution" is only allowed when the flat is, in reality, equipped and used for daily living. Occasionally, this may be controlled by the local authority, and nothing is permitted that would enable outsiders (including the neighbors) to be able to recognize that the accommodation is being used for the purpose of prostitution. This means that any form of advertising on the outside of the apartment is strictly forbidden. The working women advertise their services in newspapers or on the Internet, for example. Potential clients phone first, and an appointment may be arranged.

The discreet, private, and intimate character of this type of prostitution distinguishes it from brothel prostitution. But this is not only a marketing strategy that might be of interest to the client and the prostitute, it is also related to the rules of the local authorities and the way legal and illegal actions are defined. Apartment prostitution is legal only if it mimics the bourgeois environment and becomes invisible (as prostitution).

So, although apartment prostitution—in contrast to brothel prostitution—is spread over the whole city, political regulation nevertheless aims at exclusion. As Phil Hubbard notes, the "social marginalisation of prostitutes is reflected in their spatial isolation and exclusion" (Hubbard 1998b: 270); but, as we have seen, the exclusion and marginalization may be quite different in kind. While brothel prostitution is kept away from the other parts of the city by concentrating it in specially defined areas, apartment prostitution "disappears" by being adapted to a "respectable" lifestyle.

The (re)production of prostitution as a "space of the other" through social control mechanisms

Social control mechanisms have specific effects on the social and geographic distribution of the field. Political strategies have—in this sense—an important influence on steering "placing-" or "spacing-processes" (Löw 2001), which we mark as the main factors in the construction and constitution of space. But as factors that construct and constitute space, they also create a specific "synthesis" (Löw 2001), that is, special perceptions of the activity of prostitution. The required adaptation to the respectable bourgeois lifestyle of the surrounding neighborhood in apartment prostitution means—if it is done to the standards set by the controlling authority—that it is no longer recognizable from the outside. On the one hand this is because it happens behind closed doors, on the other because of its nearly perfect adaptation to its supposedly respectable surroundings. As a side effect of their successful control policy, even local authorities have very little information on apartment prostitution.

In the case of the brothel prostitution in the "Bahnhofsviertel," prostitution is kept away from other parts of the city by concentrating it in small well-defined areas of tolerance. On the back of the "restricted area policy," prostitution here establishes itself as a high-profile and exposed "space of the other," which defines the public image of the whole field, especially because of the invisibility and low profile of the much more "normal" apartment prostitution.

But the perception of prostitution in the Bahnhofsviertel—which in this way has a strong impact on the common perception of prostitution—is, in addition, highly influenced by processes of spatial synthesis combined with effects of social stigma. As an example, the close proximity between legal and illegal forms of prostitution may be cited. Legal brothel prostitution in the Bahnhofsviertel is situated very close to illegal street prostitution, where mainly female drug addicts work. Drug-related street prostitution in the Bahnhofsviertel is tolerated by the city authorities. They argue that with their limited resources they would not be able to prevent this from happening anyway. But for this reason both forms of prostitution share the same space in the city: On the streets it is hardly possible to distinguish systematically between legal and illegal (drug-related) prostitution. Therefore the publicly known and clearly visible—but illegal—street prostitution in the Bahnhofsviertel underlines the basic image of the area not only as a "red-light district," but also as a "problematic red-light district." Furthermore, the clearly visible measures taken to prevent dangers in the Bahnhofsviertel—for example a strong street presence of police and regulating bodies—does not always improve the sense of security. Instead it marks out and symbolizes a feeling of insecurity, regardless of the real level of danger. In this way it confirms the construction of a socially problematic space of the other. Prostitution is included in this because it is located in this area of the city.

Conclusions

Comparing Vienna with Frankfurt on the Main, we find in Frankfurt that many stagings are more clearly addressed to specific milieus. Here, distinction is the principle behind the designs. Here we find façade designs that include flowerboxes and fir sprigs that remind the observer of Christmas family idylls, and yet red lamps, supported by red ribbons in the fir sprigs, clearly indicate what the building contains. A clearly observable threshold enactment points unmistakably to the building's acquired public character as a brothel.
Vienna lacks a "place of the Other" that is at once visible for all and familiar to every child. Vienna has many scattered places of the Other that together form a space of their own that refer to and complement one another. In Vienna people still tell the story of Kaiser Joseph II, who, asked to lift the ban on brothels, is said to have responded: "What, brothels? All I'd have to do is build a big roof over the whole of Vienna…" (Anwander/Neudecker 1999: 67).

So it is that the structure of the trade reproduces itself at the city level. The game of hide-and-seek, a favorite of modern society, is perfected in sexwork. Both social workers and customers report again and again on the "other world" that they encounter in relevant bars. Many of them have trouble describing this other world. In interviews they refer to it as "mysterious" or note that "it's the clandestine that shapes the atmosphere." If they are to survive, secrets may not be allowed to become public. In the field of prostitution male customers and sexworkers/"clandestine prostitutes" work hand in hand in preserving the secretive, mysterious. Women who are not part of paid sexwork are simply members of the bothersome public. Prostitution reverses the middle-class logic that assigns women to the private sphere: It opens up a subcultural field of public female "bodies" (the prostitutes) and a public "sphere," which is represented by "middle-class" women.

But what is it that is enacted here as a secret meant to be kept? Male sexuality? Sexuality in general? Male insecurity? Few studies have been written on male customers. And these are mostly based on reports of prostitutes, not on what customers themselves have to say (Girtler 1990: 143ff.; Bilitewski et al. 1994/1991). There is little founded information available on the films—including films of different types—in which men set out to play the leading role by setting foot in a brothel. It is a striking fact that (surprisingly) many elements of the love film crop up in the world of anonymous sex. "Ring the bell and step into bliss," announces one sign on the door of a Vienna brothel. Others place little hearts and arrows in clearly visible spots of the entryway, or use neon signs blinking out the call "Love me."

In a forthcoming interview study, Sabine Grenz (2004) shows how important it is for many men not to be nagged by the sense that "it" is all done for the money. And if it still feels that way, these men tend to believe that they have simply not paid enough. Despite this explicitly "the more expensive, the more genuine" logic, many men are convinced that their favorite whore is really happy to see them in person; that a domina is a woman who really likes to deal out blows; or that "certain reactions" show them that there are "things" that "you just can't put on" (original quote from Grenz 2004: 7). The ideal of the private relationship, Grenz notes, assumes an unadulterated form in prostitution: an exchange based on give and take. "In Germany over one million men avail themselves daily of the services [provided by prostitutes]" (Deutscher Bundestag 2001: 4; cf. also Laskowski 1997: 80). The Berlin Hydra prostitute project even estimates that every day up to 1.5 million men make use of the services of prostitutes (see Mitrovic 2002: 70). In Vienna alone, every night some 15,000 men are reported to look up sexworkers.

In this connection, the definitions of prostitution typically offered by the social sciences may be "summed up as 'sex for money' with various modifications" (Laskowski 1997: 46). Accordingly, prostitutes are referred to as persons or "individuals who receive payment (whether financial or otherwise) for sexual services" (Hubbard 1998b: 269). Only a sound consumer research would be able to determine whether or not this definition does not more than oversimplify the field of prostitution. It is likely that in the end no secrets will be revealed; instead, the enactment of the secret opens up the possibility to step across a threshold. Nothing happens on the other side that is not concealed by the one side as well, but the enactment of an "other side" opens up fantasy spaces, shifts in the staging and practices of desire. Furthermore, it is precisely the enactment of the male and the female as its object—a far more fragile experience in everyday life—that is used to learn and practice a basic social structure that serves to stabilize power relations, as it were, despite the fragility of everyday experience. The examples of Vienna and Frankfurt have shown us that prostitution is a very exclusive and excluded social field. The background of the exclusion of prostitution is that this is a field seen as abnormal, immoral, and potentially dangerous. The "restricted area decree" of Frankfurt, for example, illustrates this by aiming to protect young people and "public morals."

Practices of separating off prostitution—as we know them today—assumed more and more importance in European cities in the 18th and especially the 19th centuries and they aimed—as spatially oriented control strategies—from the very beginning to exclude immoral, stigmatized prostitution from the morality of developing bourgeois everyday life. The exclusion of prostitution was strongly connected with the general separation and exclusion of sexuality as bodily experiences in everyday life, which was established at the same time. However, this separation manifested marked sex-specific differences: in the context of bourgeois gender structures, the dichotomous concepts of "male" and "female" limited the sexuality of "respectable" women to the monogamous intimacy of marriage, while the bourgeois men experienced two opposite types of love and sexuality: On the one hand there was the spiritual love of the bourgeois woman, who had to be more or less passive and without any desire (Schulte 1984: 154), and on the other hand there was the convention of prostitutional sexuality as a "valve" (Schulte 1984: 151).

Both forms are divided into different areas of social life. By using measures of social control—in much the same way as perceptions, glances, and corresponding body technologies, for example—prostitution is, as we have seen, constructed as a "space of the other," where deviant and "abnormal" forms of heterosexual relationships—like actively courting women or "insecure" men—are excluded and hidden. In this way the social construction of prostitution is included in social structures like gender relations. The "space of the other" protects and stabilizes the recognition of a strictly divided concept of opposite sexes, with the "moral" and "respectable" bourgeois lifestyle defined as "normal." Perception and placing practices, material and symbolic arrangements, forms of social control, and boundaries etc. have been used to ensure the reproduction of social patterns of order and to stabilize (gender-) specific constructions of identity.

But the processes of exclusion are by no means restricted only to the gender regime, they produce "the other" in different variants. In sharp contrast to an increasingly self-determined picture of women, even in prostitution we today find images and reports of ill-treated, battered, raped, bound, alien female bodies that—far from being merely "victims of circumstances"—often also assume the character of a symbol of threats to the nation. Under the influence of unfocused globalization anxieties, traditional power relations of the "national project" nowadays appear to be up for renegotiation. Threats from diseases like Aids, for example, and feelings of guilt regarding the North's and the West's exploitation of the South and the East being negotiated in terms of a foreign and alien "migrant identity" that is at the same time marginalized. In this context the field of prostitution shows us that demarcations of social order can change and that the "wardens of social order" change along with those they are in charge of.

References

Anwander, Berndt/Neudecker, Sigrid (1999) *Sex in Wien*, Wien.
Bilitewsky, Helga/Czajka, Maya/Fischer, Claudia/Klee, Stephanie/Repetto, Claudia (1994/1991) *Freier. Das heimliche Treiben der Männer* [ed.: Prostituiertenprojekt Hydra]. München.
Colomina, Beatriz (1997) "Die gespaltene Wand: häuslicher Voyeurismus". In Christian Kravagna (ed.) *Privileg Blick. Kritik der visuellen Kultur*. Berlin: Edition ID-Archiv, pp. 201–222.
Deutscher Bundestag – 14.Wahlperiode (2001) "Begründung des Gesetzes zur Regelung der Rechtsverhältnisse der Prostituierten". Drucksache 14/5958, pp. 4–6.
Domentat, Tamara (2003) *"Laß dich verwöhnen". Prostitution in Deutschland*, Berlin.
Feige, Marcel (2003) *Das Lexikon der Prostitution. Das ganze ABC der Ware Lust – Die käufliche Liebe in Kultur, Gesellschaft und Politik*, Berlin
Girtler, Roland (1990) *Der Strich. Sexualität als Geschäft*. München.
Grenz, Sabine (2004) *Sind es nur die hässlichen Männer, die Sex von schönen Frauen kaufen? Die Beziehungen von Geld, Macht und Potenz in der Prostitution* (Unpublished Manuscript).
Hentschel, Linda (2001) "Die Ordnung von Raum und Geschlecht in der visuellen Kultur des 19. und 20. Jahrhunderts". In Marlis Krüger/Bärbel Wallisch-Prinz *Erkenntnisprojekt Feminismus*. Bremen: Donat, pp. 150–164.

Hubbard, Phil (1998a) "Sexuality, Immorality and the City. Red-light districts and the marginalisation of female prostitutes". In Gender, Place and Culture, 1, pp. 55–76.

Hubbard, Phil (1998b) "Community Action and the Displacement of Street Prostitution: Evidence from British Cities". In Geoforum, Vol. 3: 269–286.

Kublitz-Kramer, Maria (1995) *Frauen auf Straßen. Topographien des Begehrens in Erzähltexten von Gegenwartsautorinnen*, München.

Laskowski, Ruth Silke et al. (1997) *Die Ausübung der Prostitution. Ein verfassungsrechtlich geschützter Beruf im Sinne von Art. 12 Abs.1 GG*. Frankfurt am Main.

Löw, Martina (2001) *Raumsoziologie*, Frankfurt am Main.

Löw, Martina/Ruhne, Renate (2004) *Das Wirkungsgefüge von Raum und Geschlecht am Beispiel Prostitution*, Darmstadt (Unpublished Manuscript).

Mathes, Bettina (2001) *Verhandlungen mit Faust. Geschlechterverhältnisse in der Kultur der Frühen Neuzeit*, Königstein.

Mitrovic, Emilija (2002) "Frauenarbeitsplatz Prostitution. Arbeitsbedingungen in einem bedeutenden Wirtschaftsfaktor". In Forum Wissenschaft, pp. 70–73.

Molloy, Cora (1992) *Hurenalltag. Sperrgebiet – Stigma – Selbsthilfe Materialien zur Sozialarbeit und Sozialpolitik*, Band 34. Fachhochschule Frankfurt am Main.

Rodenstein, Marianne (2000) *Hochhäuser in Deutschland: Zukunft oder Ruin der Städte?* Stuttgart.

Ruhne, Renate (2003) *Raum Macht Geschlecht. Zur Soziologie eines Wirkungsgefüges am Beispiel von (Un)Sicherheiten im öffentlichen Raum*. Opladen.

Schulte, Regina (1984) *Sperrbezirke. Tugendhaftigkeit und Prostitution in der bürgerlichen Welt*, Frankfurt am Main.

Weigel, Sigrid (1990) *Topographien der Geschlechter. Kulturgeschichtliche Studien zur Literatur*, Reinbek.

Yiftachel, Oren (1998) "Planning and social control: Exploring the 'dark side'". In Journal of Planning Literature, 12/2, pp. 395–406.

III. Imageries of Cities

Between Refeudalization and New Cultural Politics: The 300th Anniversary of St. Petersburg

Elena Trubina

In this paper, I look at the celebration of the 300th anniversary of St. Petersburg in order to show that certain elements of public memory and cultural politics can be seen as counterbalancing the tendencies of "state image promotion".[1]

Introduction

The dissemination of a positive image of Russia has been implemented both nationally and internationally. The celebration of capital cities that comprises an important part of the Russian political culture has also been involved in the ongoing state image promotion (cf. Boym 2001). With this in mind, I will first trace the continuities between pre-Soviet and post-Soviet cultural practices in the light of Habermasian work on public sphere. Second, I will outline what I believe are the promising approaches and strategies of the new cultural practitioners. Finally, I will touch briefly upon the methodological problems related to a researcher's wish to retain both the normative and the descriptive dimension of his or her work on a particular case. By applying the notion of "refeudalization" to the discourses and signifying practices through which a number of officials have constructed dominant representations of the city and its inhabitants, I hope to emphasize the complexity of the constellation of historical epochs, temporalities, mythologies, ways to sustain state power, popular participations, and cultural imaginations that historical developments of transition result in. If in their everyday life city inhabitants remain relatively

---

1 For an extended version of this paper, cf. Trubina 2005.

immune to this complexity, it is the state-organized celebrations that make them reflect on both historical continuity and disjuncture in the relationships of political elites and the general public.[2]

The ambivalence of imperial heritage

In countries in transition we witness the growing role of cities in the development of capitalism, their function as hubs allowing productive links among the various markets and controlling investment in services, broadcasting, transportation, commodity manufacturing, built form, advertising, department stores, and so forth. The ambitions and spending habits of high earners seem to have been the major driving force in the development of many cities. And it is urban landscapes that give the economic, social, and political tendencies particular configurations when the mindsets and the systems of values of the ruling classes confront particular urban traditions.

The more actively the Russian state reduces and eliminates subsidies, deregulates prices, and ceases to provide services people had come to expect, the more eagerly it tries to position itself as a basis of social solidarity, as an entity with which people might identify. The capital cities may be counted among the most powerful stately images. In part, their efficiency as vehicles of political power has to do with the narratives they embody or represent. I want to emphasize, however, that urban narratives have not always been successfully appropriated by the state. Sometimes the multilayered story that a city embodies comes into conflict with the state's implementation of particular kinds of politics.

During the three hundred years of St. Petersburg's history, the city has been used for the dissemination of narratives of national identity. They range from those about defeating nature by means of building this most beautiful city on a swamp, over the story of the city as the cradle of the Bolshevik revolution, to its conception as the genuine and the most European city in Russia. Most narratives turn the long process of energetic modernization into romantic myths, with little attention to human costs. The abundance of sites related to the days of the Russian Empire, and the fact that its core was quickly built according to a plan, give the city its formal, strict, elegant, and noble look, and St. Petersburg persists in carrying on its historic role as the site of royalty and aristocratic society. However, the city seems to resist attempts to interpret it simply as a historic citadel of the highborn living in sanctioned aloofness

---

2 My empirical material consists of four taped semi-structured interviews and field notes of some 10,500 words from numerous informal talks. There are about twenty respondents in the sample that originates from field studies in St. Petersburg in June 2003.

while the silent majority hardly scrapes by. The complex history of the city resulted in the development of a characteristic (and heavily mythologized) mentality of its inhabitants, a combination of self-reliance, bohemian suspicion towards material values, undemonstrative manners, and a sense of belonging to a past that is not rigid and finalized but so vitally connected to the present that it seems to question the present. Today the flats in the old buildings with characteristically "high ceilings" (six meters and higher) are likely to be occupied by both well-off people and those whose families lived here for generations. The striking contrast between what is outside (glorious facades) and what is inside (crumbling stairways, decaying plumbing) is not only often shared by people with totally different levels of income, and has not only come to signify one of the city's peculiarities, but also has even become a source of local pride. This contributes to a sense of democratic city life that consists of people of nearly all backgrounds sharing a common predicament.

St. Petersburg has a long history of public celebrations, which played a mediating role between its collective urban memory and the nationalist politics of history. Starting from the royal entry (already by 1712 St. Petersburg was the official capital of the Russian Empire) to the Soviet celebrations of May Day, to celebrations of cosmos exploits, of endless centennials and bicentennials of Russian writers, the festivals and celebrations encompass an important way of memorializing significant events. Although Soviet public celebrations were, as a rule, initiated by authorities, they have made their way into people's memories and managed to generate quite powerful public emotions. They also had to do with the authorities' desire to mobilize people emotionally and to educate them Similarly, the celebrations in cities that originated in pre-Revolutionary times were an efficient way to fuse local and regional identities with national identity. As a result, the festivals have definitely become a part of national culture. What differentiates St. Petersburg's recent anniversary is that it signifies a development of the city festival from being part of national and city culture to being a constructed event designed not only to attract tourists but to turn the city into a presidential capital.

A few cities have celebrated their anniversaries during the past few years (the 400th anniversary of Smolensk in 2002, the 400th anniversary of Tomsk in 2003, etc.). But in striking contrast to St. Petersburg, the amount of their funding by the federal government was negligible. The degree of importance presently being attached to everything related to "Pieter"—this is what St. Petersburg/Petrograd/Leningrad/St. Petersburg is called by its inhabitants in local parlance—can be quite easily explained. The Russian president, Vladimir Putin, had been a member of the city administration for some time, and, as president, he repeatedly expressed his concern for his home town. Thus the 300th anniversary of St. Petersburg (celebrated in 2003 at the end of May) came in handy both for the city's authorities and for the so-called "pieterskie"—those working in the Kremlin administration who came from this city (Putin has a record of appointing his former colleagues to key government positions). There is a sense in which the way the celebration was designed and executed betrays the real attitude of authorities towards perspectives of democracy in Russia.

While being exposed for months to all sorts of inconveniences related to the major face-lift their city was given prior the celebration, the city inhabitants were not shy to point out that this event was not actually "for them." As one of my interlocutors put it, "For some it is a good chance to make a fortune while for the others it all is about politics." He said that the city celebration concerns all its inhabitants, but when asked how he thought it would be possible to make the celebration "for all," he had difficulty answering. It seems that the post-Soviet public's image of itself remains vague and elusive. Indeed, what establishes the public presence of "simple people" when it comes to national celebrations? The collisions between ongoing politicization of urban and national memory and city publics take place along the evolution of the Russian political regime from representative democracy through a "managed" one to bureaucratic authoritarianism. With the celebration, an ambiguous attempt was made to promote an image of Russia as a country that was undergoing democratic reforms (in his speeches Putin repeatedly pledged allegiance to democracy) while emphasizing those components of the city heritage that are related to the fact that St. Petersburg was a capital of imperial Russia. It did reveal both the intriguing play of patterns of the past and the hybridity of Russian political culture. What I mean is that for the Russian Federation, as one of so-called new independent states, it was necessary to construct a national identity, to strengthen national traditions and values, and to amplify understanding of a historical continuity in people's minds. On the other hand, economic globalization and transnational political interaction caused rapid change of people's identities. Against this background, the traditional national rhetoric implying loyalty to the roots, patriotism, etc. is losing its effectiveness and needs to be re-invented in order to be effective.

When a once-great power loses its political and economic dominance and rapidly moves to the periphery of international politics, imperialistic nostalgia enables the nation to retain a certain dignity. St. Petersburg is considered by many to be the most European of all Russian cities, but this is not what captures the imagination of the Russian political elite. According to one observation, "Along with the rest of society, the elite consider the Russian Federation as a successor not only of the Soviet Union but, even to a greater extent, of the Russian Empire. Subconsciously, Russian elite […] aimed to come back to pre-Communist past" (Trenin 2004: 10). Numerous palaces, buildings, and museums were renovated as the celebration approached. For one, the Konstantinovsky Palace, a former tsarist residence on the outskirts of St. Petersburg, was renovated because Putin supposedly needed a "sea residence." Today this site has a double name: it figures both as a presidential residence and as the state complex Palace of Congresses.³ The most contemporary artistic forms were mobilized for the celebration. Niro Yamagata's laser show took place. The lavish water festival on the Neva River, organized by a French company, *Aquatique Show International,* which specializes in organizing large-scale water spectacles around the world, was surely impressive, and, incidentally, it consisted of two separate water shows—one for the political leaders and other VIPs, the other for the general public. City residents, during the week-long celebration, were "recommended" to postpone visiting renovated city-centre sites and attending festivals. The concentration of police per square meter beat all records. Pulkovo, the city airport, was closed on celebration days. There was a sense in which it was not the leader and the masses who were supposed to unite during the celebration but the president and those European leaders with whom he declared to have a "special relationship."

In a sense, the present St. Petersburg authorities followed two paths. The first was that of eighteenth-century authorities who used to close public celebrations and public places to people. The second was that elaborated by Soviet-era authorities who, as a rule, "cleared" the capital of all undesirable elements during major events (e.g. the 1980 Olympiad). Surely, some of these unpopular measures had to do with security concerns that are at their height everywhere. But if one is allowed to be, so to speak, historically contemplative, the underestimated potential of the older political systems comes to mind. While some researchers emphasize the effectiveness of monarchy in terms of maintaining security (cf. Ankersmit 2002), the symbolic and ceremonial potential of feudalism and absolutism should also be remembered.

Refeudalization of the public sphere and "feudal" tendencies in the cities

It was Jürgen Habermas who was most succinct in expressing the common intellectual's suspicion towards a society of spectacle and turning politics into performance and show. This attitude has to do with the realization that whatever is rendered as spectacle is deprived of the critical potential for imagining a different organization of society. The strong distinction between private and public domains that he draws allows Habermas to picture the genuine, ideal public sphere for which uncoerced deliberation is characteristic (cf. Villa

---

3 Cf. for instance the following Internet site: http://www.konstantinpalace.com/en_kd.php.

1992). Contemplating the predicament of the mass democracies of advanced or "late" capitalist society, Habermas sees the return of "representative publicity" characteristic of the Middle Ages and of absolutist society, with the organization of society as a social hierarchy of orders or estates and the king at the top. Thus the metaphor he uses for the contemporary erosion of the spaces of participatory democracy and the disintegration of the public sphere is "refeudalization." Describing how a "culture-debating public" irretrievably turns into a "culture-consuming public," Habermas argues that this leads to the transformation of publicity from a critical to a staged one. Tracing the development of the public sphere in Europe from 1640 to 1960, Habermas speaks of its "refeudalization," which occurs when the illusions of the public sphere are maintained only to give sanction to the decisions of leaders (Habermas 1989: 164, 195, 206).

Having read this sketch today, one can't help thinking that however relevant this model is from the point of view of critical theory, it seems to be very much at odds with the present moment when nearly everything in politics tends to be connected to performance or spectacle. It is not by chance that much of the criticism directed against the notion of the public sphere and its subsequent refeudalization comes both from urbanists and media scholars. They emphasize that the spread of mass media has radically changed the functioning of the public sphere, rendering Habermas' model "both backward looking and too literally spatial" (Donald 2003: 51). Rather than feeling deprived of their share in the process of political deliberation by all sorts of imaginers, rather than mourning over face-to-face interactions in specifically designed public places, citizens seem happily to embrace the opportunities that television, the Internet, and shopping malls offer. Yet I believe that it is exactly in the field of political culture that Habermas's concept possesses a sufficient theoretical interest and may result in creative interpretations of the current Russian transformations.

However, with all the reservations and doubts that come to one's mind about the extent to which the conclusions and qualifications that Habermas drew from his normative consideration of late capitalist societies are applicable to Russia, at least stylistic affinities between his description of refeudalization and present day commemorative practices are obvious. The pompous ceremonies of celebration marked the point in contemporary Russian history when even the rhetorical endorsement of democratic values has stopped being necessary and when personified power has come to the fore. Refeudalization of the public sphere thus coincides with the ongoing re-centralization of power. The self-reproducing body of high ranking officials, by cleverly channeling generous federal donations and by managing the public during the celebration, has impressively shown its growing independence from, and indifference toward, society.

Although Habermas does not concern himself with the connections between the practices of commemoration and contemporary publicity, his description of refeudalization nevertheless raises fundamental questions about the functioning of "image-making" in the contemporary politics of memory. Are we to assume that most contemporary national commemorative celebrations are supposed to be spectacles designed to impress rather than events to take part in? Cultural memory is undoubtedly prone to manipulations. The point to emphasize here is that politically informed, instrumental ways of "image-making" penetrate the private realms of residential architecture and interior decoration. The restored sites of imperial splendor that are imposed on people by the present authorities seem to be enthusiastically imitated, albeit on a smaller scale, by well-off people in their apartments and mansions. Red wood and golden ornaments, intricate parquet work, fine vases, and other cultural objects of recognized material value that are predominant in carefully created interiors not only signify changes in spending patterns but also betray the owners' sense of the epoch they want to relate to.

It is only when cultural, social, and economic processes are seen as mutually essential that it is possible to render the complex and interwoven tendencies of urban living. The cultural logic of late capitalism (to borrow the title of Frederic Jameson's book) presupposes that it is the capitalist economy that is in the center of urban development. And in post-Soviet cities one can see many corporate buildings, commercial centers, and shopping plazas signalling the accumulation of capital. On the other hand, the irrational, pompous lavishness of these centers and plazas, and a great deal of conspicuous consumption, makes one think of a totally different cultural logic, namely a feudal one (cf. O'Connor 1995). It is not the accumulation of capital but a status differentiation that finds its expression in closed enclaves and ever-present surveillance, innumerous borders and walls, both physical and virtual, that were erected during the last decade in cities, from face control in expensive nightclubs, to "fortress" buildings and villages, from the frequency with which the word "exclusive" is used in real estate and services ads, to the growing sense in which it is the urban elite that builds new parts of the city for itself.

There is one more striking similarity to the feudal structuring of court and society in general that can be traced in the present-day workings of power, namely, the growing importance of one's loyalty to the president, a regional governor, a mayor, or the head of a corporation, and one's astute sense of subordination and expectations to receive compensation in return for being loyal. In a sense, "gated communities," themselves reminiscent of feudal cities, which are becoming plentiful in Russia, can be seen as the most tangible embodiment of one's loyalties. The meaning of refeudalization can thus be expanded. It can serve as an indication of a number of social and cultural trends that might not necessarily originate in "feudalism" historically but may be perceived as similar to "feudal" by contemporary standards. What I imply is that the growing importance of one's status, which is so characteristic of post-Soviet urbanity and the obvious sophistication of the imaginers in organizing events in which even the symbolic participation of the public has stopped being necessary, is perceived by some parts of the public as the closure of the narrative of liberation under the spell of which many have lived during the last couple of decades. The teleological promise that this narrative contained (a blessed capitalist freedom to pursue one's self-interest) has led to nothing, the hopes proven lost. In this vein, speaking of the East European countries and Russia, one can easily recall how the revolutionary energy of the big cities's populations became thwarted during the last decade. Today, pragmatic urbanites are rather politically disenchanted. Busily pursuing their individual interests, they recall their romantic expectations and democratic aspirations of the late 1980s with a touch of irony. Squares—the former meeting places of the perestroika years—are now deserted, while department stores are crowded in the cities that are undergoing free-market reforms.

Whether the rendering of the current tendencies as feudal has to do with a particular appeal of egalitarian ideas that many have successfully absorbed (and thus it is especially worrying for them to contemplate the return of a social hierarchy reminiscent of the Soviet-era party-state) or with a failure of "monarchic" sentiment mobilized by those who want to give dignity to their positions and property by constantly evoking well-worn narratives, this needs to be further investigated. What is clear, though, is that the ongoing conversion of the "seats" in the present hierarchy of governmental power into enviable pieces of real estate that are camouflaged from time to time by pompous nationalistic spectacles should be viewed as something very different from the capitalist culture of spectacle.

Sand sculpture festival: persistence of vernacular

In the Peter and Paul Fortress (*The State Museum of the History of St. Petersburg*) the 3rd international sand sculpture festival took place. It managed to alter the content and the image of the sight and attracted a considerable audience. The fortress was erected by Peter the Great to protect St Petersburg, but, almost immediately after its inception it started to be used as a prison, where, for one, Peter the Great's son was imprisoned and died. In the nineteenth century many political prisoners were imprisoned in the Trubetskoy Bastion, now the Prison Museum. The fortress' granite-covered bastions, located on an island, are surrounded by the strip of sand shore. Inside the fortress, various buildings have been converted into museums. Outside, there is a sand beach that served as ground for the festival. Inside the cathedral are the tombs of

Romanov emperors and empresses, including Peter the Great and Catherine the Great. In a small room to the left of the entrance are the tombs of the last tsar, Tsar Nicholas II, and his family.

Because it is located on the island, the site has been somewhat separated from everyday city life and thus meets the definition of a tourist site as "predicated in a binary opposition between ordinary/everyday and extraordinary" (Urry 1990: 11). The sand sculptures festival was, I thought, a nice mixture of ordinary and extraordinary. As a rule, it is the public monuments that, by virtue of their durability, comprise an eternal part of city landscape that we tend not to pay much attention to. Impermanent sculptures seem to arouse more fascination: they are expected to disappear because of wind and rain; hence one must hurry to see them. Besides, they are not overloaded with heavy historical meanings, their similarity and seriality is fun to watch. The important part of the process of visual consumption that the sculptures prompted was that the site of the exhibition remained crowded almost all the time that the show was on (about one month). The sand sculptures' appeal to the visual fascination of an audience was enhanced not only by the popularity of the event but also for one more reason. People sensed that these ephemeral sculptures, although undoubtedly devoted to the 300th anniversary (just like everything else last summer in this city) had something to do with subverting the conventions of the monument. As one of my interlocutors put it: "Here you don't feel oppressed, you don't feel that you're supposed to pay respect to somebody noble and famous, you can just stroll by and compare, which is also very important—to ask myself which one I like better."

It seems that it is a sense of being free from imposed cultural and national values as well as of being free to choose between similar, yet nevertheless different, objects is what gave people a peculiar pleasure. Some of the sculptures clearly had ideological content (e.g. a concern with the environmental situation on the Baltic Sea), while others conveyed the sculptors' familiarity with the latest trend in the monumental aesthetic, namely, minimalism. Most of all, they succeeded in creating something like an informal public place where people obviously found it very enjoyable to be surrounded by other spectators. This sort of art produces social processes rather than objects. It is in this context that the organization of the sand sculpture festival can be seen as a significant act of counterbalancing a pompous spectacle of the 300th celebration with community-oriented art. The festival was a vehicle for capturing locally relevant imagery in a deliberately "low-key" way. Many interlocutors also recalled their fond experiences at the ice festival that took place in winter, while others asserted that the event was "entertaining," "funny," and had "a sense of competition". One woman in her late forties put it in typical terms:

I guess living in this historical city we all are a bit tired of now predominant ambition to build 'for ages' and of related irony that not everything that is supposedly built for ages lasts long enough. So when you see these things, it gives you a totally different perspective: they are here for months, then the material they are made from returns to where it belongs. Nothing is taken from anybody. Nothing is going to turn into an eyesore that is going to stay there forever.

I personally liked most a "politically correct" replica of Michail Schemyakin's monument to Peter the Great in which Peter had distinctly Yakutian features. The author, coming from Yakutia, not only claimed his people's—who live deep in Siberia—right to the national holiday, but also, by re-appropriating the problematic Schemyakin's monument, managed to suspend the authoritativeness of it. The festival also gave reasons to think that there is an important link between reception of public art objects and photography. Photographing themselves with the sculptures in the background was what the visitors to the festival mostly did. One is tempted to recall here what Susan Sontag says with regard to the reassuring effect of photography: "The very activity of taking pictures is soothing, and assuages general feelings of disorientation. Unsure of other responses, they take a picture" (Sontag 1977: 10). In the context of an open-air exhibition, these photographic rituals, again, served as a way to connect people's experience of public place with their everyday activities, with sharing their leisure time with friends and families. In a sense, what those sculptures were depicting was not important since people seemed to take their viewing of the sculptures as part of the overall weekend experience.

Interestingly enough, in some of the regular St. Petersburg courtyards that are slightly embellished in the tradition of trash art, we can see even more vernacular versions of the celebration. The pieces installed are made from the relics of Soviet times: vinyl discs, old radios, tires, children's clothing, etc. These courtyards, however gloomy, unpolished, and sometimes plain crumbling they might seem to a stranger, are something that the locals cherish and are not always ashamed of. As the process of globalization extends, the language and rhetoric of advertising becomes more and more universal. It sets, as Malcolm Miles is certainly right to assert, "a conceptual as well as technical standard against which public art is not always successful in competing" (1997: 25). The circulation of video clips and desires, the traffic of people and signs, the world bazaar of commodities—all this seems to render local peculiarities and struggles obsolete. Nevertheless, under these circumstances it is getting even more important to look for the ways in which the now predominant ideas of globalization are taken with a grain of salt. They are not resisted since, in fact, there is nothing to resist: the practices of transnational corporations are increasingly obtaining a force comparable with that of the laws of nature. They are either simply ignored or rearticulated within what might be called counter-narratives or countersites in which both the oddness and sheer familiarity of traditional local life, with its outdated artifacts and useless items, is preserved.

If St. Petersburg authorities tend to exploit once-held stereotypes of their city and its "cultural treasures," other agents of cultural industry look for different ways to enhance the residents' sensibilities and provide them with new ways and spaces to experience the city.

Conclusion

The challenge one faces in describing politics of memory is to keep an eye both on macrosocial structures and microsocial behaviors, both on "hard" facts related to finances and politics and imaginative investments in cultures past and present, both on iconological data and the impressions of the passers-by. What I've tried to do is exactly that, a sort of juxtaposition of meanings that can be excavated from, on the one hand, an officially arranged and officially celebrated St. Petersburg anniversary, and, on the other, its vernacular forms. I have suggested that spatial, memorial, and artistic practices employed by the authorities betray a growing traditionalism of the Russian political regime. The post-modern eclecticism the celebration embodied seemed quite compatible with strategies of managing the public by the authoritarian leader and his bureaucratic environment. On the other hand, in spite of the growing authoritarianism and hierarchy in social and political relations that enact distorted, negative publicities (rendered by Jürgen Habermas as "representative ones"), other lines of influences and modes of interactions with the past could be discerned in the context of celebration. "Low-key" art forms that were introduced by several groups of city artists and curators may be seen as defying both appropriation of urban and national past by the state and cultural elitism. Thus this kind of public art figures as genuine urban practice capable of producing an engaging, informal, even witty response to the concrete event. It remains to be seen whether future political developments will allow the combination of state-imposed national narratives with other stories, and whether submerged memories will be able to continue rising to the surface of public interest.

References

Ankersmit, Frank R. (2002) "Representational Democracy. An Aesthetic Approach to Conflict and Compromise". Common Knowledge 8/1, pp. 9–22.

Boym, Svetlana (2001) "Nostalgia, Moscow Style". Harvard Design Magazine 13, pp. 1–8.

Donald, James (2003) "The Immaterial City". In Garry Bridge/Sophie Watson (eds.) *A Companion to the City Reader*, Oxford: Blackwell, pp. 46–54.

Habermas, Jürgen (1989) *The Structural Transformation of the Public Realm*, trans. Thomas Berger, Cambridge: MIT Press.

Miles, Malcolm (1997) *Art, Space and the City. Public Art and Urban Futures*, London: Routledge.

O'Connor, Richard (1995) "Indigenous Urbanism: Class, City and Society in Southeast Asia". Journal of Southeast Asian Studies 26/1, pp. 30–45.

Sontag, Susan (1977) *On Photography*, Harmondsworth: Penguin.

Thrift, Nigel/Crang, Mike (2000) "Introduction". In Mike Crang/Nigel Thrift (eds.) *Thinking Space*, London and New York: Routledge, pp. 1–27.

Trenin, Dmitrii (2004) "Identichnost i integratsia: Rossia i Zapad v 21 veke". Pro et Contra 8/3, pp. 9–22.

Trubina, Elena (2005) "Dreihundertjahrfeier in St. Petersburg". StadtBauwelt 24, pp. 24–34.

Villa, Dana R. (1992) "Postmodernism and the Public Sphere". The American Political Science Review 86/3, pp. 712–721.

Urry, John (1990) *The Tourist Gaze*, London: Sage.

Reflections on a Cartography of the Non-Visible. Urban Experience and the Internet

MARC RIES

In the first part I will investigate the intertwining of modern, conflict-ridden urban experience with the non-visible, defined here as both motor and effect of urbanity. In the second part, diverse "illumination techniques" will be discussed in a historical perspective. In the third and major part, the Internet will then be analysed as such a technique of visibility, together with city representations on the Web as a media performance of the urban and its conflict management.

This text tries to trace the present urban experience and the conflicts it copes with in relation to the medium of the Internet in two ways. First, urban experience will be discussed as a confrontation with the non-visible, the invisible. Then urban experience and its conflict management will be sketched as a—possible—performance of a media urbanity of the Web.

I

The city represents the central settlement point for all driving forces of modernity. *Invisibility* is one of its essential properties, it is at once motor and result of urban development. I will briefly sketch a few invisibilities: The influx of ever more people into towns leads to concentrations of urban building, to proliferation at the peripheries, but also to the founding of new—so-called—industrial towns. Planned and shaped from other social viewpoints, their large proportions are not comprehensible for the individual. One neither knows nor travels in other more distant parts of a town; one has merely a vague inkling of their size and density, much remains unknown, unfamiliar. This experience is one of constructed invisibility.

"The inclusion form of the modern also brings out a specific form of invisibility which is expressed in the structural alienation of town-dwellers from each other," Armin Nassehi (2002: 228) writes, thereby formulating a basic ambivalence of modernity. In the creation of large spaces—represented by railway stations, shopping streets and malls, stadiums, and parks, which imply a coexistence side-by-side of completely different people—no scenarios of togetherness, participation, or coincidence are considered during the planning process. This social invisibility is the cause of endless tensions, anxieties, and phobias, and is revealed in the socio-architectural extremes of gated communities on the one hand and slums on the other.

Cities endow capital with a face. The abstractness and lack of quality of money, of the universal equivalent, is brought to an unusual sensuality in the exhibited surplus of the trading centres, in the extravagance of the shops and malls. But the staging of goods is at the same time evidence of powers that remain incomprehensible for the individual. Behind the illusion of merchandise ticks the invisible regulation mechanism of accumulation, the capital markets.

As the last invisiblity I would cite that of the political powers and their institutions, that of the administration apparatus, which, following the foundation of nation-states, cultivate their ugly displays of Moloch-like bureaucracies. Life is administered by invisible forces.

Together with the non-visible, something else features large in modern urban life—the secretive. Georg Simmel points out that the "secret – the concealment of realities by positive or negative means – [...] is one of the greatest mental achievements of humanity. [...] The secret offers so to speak the possibility of a second world beside the manifest one, and the one is influenced by the other in the strongest fashion" (Simmel 1906).

At the start of modern urban development, Leibniz draws on the concept of the city to relate his philosophical system's qualities to an experience of the real world. In his "Monadology" the city acts as a metaphor for the existence of different and manifold universes.

The same town looked at from different angles appears completely different, and is, as it were, multiplied *perspectively*. In the same way, it emerges that, because of the infinite number of simple substances, there seem to be as many different universes as there are substances. However, these are only different perspectives on a single universe, according to the different *points of view* of each monad. (Leibniz 1999)

The scheme of urban experience is possibly most clearly depicted in the "cubistic town." Its rendering, like Robert Delaunay's "Simultaneous Window on the Town" (1912), rejoices in the dissolution of the directed gaze, of the promise of survey and order; it is a direct illustration of the constitutive modern experience of withdrawal of orientation in living space, of forsaking tradition, of the entry of contingency into the world's inner space. The picture celebrates complexity and lack of clarity, affirms the removal of limits and destabilisation.

The multiplicity of a city's perspectives, that is, the awareness of its own "secretive" life, makes it impossible for the individual inhabitant to see the city as a whole. Many parts of it—whether in fact town-parts or rather urban processes and differentiations—necessarily remain invisible to the individual gaze. The urban product is *per se* set in a dialectic of visibility and invisibility. To summarise: the city also spans all that cannot be seen; better: that cannot be experienced. Invisibility means inability of experience, means ignorance as an epistemic fracture

II

In order to counteract this, the early modern age already programmed numerous techniques of visualisation, of rendering visible, and also of rationalising. They were intended to at least help to simulate—or to substitute for by means of sign systems—a view of the whole. However, this development is always one between enlightenment and hegemony. In answering the question "By what results can the truth of enlightenment be recognised?" Martin Christoph Wieland replied:

> when it becomes altogether brighter; when the number of people thinking, inquiring and searching for light in general [...] becomes larger and larger, and the mass of prejudices and illusory concepts visibly smaller and smaller; when, unnoticed, the shame of ignorance and irrationality, the longing for useful knowledge and particularly respect in the face of human nature and its rights grows in all classes (Wieland 1996: 81).

This leads us to illumination techniques, which, and this is essential for me, are always techniques of space as well. They evoke a redefinition of urban space, expand, and indeed establish its specific use. To begin with, the first town maps are worth mentioning, for instance the "New Plan of Rome" of 1748 by Giambattista Nolli, the first modernist among town planners. Compared to city views in earlier maps (for example, Michel Turgot's Paris map of 1734), Nolli created desensualized, objectivised overviews. His map shows the town as an abstract ground plan for the planner's eye. The plan divides space into a texture by dichotomy, into a mass of places for living and working defined by similarity and repetition, which he depicts in *black*, and into a certain quantity of objects, monuments, and traffic routes, which accommodate all forms of public in exterior and interior space; these he depicts in *white*. These actually appear empty and unmarked; one could also say they are "invisible." On the one hand, Nolli's plan is a first attempt at introducing visibility by means of a rational order, allowing the inhabitant to find orientation and an overview. On the other hand, the cartographic description of public space as indeterminate is an uncertainty relation, an organism of unknown variables. The public nature of the street is charted here as a space for moving and conveying, which brings about for the user contact with an unpredictable number of what are for him surprising, unknown and foreign elements engaged in constant change (cf. Ries 2002).

Peter Eisenman's study of an "Architecture of Absence" also revealed elements of an "Architecture of Invisibility." As in Giovanni Battista Piranesi's "Plan of the Campo Marzio" of 1748:

> Piranesi uses the Rome that was extant in the 18th century as a starting point, but it possesses no original value; it is merely a being in the present. From this existential moment of being, he takes buildings that existed in the 1st and 2nd centuries, in Imperial Rome, and places them in the same framework of time and space as the 18th century. Next, Piranesi moves monuments of the 1st century from their actual location to other locations, as if these were their actual sites in the 18th century. Piranesi also proposes buildings that never existed. They seem at first glance to be memoires of buildings that could have existed because they look like buildings until one examines them for their function. [...] the ground becomes an interstitial trace between objects, traces that exist in both time and space. [...] it is a multiple palimpsest, a series of overlays that mix fact with fiction. (Eisenman 2004: 84-85)

Eisenman redefines the map as a "diagram," which comes into operation as a "template of possibilities" against a "metaphysics of presence."

Not only the city plans are of interest; the empirical, statistical procedures introduced by the administrations, the tables, lists, and diagrams (the birth and death statistics, the map of the metro, the telephone directory etc.) also create regulation systems. Maps, lists, and diagrams do not make a town easier to experience, but by *showing* some of its measurable and decipherable characteristics they can offer the inhabitant at least a partial orientation by means of these visualisations.

It is *analytical images and data, functional images* that help to make the "the city's space system" accessible, that attempt to convert the invisible into legible, visible values.

I will not look into all the other countless illuminating techniques that make the city brighter, more readily available, and meaningful, for example electrification, the visual guidance systems that run through towns, or video surveillance. Rather, I concentrate on the "absolute" image of the city as offered by the Internet today. Websites are functional images that are capable of more than of just providing data. As media performance, they help to redefine urbanity and offer completely new models of complexity of experience, while simultaneously enhancing the status of social space.

III

Nowadays everything social is represented on the Internet, or potentially available there as the medium's artefact. In this respect the Internet is a universal medium permitting the reverse argumentation: The Web embodies the totality of everything social, it is the "pure social."

The same applies to cities: Today each and every one of them is functionally duplicated in manifold ways. It is, however, important that instead of merely doubling reality, new spaces of perception and action are created. Only the Internet—as a participatory medium aiming at a rich diversity—is capable of comprehensively exhibiting the different urban systemic spaces and of influencing them. In a common argumentation of sociology, the category of projection is used to extract correlations or derivations, as in the following thesis: "Residential segregation is the projection of social inequality into (urban) space" (Häußermann/Siebel 2002: 33). It could also be said: *Segregation is the representation of inequality in space.*

This way of thinking presupposes that space itself is inactive and "enduring" something. The same happens in argumentations within media theory that reduce media to simple representations of society. When applied to the Internet, the conclusion could then read: social inequality is projected into the Internet and likewise shapes segregation there: Migrants have their own little sites which stand in the shade of the mighty, official sites. So is the Internet just a static mirror image of society or the urban? I would suggest four counterarguments to that.

Universal medium: in its capacity for displaying the social and making it visible world-wide, the Internet is a universal medium. Based on its universal availability and on its omni-perspective and dialogic constitution, the Web embodies the pure social. The Web is always larger than its individual usage.

Space differentiation: Internet practice aims at a variety of space, at space differentiation—but without hierarchies, without ownership structures or inequalities. It fosters a media juxtaposition, a coexistence of individual, communal, institutional, and capital interests that facilitate other, and considerably more, things than any factual coexistence in the "real" town or "real" world does.

Process differentiation within space differentiation: the Internet offers the most diverse programmes of exchange, communication, coincidence: from correspondence by forms to P2P, from mailing lists and chat rooms to Web logs. This interaction differentiation advances specialisation and individualisation to an extent no other medium previously did.

Contingency: on account of its link structure, that is, its hypertext logic, the Internet is in a position to deliver the unwanted, the unpredictable, the new to its user. It introduces him to the understanding that, as Luhmann noted, "everything can also be different."

With this argumentation the Web establishes its own space, a socio-media space that is part of *the geoaesthetics of the media*. The geoaesthetics of the Internet relates to the audio-visual construction and communicative linking of social spaces, their perception, and dealing with them. Every city representation is the expression of such geoaesthetics of the Web. Like no other medium, the Internet potentiates *a media performance of the urban*. I will focus on the official city representations on the Web. It is necessary to distinguish between three characteristics of the Web.

City representations on the Internet are *self-presentations* in the sense of a demonstration of *administrative complexity* on the one hand and of *function differentiations of the urban* on the other. The entire administration of town institutions is made visible. At the same time, societal forces, which help constitute towns, are displayed: the economy, together with work and the labour market, the culture and the spectacle, the history of the town with its housing, living, and progressing.

In parallel to these representation scenarios, individual *action potentials* are offered for navigation within the complexity and the differentiation. First, *orientation* is promised: What are the overall possibilities and institutions, what services are at one's disposal? Second, *knowledge* is provided: What do the individual sections provide, what contents do they offer? And third, *operating guidelines* are offered: How must I organise myself, how must I behave in order to achieve this or that?

These three action potentials mainly concern contact with administrations or public services, but also those areas dealing with troubles and problems, such as emergency services, self-help groups, certain associations. Navigation, however, also needs a search function connecting to a database whose keywords can be called up by a "search" or "research" function. These databases quickly reveal whether the sites do in fact cover the full extent of the urban, civil landscape and also include fields of conflict, or whether the political interest merely consists in vain self-representation. Consequently, this function brings about a change of direction: not what one does not know is searched for, but rather what the database does not know, or does not want to know, is scrutinised.

Apart from these Web offerings, another quite different innovative function comes into play: that of a new public space. For the first time in the history of mass media, the Internet comes forward as a media system that turns all receivers into producers and transmitters, and its participative dimension inaugurates a "media world public," developing completely independent, sovereign structures of interchange and communication. This concerns the messaging boards, the mailing lists, the chat forums, the websites built up by individuals, groups, communities, the content management systems, the Web logs, the P2P systems. These "coincidence techniques" turn the netizens into an audience, a media public whose sovereignty affirms the Web as a democratic institution.

Official city pages are thus intended to offer discursive interfaces for political communication, but also to grant visual access to all those pages that reflect town life and urban conflicts on the part of civil actors. It is astonishing to observe that official city sites almost entirely reject this participative dimension of the Web—they represent and give directions, but are not prepared to enter into a discursive, public debate on the multiplicity of urban conflicts with individual citizens, associations, or initiative groups. Apart from providing necessary resources politicians and officials need to prepare for an active communication with citizens—and not just to summon them to the ballot box. The urban landscape of conflict is in need of just these media interfaces in order to counteract the one-sided power gradient—in the sense of a genuine participatory democracy (Claus Leggewie).

But is there not an error here in my own observation and expectation? Why should the town of Darmstadt's administrative website want more than to keep with its designated definition of just being administrative? On the other hand: Is this not a somewhat abbreviated concept of politics? The Web is per se a decentrally configured structure, and so there will always be various manifestations, opticns of visibility, alternatives to the "official clearing," which in fact also leaves much in the dark, or proceeds to place it there. Many conflicts do not take place on the local level alone, or cannot be represented there; rather, they expand out into many regions and towns, and, above all, they hardly are of local origins. Problems like migration, segregation, unemployment, poverty, and gender inequality are global issues and concerns. The Internet is at its most impressive when interconnecting translocally.

IV

For it is the decisive nature of the metropolis that its inner life overflows by waves into a far-flung national or international area. [...] The most significant characteristic of the metropolis is this functional extension beyond its physical boundaries. And this efficacy reacts in turn and gives weight, importance, and responsibility to metropolitan life. Man does not end with the limits of his body or the area comprising his immediate activity. Rather [it] is the range of the person constituted by the sum of effects emanating from him temporally and spatially. In the same way, a city consists of its total effects which extend beyond its immediate confines. (Simmel 1950)

When Simmel wrote this, the city represented the only "expert system" for the non-visible, the complex, the differentiating out of systems. Today things are different. The "web of the webs' is no town. Yet it has become an expert system for the non-visible. The "inner life" of the Internet consists of all the computers connected worldwide, of all the sites on all the computers worldwide. That is, the Web possibly epitomises the formula of "world inner space," as reported by Hardt/Negri's political philosophy, or by Peter Sloterdijk's historical anthropology. To rethink the whole world as an inner space, as an interior which we can never look at from the outside, but in which we should freely roam. By means of the Internet, for example. Its "functional extension" results from the possibility for a connected individual to perceive all other connected individuals or institutions or power centres, and perhaps to communicate with them. The Internet does not function like geographical space with a Here and There, but rather like a purely relational space where there is exclusively a Here and Now. For the data stream every individual interface is at every moment the centre of the world. Yet every Internet site can indeed be measured by the "sum of effects emanating from [it] temporally and spatially." A site like *blogsbyiranians.com* thus obtains its legitimacy from its urban quality of reaching as many people in the world's inner space as is possible—not only in Iran, but also world-wide. Being part of the Web means being part of an urbanity, understood as a life form.

References

Eisenman, Peter (2004) "Giovanni Battista Piranesi. A critical analysis". In Peter Noever (eds.) *Peter Eisenman. Barfuss auf weiss glühenden Mauern/Barefoot on White-Hot Walls,* Wien: Hatje Cantz , p. 84–85.

Häußermann, Hartmut/Siebel, Walter (2002) "Die Mühen der Differenzierung". In Martina Löw (eds.) *Differenzierungen des Städtischen*, Opladen: Leske + Budrich, p. 27–67.

Leibniz, Gottfried W. (1999) *The Monadology.* Trans. George MacDonald Ross. http://www.philosophy.leeds.ac.uk/GMR/hmp/texts/modern/leibniz/monadology/monadology.html#m56.

Nassehi, Armin (2002) "Dichte Räume. Städte als Synchronisations- und Inklusionsmaschinen". In Martina Löw (eds.) *Differenzierungen des Städtischen*, Opladen: Leske + Budrich, p. 211–232.

Ries, Marc(2002) "Wrong Way. Zur Darstellbarkeit nachmoderner Städte im zeitgenössischen Hollywood-Kino am Beispiel Los Angeles". In *Medienkulturen*, Wien: Sonderzahl, p. 158–171.

Simmel, Georg (1906) "Das Geheimnis. Eine sozialpsychologische Skizze". In *Aufsätze und Abhandlungen 1901–1908 Band II*, Frankfurt am Main: Suhrkamp, p. 317. See also: Simmel, Georg (1906) "The Sociology of Secrecy and of Secret Societies". In *American Journal of Sociology* 11, p. 441–498.

Simmel, Georg (1950) "The Metropolis and Mental Live". ed. and trans. by D. Weinstein/Kurt Wolff *The Sociology of Georg Simmel*, New York: Free Press, pp. 409–424. http://condor.depaul.edu/~dweinste/intro/simmel_M&ML.htm.

Wieland, Christoph Martin (1996) "A Couple of Gold Nuggets, from the Wastepaper, or Six Answers to Six Questions". In James Schmidt (eds.) *What is Enlightenment? Eighteenth-Century Answers and Twentieth-Century Questions*, Berkeley, CA: University of California Press, p. 78–83.

Picturing Urban Identities

SERGEJ STOETZER

Images of cities play a key role in the formation of urban identity, producing specific spaces and sometimes leaving traces of that process behind, inscribed in material artefacts specific to places. Picturing urban identities is a new method of mapping the linkages between specific places, the production of space, and visualising the basis of the construction of urban identity as highly specific to place, media image, and acting.

The images of cities created by professionals, as well as by individual actors, play a key role in the formation of urban identity. Professional images are oriented towards media distribution in campaigns used to convey a precise picture of what should be regarded as specific to the city in the eyes of the beholder.

Besides these intended images, subjective ones arise from the perception of urban space, experiences, memories, and ideas, building tension between the individual constitution of urban space and the adoption of a pre-arranged mixture of symbols, historical issues, visual artefacts, and narratives produced intentionally. The individual actor's urban identity, his/her mental image of the city, is formed from this tension.

The subjective image of the city is reconstructed using visual and narrative empirical data from students at Darmstadt, where these processes of negotiating identities are studied. The city's official imagineering is analysed utilizing its Web presence, focusing especially on Darmstadt as a "city of science."

The theoretical aim behind this is to integrate concepts of place-based identity with a sociological perspective on the constitution of space as a social process that involves action and structure, materiality and atmospheres, ascribing both subjective and perceived preconfigured characteristics to places —to the urban realm.

Four main aspects will therefore be addressed here: place-marketing, with a tendency towards homogenisation; concepts of identity and place; the newly elaborated methodical framework for analysing processes of attributing meaning to specific places while constituting space, and, finally, first findings about a way to integrate the different theoretical approaches to place, space, and identity.

Place-marketing and homogenisation

Place-marketing as a metaphor describes a promotional strategy that arises from the quest for locational competitiveness with the shift from the managerialist mode of urban governance to the entrepreneurial one caused by the decline of the Fordist model of mass production—but it is not its hour of birth:

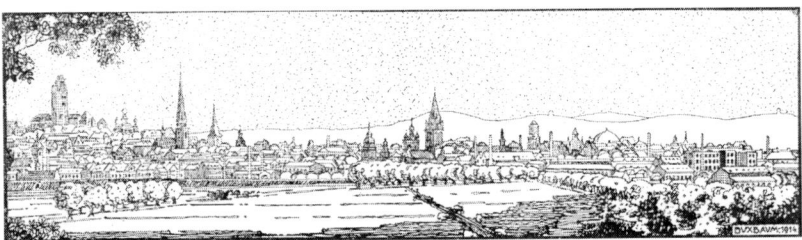

Figure 1: Darmstadt 1914
(Darmstädter Kunstjahr 1914, Reclams Universum Sonderheft, Leipzig 1914)

Portrayals of Darmstadt in 1914 intend to address cultural and recreational aspects of a city beautifully integrated into the natural environment, mediated both textually as well as pictorially—with the smokestacks of the industrial complexes deliberately minimized to near insignificance (Schott 1999).

Place-marketing is aimed at the projection of intentionally produced images to external audiences and local populations, bringing together two not always compatible objectives: Next to the attraction of capital investment, consumer spending, and highly skilled migrants, it is also addressed to the internal audience, the citizens, seeking to legitimse regeneration and development policies and increasing social cohesion in times of an increasingly divided an segregated city (Griffith 1989).

Place-marketing becomes difficult in a globalised world, with communication technologies making the functional differences between places less important, while reducing the "quality of authentic places" to simple location factors (Hassenpflug 1999), so greater effort is spent on differentiating them by increasing their symbolic value: The fear of not being noticed drives the quest for achieving symbolic advantage over other competing cities. This is done by creating city-myths—reimaging or visionary strategies, or referring to the city's great narratives (Griffith 1989).

Publicity and advertising have been important factors in place-marketing, though the budget used for them seems to be very small compared to other forms of commercial advertising, and local authorities seem to be the main actors here, not international advertising agencies. They tend to communicate less information about functional qualities and emphasise material artefacts (or the materiality of the city) for its symbolic loading. The logic behind this idea is that "rooted" materiality gives competitive advantages in a "space of flows" (images of cities, information about them) because of its (relative) immobility.

A strong tendency towards homogenisation and convergence in the advertising strategies can be observed, both in what is included and excluded from the imaginary created for these purposes—downplaying or silencing problems and portraying only highly selective versions of a place's history.

The creation of new urban landscapes by flag-ship buildings supports this tendency, as the services of very few superstar-architects are used to create the symbolic and material atmospheres desired for creating upscale lifestyle enclaves. The gap between anticipated and preferred living conditions, however, has been revealed in different studies, e.g. by Peter Noller and Klaus Ronneberger (1995). Next to the architecture of superlatives, more subtle ways can be found by renaming places, or by theming urban landscape from a selection of "premixed design packages that reproduce pre-existing urban forms," as Boyer (1992) describes it (p. 184; cit. from Griffith (1989)). (Re)arrangements of people and social goods found in architectural drawings showing the intended "users" and trying to locate the virtual building in its later environment may lead to homogenising pictorial representations of buildings not even built yet by the use of templates provided within the software used during the design process (Löw 2003). This thesis can be extended to visual representations of an actual built environment, the city, in electronic media in the context of professional production of images for place-promotion purposes.

From a critical point of view, place-marketing has been targeted because of its ideological effects, its highly speculative nature, and the socially regressive consequences. The criticism of its ideological bias is rooted in the virtue of the idea itself: the manipulation of meanings and perceptions in order to suggest specific prearranged ensembles of people and social goods said to be specific to the promoted place for the individual's production of space.

There is, of course, a tension between the desired effects and the way the addressed local publics perceive the strategies developed by the city's authorities, making any simplistic assumptions of cause-action impossible: Given the possibility of different "readings" from the local public, it is nowadays even easier for individual actors or marginalised groups to address electronic image campaigns, showing their rejection of the official portrayal, and to make their own interpretation of the places' history visible,[1] even if this includes showing the opposite of what official image campaigns try to do: to make the city look good.

A shimmering example of that conflict can be found online: Halle is a quite old city with a remarkable history in (higher) education and fine arts, known for its reform university during the Enlightenment. It is also known for the environmental problems caused by a huge chemical industry located nearby—and an increasing rate of unemployment caused by the decline of that industry after the Wall came down.

The conflicts arising between the official representation of the city (showing cultural and historic sites on virtual tours: www.halle.de) and a group of six people targeting this representation in quite cynical ways, starts with the name of the city's "different" representation, connecting the city's name Halle with a phonetically similar one, Hoelle, meaning hell (www.hoelle.de).

Starting with pictures of incivilities, desolated buildings, and characterising the city's problems as one of shrinkage, the website shows a counter announcing the estimated number of citizens, but going backwards, extrapolating that the last citizen will have left in 11959 days due to a decline of nine citizens per day. It is no wonder that the city has tried several times to shut down this website, though it has had only temporary success.

Given the uncertainty of place-marketing, it is reasonable to limit these risks by re-using concepts that seemed to be effective elsewhere—leading to the homogenisation of media campaigns and to pictorial representations of cities using very similar visual methods. This logic of careful competition may seem reasonable at first, avoiding spending (public) money on speculative promotion strategies when it could be very well used elsewhere, but it is compromised by a deep internal contradiction:

In a globalising world, with the importance of being noticed, cities need to stress their specificity on the one hand, while being careful in doing so on the other because of the highly speculative nature of place-marketing, allowing only slight changes from the path other cities seemed to have walked successfully. They find themselves between the poles of an *imperative for differentiation* and an *imperative for uniformity* (Griffith 1989).

---

1 Cf. Escobar (2001) trying to leave the dichotomizing debate on the local and the global behind by introducing "concepts that are useful for ascertaining the supra-place effects of place-based politics, such as network and glocality" (p. 142) and empowering the defence of place-based identities and practices in contexts of globalization.

Theoretical conceptualisations of identity and place

In the same context of globalisation that is said to have an intrinsic potential of homogenising images of places, they themselves are contemplated with different importance both theoretically in the discourse as well as practically in everyday life. Abstract connections between specific places, highly networked cities constitute powers of a different scale and quality, the global cities, on the one hand, while others disappear from the scene, forming the hinterworlds (Taylor 2001).

Theoretical conceptualisations of place often refer to four interplaying phenomena: to *non-material ones* as atmosphere, meanings, feelings, or memories of experiences specific to places, to *activities*, to the *social environment*, and to *materiality*[2] in situ (models of: Relph 1976, Canter 1997 with an emphasis on materiality, action, experience, and scale, Agnew 1987).

Place identity can then be understood as the person's socialisation with the physical world, which is an intrinsic characteristic of a general socialisation process, not as two opposing or non-related processes.[3]

Peter Gerlach (1997) describes an empirical study of spatially related processes of identity formation conducted in Berlin. Profiling the constitution of individual identities in relation to spatial contexts, he identifies three different levels of complexity of people's spatial appropriation, identifying spatial appraisal patterns as playing a key role in the process of an emerging identification with a place.

Doreen Massey (1994) warns about the misleading potential of common-sensical conceptions of place that can result in even reactionary conclusions—especially when thinking about place and identity in spatial terms of territorial boundaries naturalising the complex processes of building and establishing spatial links to a blood-and-soil theorem. She suggests a "progressive sense of place" that considers places as networked intersections, characteristic because of its local intrinsic specificity as well as its links in different spatial scales.

Her idea harmonises with the concept of space Martina Löw (2001) has elaborated, and which is the theoretical framework for the analysis presented: By conceptualizing space as a relational setting of human beings and social things with the power of structuring social behaviour, while at the same time being structured and modified itself by perception and action, Löw found a new way of thinking about space. The sociology of space goes beyond the

---

2   Hidalgo/Hernández (2001) stress the importance of analysing them in conjunction with each other since most studies about attachment to place(s) have only considered the social environment at a spatial scale and concept of neighbourhood only.
3   Cf. Twigger-Rosss/Uzzell (1996) for details on their critiques about this separation of a socialisation process.

dualism of absolute versus relativistic definitions of space (space as a container; space as constructed in the human mind only) and differentiates between two primary processes—synthesis and spacing, both recursive and interwoven, representing the two dimensions of space: structure and agency. Places are simultaneously the sources and the intention of the constituting processes: Meanings and attributes are attached to places by spatial links: Elements and people found in situ are synthesised along with perceptions of the materiality, memories, thoughts, and feelings according to their significance for the individual actor—interwoven with placing oneself in the situation in relation to the rearranged elements found there.

As a consequence, a new methodical design was developed to be able to capture specific fragments of this highly complex and perpetuating process—dealing with the inscription of meaning to places by establishing meaningful connections ("links") between elements found in situ, every day experiences, memories, ideas, and prearranged images—for analytical purposes.

Methodical and methodological issues

Reconsidering methodical issues related to the reconstruction of the individual, subjective "image of the city" (Lynch 1965), a wide range of visual methods such as video documentary, ethnographical description of visited places, and mental maps is applicable. Kevin Lynch used the latter one combined with interviews and observation of places in his prominent five-year study of Boston, Jersey City, and Los Angeles in the 1960s, identifying five key elements shaping the spatial mental representation of a city: paths, edges, districts, nodes, and landmarks.

Due to the methodical uncertainties involved in using mental maps or sketch maps as empirical data,[4] the crucial element of the reconstruction process is to achieve a visualisation based on the individual actors' mental image of the city, which includes pictorial definitions of urban space significant for identity formation next to narrative representations (interviews) of the city.[5]

Visual representations of cities are of course an important discourse in architecture, arts, and geography and have become more important in other dis-

---

4 Mental maps, however, suffer from reliability issues and are quite problematic to analyse, since tracing contortions between the city-map and the drawn sketch map as a material representation of the internal mental map to underlying causes is highly vague (Downs/Stea 1982; May, 1992). Thomas Sieverts (1997) argues similarly and urgently recommends review of the literature from other involved disciplines as well, especially the psychology of perception.
5 Dietrich Hartmann (1989) identified three main techniques of narrative description of cities: the list, the map, and the imaginary walking tour (p. 80)—differentiated by their spatial knowledge.

ciplines over the last years, e.g. informatics and computer science. Their interests lie in the realisation of digital, visual representations of actual cities and the simulation of vital functions provided within them.

There are a number of ways to realise digital representations on the Internet, ranging from complex rendering approaches based on the geometric data of buildings to the use of panoramic scenes from a static viewpoint.

The approach used in this study is based on a network of photos derived from the actual town, an interactive collage with links between the pictorial representations of actual places. It was intended for the creation of digital cities by individual actors, allowing them to share their own experiences moderated visually, or show memorable sights to other people publicly on the Net, allowing the building of digital representations from scratch with the fewest barriers possible – like a grass-roots visualisation of the actor's city (Tanaka/Arikawa 2001).

To analyse subjective images of the city, students were asked to take photos of their town, Darmstadt, and to link them with this software to create an interactive collage.

Linking the pictures is done by identifying persons, objects, or even parts of the picture itself on at least another one: The corresponding areas of the photo are chosen by the actor and then linked according to the persons or objects they both have in common—or that should be considered as belonging to each other (symbolic loading).

Figure 2 a/b: Linking corresponding areas
2a) detaillisction purpose,   2b) shift of atmosphere
(both taken from empirical basis, second collage presented). © Sergej Stoetzer

The links between the pictures are spatial relations, attached with meaning by the actors' selection (of what to link and in which ways).

Following the links, the photos will be crossfaded, allowing the impression of walking through the collage, or the city, just by choosing the next among the linked pictures. The possibilities of navigating and exploring this digital city are framed by the structure of the collage itself, by the shape of the network emerging from the links between the pictures.

The task given to the students as participants explicitly dealt with the specificity of place and the need for a kind of serial photography, allowing easier linking afterwards. Similar to film-making, they had to prepare a storyboard beforehand to sharpen the idea of what to show of "their Darmstadt" for its digital representation. Considering the complex possibilities of overlapping constructions of space, the chosen topic was anticipated while the serial photography took place, assuring that the range of choices—which elements between different pictures could be chosen for the collage later to fit the topic—would be narrowed down while being at the specific place taking pictures. This instant selection at the "place of action" is a methodological trick to keep influences (e.g. atmospheres, conflicting or overlapping spaces) on this process place- and time-specific, meaning that the subsequent linking only "mechanically" reproduces the selection processes that took place in the city's realm, adding no further complexity to the production of space.

In order to be able to compare the levels of analysis between the *reconstruction* of the actor's image of the city based on the visual data (photos, collage) and the *actor's own* description of that visual representation and its intended effects, an interview was conducted after the photos were taken and the intention (the "storyboard") was requested in writing. Triangulating the pictures taken by the students with the collage and the interview itself is now possible.

Analysis of the webpage is done on three levels, starting with *formal arrangements* and *contents*. In the *final step*, content and formal analyses are cross-referenced, identifying the support or lowering of intended meaning(s) and structure.

In the following, that comparism will be narrowed down to the image of Darmstadt as a city of science, an official title that was granted to Darmstadt by the Ministry of the Interior of the state Hessen in 1997. The official website of the city devotes one navigational reference to Darmstadt being a city of science, listing the research centres located in the city, as well a the research carried out in local enterprises. Interestingly, the students are excluded from this conceptualisation, they are not perceived by the local public or the press in this context—notwithstanding their contribution to a city of science as revealed by a recent study from Beate Krais and Maja Suderland (2004)—just the university is mentioned, of course, among the other research centres. It will therefore be interesting to find out what references students draw from this concept of their city.

Examples from the empirical base of the study

The two portraits of Darmstadt that are introduced in the next passage have the following in common: First, Darmstadt was attributed with negative imaginations, like "ugly city" or the buildings were described as "architectonic malformation"[6], but as time passed this attitude changed.

Instead of using the interactive collages themselves, an overview of them will be used, generated by extracting the linkage information. This overview is static, but gives significant insight into the structural conceptualisation and uses a graphic representation that is energy-minimized by placing a "virtual" spring between the photos so that, by iteration, an arrangement can be found that allows minimal overlap between pictures and links. Even pictures excluded from links with the other ones can be identified, showing what was included in the collage as well as what was excluded from the original material.

Starting with the first collage, five segments can be identified, representing different themes and paths connected to each other by one picture in the middle, a photomontage that looks like a postcard. The starting pictures of each of these five walks through Darmstadt's imaginary space are situated here.

1. Labour and Internment camp
2. "Kavalleriesand-Kasernen"
3. Formerly private bank ("Bank für Handel und Industrie")
4. Houses and courtyards at the Magdalenenstraße
5. Residential Castle

Figure 3: Collage from empirical base; generated overview. © Sergej Stoetzer

---

6   Quoted from the interview with F.O. (with reference to the first collage; line 180).

The labour and internment camp was located on the property of the Telekom's research centre directly after WWII (by Allied forces), and fragments of it, like the old gatehouse with the main entrance, still exist, but usually do not get noticed, even by people who have worked there for ten or more years, like the student taking these pictures.

The second theme shows a view of a barracks square in the same area as the internment camp, the Kavalleriesand-Kasernen. The original picture was taken after the war and the participant tried to relocate the exact position from which the old photo was taken, trying to show the relationship of tension between similarities and changes that occurred over the decades.

The first two motifs have a very close relationship to the biographical background of the student, who had worked at these locations for about a decade before studying again. They represent the main idea of this collage, identifying places from which old pictures were taken and trying to show what remained, was altered, vanished, or which new elements appeared on the scene—inspired by a publication doing just that and evoking a first interest in the rest of the city, not just the place of work.

The third tour shows a formerly private Bank (to 1932; built 1873-1875), the "Bank für Handel und Industrie." It is located quite close to the inner city, next to a former railway station that was relocated to its present location in 1912. The roof was damaged during WWII and two storeys were added afterwards, with very little architectural sensitivity—thus the student's accusation: The building is protected as an architectural monument, but the reconstruction of at least the façade could have been made better to be fair to the building's architectural and aesthetic roots.

The houses and courtyards at the Magdalenenstraße were chosen because their old fabric is still intact. The old half-timbered houses created a specific flair that could be (at least partly) preserved.

The Residential Castle, along with the university, constitutes the second main biographical reference: the place of study. Similar to the motive before, the castle's courtyard is shown, too, as well as references to the underlying theme of similarity/change and references to destruction caused by war (and buildings in the post-war period): A single house was discovered close to the university that still shows signs of another building that must have been next to it, but was destroyed by the bombing of the city in September 1944.

Engaged with pictures of pre-war Darmstadt, the city's history holds great potential for explaining what was perceived as "architectural sins," leading to a more forgiving judgement of the city's present appearance: The formerly nice-looking city with a lot of Jugendstil buildings was nearly completely destroyed on the 11th and 12th of September 1944, making rapid rebuilding necessary after the war. The buildings of the post-war period were perceived as sterile, but knowing the city's history lead to the reinterpretation of Darmstadt's outer appearance, the victimising of the city by historical circumstances beyond its influence in times of global conflict.

The second collage consists of three main topics: the private sector with the shared flat, or student's residence, leisure time activities and, the university itself. The latter can be differentiated into five subtopics:

3. university campus outside the city, the Lichtwiese
   3.1 workrooms
   3.2 everyday-life events and communication at the university
   3.3 the university canteen
   3.4 artwork on the campus
   3.5 "connectors" inside the building

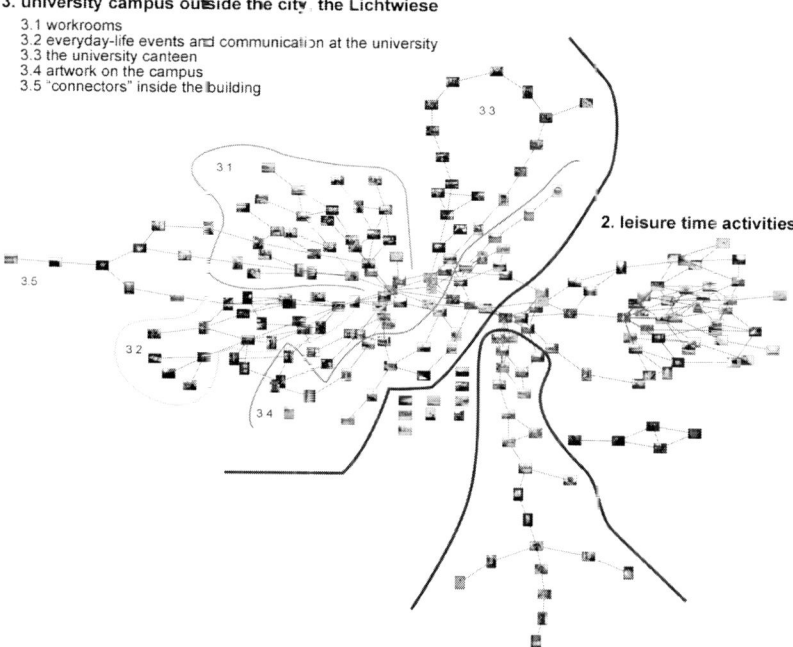

2. leisure time activities

1. shared flat/student's residence

Figure 4: Second Collage. © Sergei Stoetzer

The collage begins with the exit from the private sector to one of the centres of the collage, an aerial picture, allowing the observer to choose between the two other main topics: the university or leisure.

The right part of the collage is about leisure activities, especially sports at the university's stadium. It can be reached from the other topics by aerial pictures and photos of a schematic map showing the different buildings at the campus. The importance of this place is due to the events taking place there, like an ironically-named doddery-triathlon with ten people working together to overcome the distance intended for one. In connection with this Olympic spirit, the people who meet there and activities with friends are what are important and load this place with meaning by peers, action, and archaic symbols. Another interesting aspect is the use of photos taken at different times of the same place, but with a different timescale: While the photo tour took place in winter, some of the important "ensembles" for the participant's production of space (and ascription of a specific meaning to this place) were missing: the peers and friends gathering around him there are substituted by using pictures where they are present.

The last five identifiable themes are grouped around the third main topic, "university." Starting with the two most complex ones, working and partying at the same location, there are very interesting descriptions of place-attributed informal rules concerning both working rooms and events inside university life: The students' workrooms are highly hierarchically ordered, with the best and most wanted places occupied by more advanced students, who spend most of their time there. Time, as a resource, has to be invested on a long-term basis to improve one's own situation.

Communicational functions inside that building are very important and are provided by a coffee shop and places intended for assembly. Even the material of the building, concrete, plays an important role, providing people with durable walls to which one can nail posters or attach different kinds of artwork, including graffiti or mosaics. In this respect, the material of the building provides communicational functions, serving as a platform for presenting ideas, exchanging them, and—technically speaking—working as a distribution machine with the corridors, elevators, and stairwells serving as connectors between different places. A cluster of pictures takes these connections as a topic. The canteen serves as a communication platform, too.

As a counterweight to the atmosphere of work and study, parties change the atmosphere by decoration, including different DJs for separate rooms and visual projections. This atmosphere provides a specific quality of freedom: the freedom to be able to do things that are very close to being illegal (just concerning safety issues) without anybody asking questions on the one hand, and on the other knowing that without responsible behaviour this freedom would vanish very soon. There is a very interesting contrast here between the highly organised way workplaces have to be appropriated by students and the freedom to organise events.

The subtopic connecting the two great poles of university and leisure in the overview of the collage is artwork. It can be found on the campus and even next to the student residence. The artwork shown in the collage ranges from huge installations (the linear house) to very tiny graffiti or mosaic patterns. For the student constructing this collage, art symbolically loads a place with meaning by inviting the observer to discover meanings and links to other places, people, or times—seeking traces other people have left behind. The presence of others is characteristic of a place. To acquire a place then means to institutionalise the perception of space at this specific place in a way that the self is perceived (by the person as well as by others) to be one "legitimate" element of the constitution process. Identity, as belonging to certain groups and places, is inscribed this way by institutionalising the process of the production of space specific to places.

Darmstadt, as a city of science, is addressed in both collages by references to the university as well as to a research centre outside the academic world. In the interviews this concept of a city of science was questioned with answers ranging from pride and identification (referring to national ranking concerning research centres in and outside academia, where Darmstadt occupies the third top place) to criticism, since this town has more to offer.

The analysis of the collages so far indicates three main visual representational techniques, addressing different levels of the process of identity-formation in urban space:

The *first technique, overview,* is a result of an unfamiliar way of orientation in the city's space, like the way the collages would be *without* these vantage points, allowing one to gain any sense of direction from the perspective of street-level *only*. Brenda Yeoh (2001: 457) explains postcolonialism next to its more known, tangible conception as a conceptual frame of reference "to destabilize dominant discourses in the metropolitan west," revealing assumptions about perception and orientation in the city (of the West).

Transferring this to purposes of orientation in Japanese urban space (leaving the Eurocentric perspective), streets seldom have names and navigation in the city is done by using some landmarks for a rough sense of direction, then depending on traffic lights, pedestrian overpasses, hospitals, schools, and other easily identifiable buildings. The intended way to build a digital city with the approach used here visualises just that: the way a certain path through the city would look like from the perspective of street-level. This would enhance the recognition of the observer actually visiting the places, preventing him from getting lost, if not helping him grow accustomed, to this kind of navigating. These collages can indeed be found almost solely with reference to the Asian region: hotels showing their anticipated customers the way from the train station, historic and religious monuments offering virtual explorations supporting an easier finding of one's way around actually visiting the site, or people visualising their neighbourhood, house, or holiday trips.

Caricaturing the other perspective used in the collages, one could say that people rooted in "Western culture" can imagine the city only after looking at a map showing them the bird's-eye view in a highly schematic and abstract way.

Combining both views in the collages looks like a workaround at first, considering the taken-for-granted assumptions about how urban space is explored. Having to work with a tool (the software was developed in Japan) that is not intended for these "overview" purposes, using this technique anyway illustrates the deeply rooted cultural bias in exploring urban space—influencing the constitution of urban identities by culturally different approaches of navigation and orientation in urban space ("needed" overview in Western cultures).[7]

The *structural arrangement* of the collage explains the highly selective choice of what to show of the city's diversity. The meanings of certain places depend on the context of the actor's intention exploring urban space, exposing the influence of context of action for the choice of places to "interact" with.

Moderating the *shift(s) in the temporal order* of the collages by integrating pictorial representations from different times using variable time-scales, the places' dependency on time is stated concerning its atmosphere and the possibilities of attaching meanings to it by integrating people and materiality.

Summary

Focussing these provisional findings, the following cornerstones of identity-formation relating to places are available:

Concurrent to a three-pole triangular model of meaning of place suggested by Per Gustafson (2001), the corner-stones of identity-formation are Self, Others, and Environment, with the possibility of mapping meanings of place between the three poles instead of assigning them to one as a sole category. Other important aspects are the scales of place and time, the cultural context, and the structure of attributed meanings.

Condensing these observations, Gustafson's model of mapping meanings of places can be regarded as what Martina Löw (2001) describes as production of space, consisting of two processes of perception (synthesis) and action (spacing). Synthesis includes the perception of self, environment, and others, depending on the symbolic and material factors in situ, the habitus of the acting person(s), the structural in- and exclusions. Synthesis and spacing are interwoven and referenced against each other.

The production of space regarding place-based identity is therefore highly dynamic, with each of the triad's components underlying the axes of time, the specificity of the places included (which changes due to the context the places are visited), and the knowledge about the cultural connotation (Figure 5). This leaves time as an ambiguous influencing factor. Mediating this triad on the one hand, while being one of the resources used on the other hand, it at least reassures what Norbert Elias (1994) said about space and time: being the two main concepts of reference.

---

7   Thomas Sieverts (1997) is thinking about ways to integrate a schematic overview for orientation purposes, while keeping the myth of the urban labyrinthine alive, making it a task for urban and regional planning.

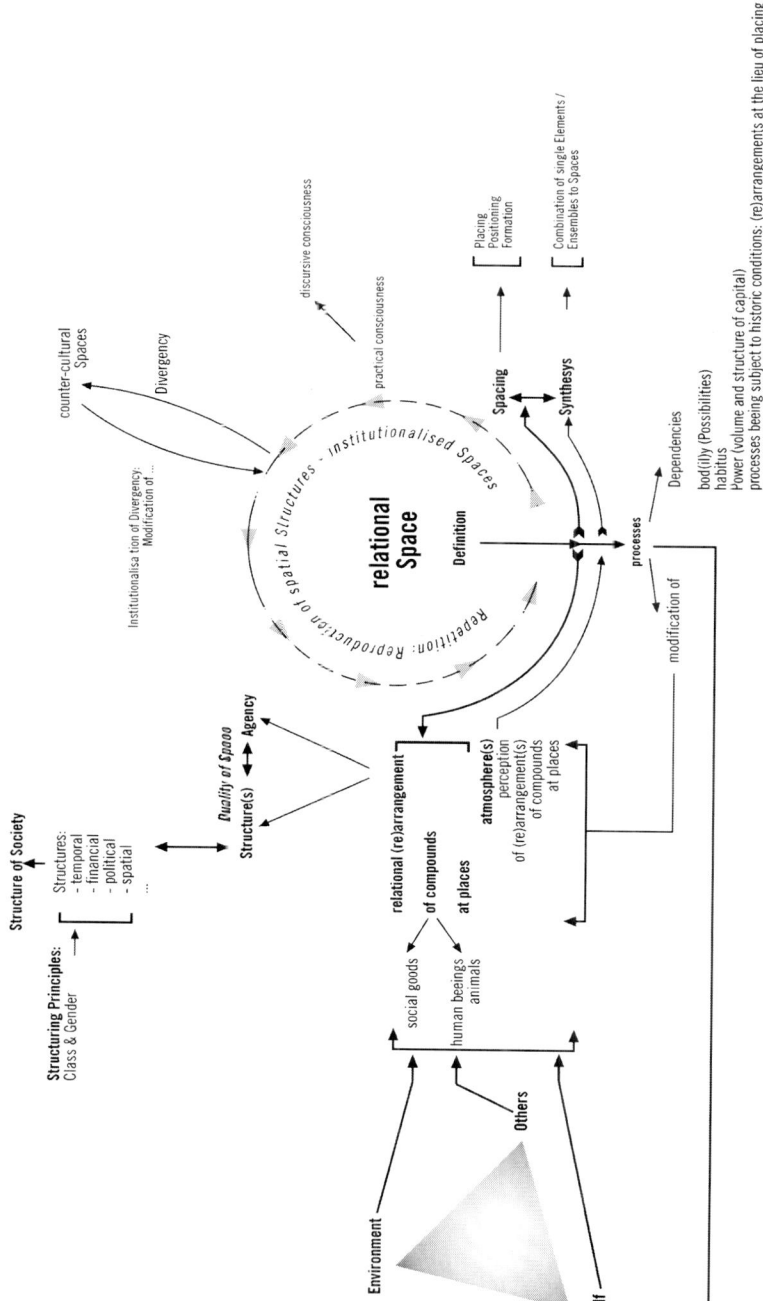

Figure 5: Model of Löw's relational space—attached with Gustaffsons tripolar model of place-based identity. © Sergej Stoetzer

Building a collage as a network of photos of specific places, the students participating were able to build their subjective image of the city as a digital one existing in medial space—like the official image production using ordinary webpages. Showing fragments of the city's space with specific importance, these iconographics (semantic network of photographic essences of places) can be analysed in order to examine the processes in which identity is bound to places by repetition, memory, imagination, and social networks. Time and the efforts for the production of space(s), as well as the place itself, artefacts, and practises are the resources in this process.

References

Agnew, John A. (1987) *Place and Politics*, Boston: The Geographical Mediation of State and Society.

Canter, David (1977) *The Psychology of Place*, London: Darmstädter Kunstjahr 1914, Reclams Universum Sonderheft, Leipzig 1914.

Canter, David (1997) "The facets of place". In G. T. Moore & R. W. Marans (eds.) *Advances in Environment, Behavior and Design*. Vol. 4: Toward the Integration of Theory, Methods, Research and Utilization, New York, pp. 109–147.

Downs, Roger M./ Stea, David (1982) *Kognitive Karten. Die Welt in unseren Köpfen*, New York: Harper & Row.

Elias, Norbert (1994): Über die Zeit. Arbeiten zur Wissenssoziologie II, Frankfurt am Main.

Escobar, Arturo (2001) "Culture sits in places: reflections on globalism and subaltern strategies of localization". Political Geography 20, pp. 139–174.

Gerlach, Peter (1997) "Raumbezogene Identitätsbildung in der Stadt: Befunde und Interpretationen aus der Fallstudie 'Berlin-Friedrichshain'. Raum und Identität. Potentiale und Konflikte in der Stadt- und Regionalentwicklung." Institut für Regionalentwicklung und Strukturplanung: Erkner, IRS. 15, pp. 29–52.

Griffith, Ron (1989) "Making Sameness: Place Marketing and the New Urban Entre-preneurialism. Cities, economic competition and urban policy," London: N. Oatley, pp. 41–57.

Gustafson, Per (2001) "Meanings of place: Everyday experience and theoretical conceptualizations". Journal of Environmental Psychology 21, pp. 5–16.

Hartmann, Dietrich (1989) "Zur Konzeptualisierung von Makroräumen und städtischer Identität." In: C. Habel/H. Herweg/K. Rehkämper (eds.) *Raumkonzepte in Verstehensprozessen. Interdisziplinäre Beiträge zu Sprache und Raum*, Tübingen: Niemeyer, pp. 70–89.

Hassenpflug, Dieter (1999) "Citytainment. Die Neuerfindung der Stadt im Zeichen des Imagineering" In Praxisreport Industriebau. *Kreative Beweglichkeit – Offene Grenzen, Wien:* Neue Partner. D. Sommer, pp. 86–105.

Hidalgo, Carmen M./Hernánzez, Bernando (2001) "Place Attachment: Conceptual and Empirical Questions". Journal of Environmental Psychology 21, pp. 273–281.

Ipsen, Detlev (1997) "Was trägt der Raum zur Entwicklung der Identität bei, und wie wirkt sich diese auf die Entwicklung des Raumes aus? Raum und Identität. Potentiale und Konflikte in der Stadt- und Regionalentwicklung." Institut für Regionalentwicklung und Strukturplanung: Erkner, IRS. 15, pp. 15–27.

Krais, Beate/Suderland, Maja (2004) *Darmstadt – Wissenschaftsstadt ohne Studierende?* Abschlussbericht des empirischen Lehrforschungsprojektes "Zur Soziologie der deutschen Universität" am Institut für Soziologie Fachbereich 2 "Gesellschafts- und Geschichtswissenschaften" der Technischen Universität Darmstadt Sommersemester 2003 und Wintersemester 2003/2004.

Löw, Martina (2001) Raumsoziologie. Frankfurt am Main: Suhrkamp.

Löw, Martina (2003) *Prinz Charles, Hollywood und Hongkong. Raumsoziologische Annäherung an Architektur und ihre Bilder.* Antrittsvorlesung. TUD-intern 5/2003.

Lynch, Kevin (1965) *Das Bild der Stadt*, Frankfurt am Main/Berlin: Ullstein GmbH.

Massey, Doreen (1994) *Space, Place and Gender*, Cambridge: Polity Press.

May, Mark (1992) *Mentale Modelle von Städten: wissenspsychologische Untersuchungen am Beispiel der Stadt Münster*, Münster/New York: Waxman.

Noller, Peter/Ronneberger Klaus (1995) *Die neue Dienstleistungsgesellschaft. Berufsmilieus in Frankfurt am Main*, Frankfurt am Main/New York.

Noller, Peter (1999) *Globalisierung, Stadträume und Lebensstile. Kulturelle und lokale Repräsentationen des globalen Raums*, Opladen: Leske+ Budrich.

Relph, Edward (1976) *Place and Placelessness*, London: Pion.

Schott, Dieter (1999) "Kunststadt – Pensionärsstadt – Industriestadt: Die Konstruktion von Stadtprofilen durch süddeutsche Stadtverwaltungen vor 1914". In: Die Alte Stadt, 26 Jg., pp. 277–299.

Sieverts, Thomas (1997) "Zur Lesbarkeit und inneren Verfügbarkeit der Stadtregion Berlin als Lebensraum. Raum und Identität. Potentiale und Konflikte in der Stadt- und Regionalentwicklung". Institut für Regionalentwicklung und Strukturplanung: Erkner, IRS, pp. 15: 53–69.

Tanaka, Hiroya/Arikawa, Masatoshi/Shibasaki, Ryosuke (2001) "Technologies for Digital Cities – A 3-D Photo Collage System for Spatial Navigations". In M. Tanabe/P.V. d. Besselaar/T. Ishida (eds): Digital Cities II. Computational and Sociological Approaches, Second Kyoto Workshop on

Digital Cities (Kyoto, Japan, October 18–20, 2001, Revised Papers)., pp. 305–316.

Taylor, Peter J. (2001) "Urban Hinterworlds: Geographies of Corporate Service Provision under Conditions of Contemporary Globalization". Geography, 86/1, pp. 51–60.

Twigger-Ross, Clare L./Uzzell, David L. (1996) "Place and Identity Processes". Journal of Environmental Psychology 16, pp. 205–220.

Yeoh, Brenda S. A. (2001) "Postcolonial cities". Progress in Human Geography 25/3, pp. 456–468.

Communist Heritage Tourism and its Local (Dis)Contents at Checkpoint Charlie, Berlin

Sybille Frank

This article focuses on a conflict that developed at Checkpoint Charlie in 2004 about the representation of the history of the famous site. It is argued that, in the deregulated Berlin heritage industry, urban streets prove to be the contested arenas in which questions of historic agency and display, as well as those of self and other, are (re)negotiated between public, private, local, and international actors, providing no ready-made scripts, but offering highly different negotiation powers for each of them.

With the Wall coming down in 1989, Checkpoint Charlie, divided Berlin's famous Allied border control point, became obsolete. Throughout the 1990s, millions of people witnessed the breathtaking transformation of the former checkpoint from a promising urban development site to a derelict symbol of the reunified city's failed investment politics, and, finally, to the former border crossing point being partially re-erected for tourist consumption by public and competing private initiatives.

Notwithstanding this continuing tourist and media interest, the disputed ways in which today's Checkpoint Charlie came into being have hardly caught the attention of the scientific community. Therefore, this article aims at identifying some of the public and private players in the politics of history and memory at Checkpoint Charlie, and at analyzing their diverging interests. To this end, the analyses will focus on a conflict that developed there between the Berlin government, the private Berlin Wall Museum, and a handful of drama students in the summer of 2004 and which led to a most controversial debate about how the history of the site should be represented. After investigating the economic, political, and cultural background of the controversy, the conflict will be interpreted as illustrating the emergence of a Berlin heritage industry, the peculiarities of which will, finally, be characterized with a view to the complex ways in which urban conflicts are negotiated in times of globalization. The term "heritage industry" is employed with reference to the works of British and US researchers such as Robert Hewison (1987), David Lowenthal (1985; 1996), or John Urry (1990), who defined the heritage industry as an increasingly diversified and globalized tourism- and leisure-based industry that has evolved against the background of post-Fordism, and in which a variety of public, and, in particular, a growing number of private actors compete to create support for and revenue from anchoring their interpretation of history in public space (cf. Wright 1985; Fowler 1992; Rojek 1993; Samuel 1994, 1998; McCrone/Morris/Kiely 1995; Kirshenblatt-Gimblett 1998; Arnold/Davies/Ditchfield 1998; Graham/Ashworth/Tunbridge 2000).

The history of Checkpoint Charlie

Checkpoint Charlie was inaugurated in September 1961 by the British, French, and US forces who had been stationed in Berlin since the end of World War II. One of the few inner-city border crossing points that connected the eastern and the western parts of divided Berlin, Checkpoint Charlie was reserved for diplomats, members of the Allied forces, and foreign travellers. However, only tourists were fully checked there, whereas diplomats and Allies were allowed to pass the control point uncontrolled, following the freedom-of-movement-agreement between the Soviets and the Western Allies (cf. Skiorski/Laabs 2003).

Until the fall of the Berlin Wall, Checkpoint Charlie developed into the city's most famous border crossing point, and it did so for five reasons: first, it became famous as a dangerously "hot" site of the Cold War. In October 1961 it was the place where US and Soviet tanks faced each other, ready to shoot, after Soviet soldiers had refused to let an American diplomat pass the border uncontrolled. Soon after the conflict had been settled, Checkpoint Charlie hit the headlines again: second, the most famous Wall victim, 18-year-old Peter Fechter, bled to death close to Checkpoint Charlie after having been shot by East German soldiers during his attempt to escape to the West. Notwithstanding this, Checkpoint Charlie, third, also became renowned for more than 1200 successful flights to the West, since many GDR citizens made use of its special status by dressing up as Soviet majors or American soldiers, thus crossing the border unmolested. Fourth, in 1963 the West Berlin Wall Museum opened at Checkpoint Charlie to document both the history of the Wall and the flight stories. Founded by refugee smuggler Rainer Hildebrandt, it became not only one of Berlin's best-visited museums, but also a centre of peaceful resistance against the Wall. Fifth, Checkpoint Charlie was heavily frequented, as it was the eye of the needle for foreign travellers wishing to enter East Berlin. Therefore, the border crossing point symbolized both hopeless division and a hopeful passage.

When the Wall came down in 1989, Checkpoint Charlie lost its function overnight. Following the ceremonious dismantling of the border crossing point in June 1990, the place, suddenly located in the "new centre" of the soon-to-be German capital, became attractive for investment. It was as early as February 1992 that the Berlin Senate sold the former borderland at Checkpoint Charlie to a private enterprise: the Central European Development Corporation (CEDC) planned to build an American Business Center on the premises that were soon meant to become the headquarters of some big service companies.

For the Berlin Senate, the sale of the land was very attractive, as it promised both a prestigious urban development project and the creation of jobs in times of public money shortage. Following reunification, Berlin had lost the generous financial feeds that both West Berlin, the "island city" of the Federal Republic of Germany, and East Berlin, the capital of the German Democratic Republic, had enjoyed. To provide the city, which was characterized by a backward industrial sector and high unemployment rates, with a new perspective, the Berlin Senate decided to attract foreign capital that should profit from a deregulated bureaucracy (cf. Lenhart 2001). Being Berlin's first major urban development project, the contract of purchase with the CEDC was signed rapidly, making no conditions as to the representation of the site of the famous former Allied checkpoint. Because of the ongoing dead calm in the Berlin real estate market, however, the project soon came to a halt. By the time the main investor left the CEDC in 1997, only three of the planned five blocks had been built, turning the former model project into an infamous urban planning torso.

As a consequence, the void CEDC grounds East of the former border were gradually taken over by hawkers who sold GDR-souvenirs to tourists. On Checkpoint Charlie's Western side, the Berlin Senate marked the former line of the Berlin Wall with cobblestones in 1997, responding to the rising tourist demand for signs of the vanished border. A year later, the previous border crossing point was further furnished with a large lighted box that displayed two photos of a Russian and an American soldier. Moreover, in 2001, Rainer Hildebrandt, still the director of the Berlin Wall Museum, donated to the former Checkpoint Charlie an exact replica of the dismantled Allied border control cabin. Garnished with fake flags and sand sacks, and combined with a copy of the famous warning sign "Your are leaving the American Sector...," the replica succeeded in re-establishing much of the former view of the once-famous border crossing point (*Figure 1*). It was this replica which set the scene for a "burlesque" (Berliner Provinzposse 2004) that developed at Checkpoint Charlie in the summer of 2004.

Figure 1: Checkpoint Charlie with picture of border official (Berlin Senate), border sign and cabin replicas (Wall Museum), seen from the east (Photo: © Sybille Frank, 2004)

The "burlesque" of summer 2004

On the 3rd of June, 2004, the German press agency broadcast the following news: "In protest against the appearance of fake GDR policemen in front of the Berlin Wall Museum at Checkpoint Charlie as a tourist attraction, the world-famous former border crossing point has been wrapped up. 'We can no longer tolerate that this symbol of division is being abused,' the initiator Alexandra Hildebrandt, member of the Wall Museum, said" (quoted according to Protest gegen falsche DDR-Polizisten 2004).

In interviews with the rushed-to-the-scene reporters, the fake GDR policemen who had provoked the spectacular veiling turned out to be a group of drama students. For a few euros, the students, who were dressed in uniforms of the former GDR People's Police, posed with tourists in front of the control cabin replica for photo-shoots, or pressed original GDR border stamps in passports. After some days of verbal clashes between the fake border officials and Alexandra Hildebrandt, who had become director of the Wall Museum after the death of her husband Rainer Hildebrandt, Mrs. Hildebrandt had ordered a building firm to veil the control building with a tarpaulin.

In Alexandra Hildebrandt's opinion, the students' activities insulted the victims of German separation. She could not bear to witness how "a memorial place is being transformed into a Disneyland" (Hildebrandt, quoted according to Müller 2004), and she declared that she would "unveil the cabin only after the degrading spectacle has terminated, or after the Berlin government has called a halt to that offence against history" (press release of the Wall Museum, June 3, 2004).

Within the next few hours a rapid development of conflict lines could be observed: The director of the memorial for the victims of the GDR state security service, Hubertus Knabe, declared that he could "not understand the careless way in which the students treat the symbols of political persecution in the former GDR" (quoted according to Pletl 2004a). At the same time, the Association of Former Political Prisoners/Union of the Victims of Stalinism insisted on the immediate end to the activities—a demand that was supported by more and more victims' associations.

The drama students, however, felt irritated by the sudden uproar. Their speaker, Tom Luszeit, argued: "In Rome, there are gladiators in front of the Colosseum as well" (quoted according to Nickel 2004), and he informed the bewildered journalists that the students had posed in front of the cabin for months. After the former East Berlin district Mitte had refused to approve their action, they had asked the former West-Berlin district Kreuzberg for permission, which was granted in October 2003. Even though this made the students in their Eastern costumes stand on the historically "wrong" side of the border, i.e. the former Western side, and although the former Eastern border officials had not worn the uniforms of the GDR People's Police, but those of the GDR People's Army, the tourists' reactions had been enthusiastic. The students wanted to give the Berlin visitors "a live impression of what had happened at the place in former times." "I want to educate, not to insult the victims," Luszeit summarized the students' intents (quoted according to Müller 2004, Pletl 2004b).

With a view to the tense situation, a comment from the district Kreuzberg, which had approved the students' activities, was eagerly awaited. The town councillor in charge, Franz Schulz (Green Party), declared that it was neither forbidden to let oneself be photographed in the streets for money nor to wear a GDR People's Police uniform in public. When enquired about the control building, Schulz dissociated himself from the Wall Museum, denouncing its cabin replica as "Disneylike": "Quite obviously, neither does this cheap copy for tourists correspond to the dignity of the place" (quoted according to Schmidl 2004).

The next day, the situation suddenly changed: The students apologized to the victims' associations, replaced their GDR People's Police uniforms with those of the Western Allies and asked Alexandra Hildebrandt to uncover the control building. However, Hildebrandt insisted that she would only let people gaze at the cabin again if all commercial activities at Checkpoint Charlie were officially banned. As a surprise, the victims' associations now declared their solidarity with the students. For example, Herbert Pfaff, a representative of the memorial site for the victims of the GDR state security service, blustered: "Checkpoint Charlie is not the property of Mrs. Hildebrandt" (quoted according to Puppe 2004), and he demanded that the tarpaulin be taken away so that the victims of German separation could once again be commemorated at the historic site.

Finally, after some more days of fierce struggle, Berlin's Senator for city planning, Ingeborg Junge-Reyer (Social Democrats), intervened by issuing a three-point-press release. In the document, Junge-Reyer clarified that Checkpoint Charlie was a place "where the division of the city is commemorated, and not a place for masquerade" (Checkpoint Charlie ist kein Ort für Mummenschanz 2004). As the first of the recommended measures, the Senator called upon Alexandra Hildebrandt to remove the veiling of the cabin immediately, since it violated the special public space use permit agreed upon with the district. Second, a higher density of traffic police controls at Checkpoint Charlie was announced, so that free traffic flow would be guaranteed. As a third instruction, a zebra crossing was to be installed next to the traffic island, in which the control building was located, in order to raise pedestrian traffic safety.

These three "traffic" instructions in fact meant a defeat for both of the contending parties: While Alexandra Hildebrandt was obligated to unveil the building, the announced traffic police controls and the zebra crossing equalled a trading prohibition for the students: they were no longer allowed to pose on the street for their photo-shoots, and the traffic island would be restricted soon as well, as trading on zebra crossings was generally prohibited. Consequently, only the narrow sidewalks at Checkpoint Charlie could be legally used by the students in the future.

Following a police raid against the students, Alexandra Hildebrandt finally unwrapped the control cabin. But the students returned, temporarily taking up position on the traffic island with the control building (*Figure 2*). Ironically enough, this decision now made the *tourists* fall victim to the intensified police guard: as it was now they who had to step on the street to take pictures of the students from a good perspective, they had to be escorted back to the sidewalks by the policemen. And, even more ironically, in doing so, it was now the "real" policemen who turned into desired photo objects. Quite obviously, the heightened police presence at the former border crossing point augmented the authenticity of the historic place, known to be a checkpoint.

While analyzing some of the economic, political, and cultural backgrounds of the conflict in the following, the focus will lie on Alexandra Hildebrandt's activities, as it was she who staged the described fight as a media event—a fight about the question of what today's Checkpoint Charlie should stand for, and who should have a say in it.

Figure 2: Drama students dressed in uniforms of the Western Allies (Photo: © Sybille Frank, 2004)

The economic perspective

From the economic perspective, the conflict can be interpreted as Alexandra Hildebrandt's fight to monopolize the profits that come with the internationally renowned place by transforming it into a showcase for her Wall Museum. To achieve this, the museum director engaged in a strategy that can be called *profit generation by spacing*. Spacing was important as it could provide for *hereness*: as the American researcher Barbara Kirshenblatt-Gimblett has noted, the successful production of a heritage destination necessitates the creation of hereness, which can be achieved either by actualities, or, in the absence of actualities, by virtualities (1998: 167). In the case of dismantled Checkpoint Charlie, hereness obviously had to be produced by virtualities, which were provided by the museum's replicas of the control cabin and the famous border sign. As these copies put the historic place back on the Berlin map, it was also, subsequently, put back on tourist bus itineraries.

Moreover, once the tourists had reached Checkpoint Charlie, spacing could *channel* them into the museum by using the replicas as signposts. For example, a board under the famous border sign informs the visitors: "This sign is a copy. The original still exists and can be seen in the Haus am Checkpoint Charlie"—which is the German name of the Wall museum. Finally, spacing could help to maximize profits through the displacement of competitors. Accordingly, Alexandra Hildebrandt used the wrapped-up control cabin as a pledge against the students who had degraded the building to a photo background and obstructed its advertising function for the museum. But, as described, the veiling of the building was also intended to focus public attention on the "commercialization" of the historic site, and to push for a grand political solution. In order to strengthen the museum's position in this process, however, the public had to take the side of the museum and its interpretation of history.

The political perspective

Hence, the political perspective shows the burlesque as a struggle about *what* should be commemorated at the historic site. In this context, Alexandra Hildebrandt was aiming at establishing Checkpoint Charlie as a *victims' place* in public memory, and at anchoring the museum as the *victims' advocate* in public discourse.

To construct Checkpoint Charlie as a victims' place, Hildebrandt set out to criticize the other commercial suppliers at Checkpoint Charlie for capitalizing on the victims' pains. This implied a scandalization of the students' activities as "a disgrace of the Berlin Wall victims" and "an offence against history" (press release of the Wall Museum, June 3, 2004)—a point of view that was soon supported by the victims' associations. As a consequence, the fact that Checkpoint Charlie had been world-famous for numerous successful escapes to the West receded into the background. At the same time, Hildebrandt's attempt to establish the museum as the victims' advocate in the public discourse could distract from the fact that, since the fall of the Wall, the former non-profit Wall Museum had also changed into a profit-oriented private enterprise that capitalized on the victims' stories. Throughout the 1990s, the museum's exhibition concept had been changed according to an event- and adventure-based dramaturgy, new rooms had been rented and a museum shop had been opened so that, after the museum officially relinquished all subsidies in 2002, it managed to establish a reputation as Europe's most successful commercial museum (cf. Engel/Konnerth 1998; Kunzemann 2002).

Nonetheless, to perpetuate the museum's acclaimed traditional image as an unselfish, courageous advocate of the oppressed, however, today's institution is promoted by Alexandra Hildebrandt as the lifework of museum founder Rainer Hildebrandt, the political activist and refugee smuggler. This message is again communicated by the disputed control cabin, which was changed into a memorial for Mr. Hildebrandt shortly after his death in early 2004: the windows of the cabin have been covered with copies of the museum's press release that informs about the local hero's life and death. Behind the windows, a huge oil-painting portrays Rainer Hildebrandt. Next to the building, flowers have been piled up to commemorate the deceased museum director.

Therefore, the students' activities did not just disgrace the victims of the Wall. According to Alexandra Hildebrandt, they also defiled the remembrance of her husband (cf. Müller 2004). Publicly staged like this, the reference to refugee smuggler Rainer Hildebrandt did not only bear the potential of identifying today's private museum with the former political non-profit organization, but also of making the discourse on Checkpoint Charlie as a victims' place more plausible.

The cultural perspective

Last but not least, the cultural perspective brings cultural value systems and practices into focus and shows today's Checkpoint Charlie as a site where local traditions of historic agency and display *clash* with traditions brought along with tourists from all over the world.

This point can be illustrated by the accusation of Disneyfication that accompanied the whole debate as a leitmotif. First launched by Alexandra Hildebrandt against the students' activities, it was later turned against the Wall Museum's cabin replica by town councillor Franz Schulz, and, finally, bundled in the press against all commercial suppliers at Checkpoint Charlie, who were criticized for reshaping the historic site as a spectacular place of event and sentiment, thereby violating the authenticity, respectability, and truthfulness of the historic site. While serving as a cultural demarcation line against the "fake" and "commercialization," the Disneyfication reproach thus implicitly suggested that there was something "original" and "inalienable" to be protected at dismantled Checkpoint Charlie—which turned out to be the locality itself.

The logic behind this is uncovered by Frank Schulz's earlier critique of the cabin replica: In stating that "Quite obviously, neither does this cheap copy for tourists correspond to the dignity of the place" (quoted according to Schmidl 2004), Schulz extended his critique of the cabin to its consumers, the tourists. Apparently, the tourists did not seem to care whether or not the objects presented to them at Checkpoint Charlie were originals or copies. To them, it was far more important that they could *experience* the famous Cold War site—which also embraced, as described, the overall presence of policemen. Therefore, the fact that Checkpoint Charlie, which had been proudly dismantled in 1990, was partly reconstructed by a set of private actors for tourist consumption a decade later, was scandalized as an undesirable change of the locality under the grasp of global tourism. Accordingly, it was provocative that the students, in defending their costumed activities, did not refer to the local tradition of flight masquerades through Checkpoint Charlie during Cold War times, but, as quoted above, to the fake Gladiators in front of the Colosseum in Rome.

In sum, the import of both the American Disney and the American *Living History* model with its historic re-enactments to Berlin, and its success with foreign tourists, confronted the city with a new—globally induced—problem that still had to be negotiated locally: the question how to integrate differing cultural values and practices at a place that had only recently been constructed as a "sacred" victims' site.

Conclusion

Putting together the three perspectives, the Checkpoint Charlie case illustrates the conflict-laden formation phase of a post-Wall Berlin heritage industry that can be characterized by the following three points:

First, the described conflict shows the formation of a Berlin heritage industry *beyond political regulations*. While most of the Anglo-American heritage research identifies national, regional, or communal governments as well-organized actors who deliberately initiate specific public-private-partnerships in the field of heritage politics to exploit it, for example, as a means of local economic regeneration or to exert power over social groups (c.f. Wright 1985; Lowenthal 1985; 1996; Hewison 1987), the Checkpoint Charlie case introduces a Berlin government that is highly disorganized. First, the Berlin Senate sold the premises at Checkpoint Charlie to an international investor without giving any instructions as to how the famous historic place should be represented. Second, following the investor's breakdown, a potpourri of private actors was invited by the two involved districts to capitalize on the history of the former control point—once more without the issuing of any regulations as to what should be presented at Checkpoint Charlie, or how that should be done. The described conflict forced the lack of concepts and ready measures of Berlin's governing bodies to address the city's Cold War history and to regulate those private actors on the public agenda for the first time, leading to it being referred to as a "burlesque."

The second peculiarity of the Berlin heritage industry is its spontaneous formation *beyond sites*. While the vast majority of heritage research describes the ongoing global heritage boom as a purposeful restaging of historic relics as *sites* (c.f. Urry 1990; Rojek 1993), Checkpoint Charlie is neither a place where historic remnants can be found nor a space that has been nominated for commemoration. Having been spontaneously resurrected by a set of actors who tried to meet a continuing tourist demand, today's Checkpoint Charlie therefore catapults the supply- and site-oriented heritage discussion to a demand-oriented level on which *urban streets* come into focus. In this constellation the addressees change: while designated sites primarily appeal to *tourist* needs, the revivification of Checkpoint Charlie at the same time needs to be conveyed, as a publicly accessible inner-city space, to *locals*, too. It is this need to create local support for the restaging of the famous place that explains Alexandra Hildebrandt's strategy to anchor Checkpoint Charlie as a "dark" victims' spot in the local perception, and to use the Berliners' subsequent *prise de conscience* for the former border control point to engage them in a Disneyfication discourse which aimed to degrade and displace the museum's commercial competitors. Accordingly, Checkpoint Charlie became connected with local discourses that separated "admissible" from "degrading" cultural practices, turning the derelict place into a "sacred site," and the replica of the Allied control cabin that had itself been accused for being Disneylike shortly before, into a symbol of local identity and pride eagerly defended by the victims' associations.

As a third point, the Checkpoint Charlie example contradicts heritage theories that lament the power of the global over the local (c.f. Kirshenblatt-Gimblett 1998). On the contrary, the urban conflict that was negotiated here shows the (re)construction of the locality as a *reciprocal regotiation process* into which both global and local images of the place have entered.

On the global-local level, the tourist demand and presence has shaped both Checkpoint Charlie's material face and local commemorative traditions. While Berlin's hitherto existing places dedicated to the Cold War victims were located at original sites, away from tourist routes, the identification of the victims' associations with today's resurrected Checkpoint Charlie shows a twofold adoption of practices that had been dismissed as "Disneylike" before the conflict: first, the victims' identification with a *replica*, i.e. the control cabin replica, and, second, the desire to anchor the remembrance of the Wall victims in a centre of international *attention*. These processes indicate the victims' turning away from the traditional European idea of the inalienability of originals for commemoration, both with a view to original historic objects and to original historic places.

On the local-global level, the rise and maintenance of the victims' perspective has functioned as a local corrective against the tourists, for whom the thrilling Cold War history of Checkpoint Charlie—with the tanks that faced each other—makes up the sensation of the place. This perspective even led to the widely-reported opening of a private Wall victims' memorial on the Eastern side of Checkpoint Charlie in October 2004, donated by the Wall Museum, which was torn down by the credit company administering the former CEDC grounds in July 2005, despite substantial local and international protest. By this, the burlesque of summer 2004 has, in the long run, also led to the public insight that reunified Berlin's governing bodies and local groups urgently need to find their position as to the city's globally popular, but locally still very unpopular, Cold War history if they want this history to be told by themselves and not by others.

References

Arnold, John/Davies, Kate/Ditchfield, Simon (eds.) (1998) *History & Heritage. Consuming the Past in Contemporary Culture*, Shaftesbury, Dorset: Donhead.
Berliner Provinzposse. Vopos am Checkpoint Charlie (2004) http://www.ntv.de/5250761.html, 3 June.
Checkpoint Charlie ist kein Ort für Mummenschanz (2004) Senatsverwaltung für Stadtentwicklung, press release, 11 June.
Engel, M./Konnerth, D. (1998) "'Wir arbeiten in Angst und Schrecken'". Berliner Zeitung, 21 November.
Fowler, Peter (1992) *The Past in Contemporary Society. Then, Now*, London: Routledge.
Graham, Brian/Ashworth, G.J./Tunbridge, T.E. (2000) *A Geography of Heritage. Power, Culture and Economy*, London: Arnold.
Hewison, Robert (1987) *The Heritage Industry. Britain in a Climate of Decline*, London: Methuen.
Kirshenblatt-Gimblett, Barbara (1998) *Destination Culture. Tourism, Museums, and Heritage*, Berkeley: University of California Press.
Kunzemann, Thilo (2002) "Kontrollen am Checkpoint". Die tageszeitung, 14 February.
Lenhart, Karin (2001) *Berliner Metropoly. Stadtentwicklungspolitik im Berliner Bezirk Mitte nach der Wende*, Opladen: Leske + Budrich.
Lowenthal, David (1985) *The Past is a Foreign Country*, Cambridge: Cambridge University Press.
Lowenthal, David (1996) *The Heritage Crusade and the Spoils of History*, New York: Free Press.
McCrone, David/Morris, Angela/Kiely, Richard (1995) *Scotland – the Brand. The Making of Scottish Heritage*, Edinburgh: Edinburgh University Press.

Müller, Felix (2004) "Ein Gespenst geht um am Checkpoint Charlie". Berliner Morgenpost 3 June.

Nickel, Veronika (2004) "Checkpoint Charlie. Wieder eine Baracke verhüllt". Die tageszeitung, 4 June.

Pletl, Steffen (2004a) "Baracke aus Protest verhüllt". Die Welt, 4 June.

Pletl, Steffen (2004b) "Checkpoint-Baracke: 'Vopos' verhüllen sich". Berliner Morgenpost, 4 June.

Protest gegen falsche DDR-Polizisten (2004) http://www.bkz-online.de/modules/news/print.php?storyid=79_9, 3 June.

Puppe, Andrea (2004) "'Alliierte' posieren im US-Jeep". Berliner Morgenpost, 7 June.

Rojek, Chris (1993) *Ways of Escape. Modern Transformations in Leisure and Travel*, Lanham: Rowman & Littlefield.

Samuel, Raphael (1994) *Theatres of Memory. Vol. 1: Past and Present in Contemporary Culture*, London: Verso.

Samuel, Raphael (1998) *Theatres of Memory. Vol. 2: Island Stories. Unraveling Britain*, London: Verso.

Schmidl, Karin (2004) "Unruhe am Checkpoint Charlie". Berliner Zeitung, 5 June.

Sikorski, Werner/Laabs, Werner (2003) *Checkpoint Charlie und die Mauer. Ein geteiltes Volk wehrt sich*. Berlin: Ullstein.

Urry, John (1990) *The Tourist Gaze. Leisure and Travel in Contemporary Societies*, London: Sage.

Wright, Patrick (1985) *On Living in an Old Country. The National Past in Contemporary Britain*, London: Verso.

Earthquake Recovery and Historic Buildings: Investigating the Conflicts

FATIMA AL-NAMMARI

As a pilot study, this paper investigates how conflicts developed during the earthquake recovery of a historic building in San Francisco. The study shows that such a building can be a contested space in earthquake recovery, as different groups push for different values. The subsequent conflict develops in phases, with roots based in the people and the context of the recovery more than in the building itself. More research is needed to investigate the process of recovery as it relates to historic buildings.

Background

Recovery after an earthquake is challenging for any community as it endeavors to repair the damages. It is a period that witnesses struggles between different groups with different priorities. As such, the recovery period is often tinged with conflicts (Berke/Beatley 1997: 27–31; Geipel 1982: 16, 171; 1991: 91; Lindell/ Prater 2003: 11–12).

Disasters have physical, social, psychological, sociodemographic, socioeconomic, and political impacts, in addition to many indirect impacts (cf. Lindell/ Prater 2003). As a community focuses on returning to routine life activities, historic buildings may not be valued and they may be unnecessarily demolished, leading to the irreversible loss of many important cultural properties (Craigo 1998: 96; Feilden 1987: 37; Kariotis 1998: 59).

Literature divides the post-disaster period into four main stages: 1) Emergency (response) period; 2) Restoration (short-term recovery) period; 3) Reconstruction I (long-term recovery) period; and 4) Reconstruction II (commemorative period) (Berke/Beatley 1997: 36; Haas et al. 1977: 279–281). This paper measures recovery as the time needed to repair a building after an earthquake.

Many factors affect the decisions made during the recovery period—the amount of damage, costs and benefits, resources available, time pressures, preservation awareness in the community, and political attitudes, which can have an important influence—especially after wars (Geva/Al-Nammari 2002; Haas et. al. 1978: 263–264). Such decisions are an outcome of social processes that have not yet been fully investigated. The dynamics of such processes are important, as they affect the decisions as well as the time and cost involved in the recovery.

In this paper, conflict follows the definition provided by Anstey (1999: 6) as a struggle over resources aimed at controlling the result. It is part of any process of decision making that affects a community or a resource, and is based on the beliefs of groups, which can be true or false (Anstey 1999: 5–13; Warner 2001: 14–16). Therefore, since resources are limited in post-disaster situations, different groups will have different stands on the best use of such resources, thus creating conflict (Bolin/Stanford 1990: 107; Geipel 1982: 171; Phillips/Ephraim 1992: 6–9).

Preservation[1] is defined by the International Committee of Monuments and Sites (Australia ICOMOS 1999: article 1.4) as a process of looking after a place to retain its cultural significance. Preservation is thus an act of management, and international charters have stressed that cultural resources should be preserved so that their tangible and intangible values are maintained and passed on to future generations (cf. ICOMOS 1982; 1987; 1999).

Historic preservation after disasters has seldom been investigated. Several studies have shown that historic buildings face special challenges (cf. Eadie 1991; Jones 1986; Look/Spennemann 2000, 2001; Merritt 1990; Nelson 1991; Spennemann/Look 1998). The old construction methods, the significance of the buildings' fabric, and the meaning they hold put them in a separate category from nonhistoric buildings, which is a situation that sometimes leads to conflicts. Noted issues are damage assessments, retrofit, and maintaining the integrity of the historic fabric.[2] Also, the specific requirements of mitigation and rehabilitation pose challenges that encourage owners to demolish and build anew (Craigo 1998: 18; Feilden 1987: 43–53; Kariotis 1998: 55–59; Look 1997: 1–7; Spangle Associates 1999: 22–26). While several studies have indicated that historic buildings face conflicts in recovery, more studies are needed to investigate how such conflicts happen. Such investigations are important,

---

1 ICOMOS uses the term "Conservation," not "Preservation," but to maintain consistency the term Preservation will be used, as it is the term used in the US.
2 Integrity of fabric is a term used by preservationists to identify a state in which the original historic building materials and systems remain intact.

as conflicts cause delays and time is an important factor in successful disaster recovery (Haas et al. 1977: 21; Wu/Lindell 2004: 76–77).

Demolitions seem to be the most cited source of conflict for historic buildings. After an earthquake, there is intense pressure on public officials for rapid demolitions because damaged buildings seem to pose a safety threat (Schwab et al. 1998: 295). In addition, damage to some buildings leads to the assumption that the historic fabric is no longer of historic value, which also results in demolitions (Spennemann/Look 1998: 3). Demolitions are also sometimes considered by the owners of historic structures due to the regulations and building codes that encourage such actions indirectly and make them more economically rewarding (Spangle Associates 1999: 23–27).

Therefore, the objective of this paper is to investigate the conflicts that face historic buildings after earthquakes. It is a pilot study to identify how conflicts develop. It is not the purpose of this paper, however, to investigate all challenges facing historic buildings in recovery. Instead, the study focuses on the roots of the conflict and how these conflicts ensue. This is accomplished by studying the recovery process of a publicly-owned building in San Francisco that was, at one point, scheduled for demolition.

Methods

As a pilot study that is part of a larger investigation of the recovery of historic buildings after earthquakes, this investigation used a case-study approach and focused on a building in San Francisco after the 1989 Loma Prieta earthquake. San Francisco was chosen because it has been through several earthquakes in its history. As a result, its codes and city processes have familiarity with post-earthquake recovery processes. Also, its most recent earthquake occurred far enough in the past to enable researchers to reflect on the effects of the long-term recovery and its issues. The chosen building, the Williams Building, faced more recovery delays than similar buildings in San Francisco. It took more than eight years to attain funding, while 75 percent of publicly-owned historic buildings needed four to five years after that earthquake to get funding (Al-Nammari 2005).

Two sources of data were used: 1) documents related to the recovery of the Williams Building; and 2) interviews with ten professionals involved in the recovery of that building and other historic buildings. Each source complemented the information attained from the other and helped develop a better understanding of the case and its context. The documents were obtained from the State Historic Preservation Officer (SHPO) in California.[3] Not all of the

---

3   Also known as the Office of Historic Preservation.

documents were found, but the documents available provided an outline of what occurred until most of the funding issues were resolved. The analysis focused on correspondences and agreements, as they show the concerns of the different parties and related decisions. The data were complemented by information attained through semi-structured interviews administered on the phone with professionals who were either involved in this project or with other publicly-owned historic buildings. The objective of the interviews was to complement the information attained from the documents and to relate the recovery of that building to recovery of historic buildings in general. The questions covered the main issues that were faced during the recovery. Probes were used to identify the sources of the conflicts.

Two main kinds of matrixes were used to analyze the data. The first matrix was time ordered, and it reflected the developments taking place across time, with subheadings identifying the different variables that were grouped as the documents were studied. The interviews were analyzed using a matrix where sources of conflict were grouped based on an interpretive analysis of the answers (Miles and Huberman 1994: 127–129).

Case study: The Williams Building

Built in 1907, the Williams Building is an eight-story building with a 50,000 square-foot area, eligible for listing on the National Register of Historic Buildings. It was constructed of a steel frame with brick aggregate concrete floor slabs and masonry cladding, with distinctive brickwork on the east and south facades. The building occupies an important corner at the intersection of two streets in downtown San Francisco. The San Francisco Redevelopment Agency, a public agency, owns the building, which lies in an area that was subject to a redevelopment project.

The earthquake of 1989 created several cracks in the walls, beams, and columns, leading to a red-tag status for the building. As a public agency, the owner applied for recovery funding from the Federal Emergency Management Agency (FEMA). Since the building is historic, it was subject to a Section 106[4] review.

According to the available documents, the project started with FEMA in October 1989, and ended in April 2001. The total funding given to the build-

---

4 Section 106 is part of the National Historic Preservation Act of 1966, which requires federal agencies to consider the effects of their undertakings on historic properties. It provides the Advisory Council on Historic Preservation, an independent federal agency in collaboration with State Historic Preservation Officer (SHPO), a chance to comment on the project in an attempt to reduce negative effects on historic properties. It also requires public participation in the review.

ing was $6,876,692. Since few historic buildings took that long to attain funding from FEMA, investigating this building is useful in understanding the possible sources of complications.

This paper investigates the process of recovery as it relates to decisions about how to repair the building, but not the construction process itself. As such, the study ends by 2001, which represents the end of the legal relationship with the funding agency (FEMA) and the major decision-making phases. Construction work was still taking place on the site when it was visited in April 2005.

The Williams Building's project went through the following stages:
1. *1989-1993: Project initiation.* This stage was the most critical, as decisions had to be made on what to do with the building; these decisions led to the conflict. Once the owner applied for funding from FEMA, the Section 106 process was triggered and several issues were raised before the funding could be provided.
    - To demolish or to repair. The owner felt that demolition was the best solution. The building was red-tagged, but that does not necessarily mean that it was beyond repair. Demolition could have been funded by FEMA, had it not been a historic building. Section 106 review brought the decision-making process to the SHPO, who did not concur with the demolition. It also allowed for interested stakeholders to be involved, thus including active historic preservation groups in the decision-making process. Since the building could be repaired, demolition was not an option. This introduced several questions, as repairs depended on the building's future use, which was not clear at the time.
    - The level of strengthening needed. The owner believed that if the building was not to be demolished, then it should have an acceptable level of seismic safety for its inhabitants. The owner's consultant had a specific level of safety in mind, but the SHPO's consultant believed that the building did not need all the strengthening proposed by the owner. This divergence in the consultants' opinions took years to resolve as the strength of the structure and its historic construction were questioned. Professionals on either side had different assessments of the seismic strength of the building, creating further delays.
    This issue launched other questions. The owner and the consultant proposed that the strengthening they suggested was required by the San Francisco Code (Section 104 (f)), which was debated until it was shown not to be the case.
    - How to strengthen the building was also an issue. The owner's consultant proposed a certain scheme that used shear walls and temporary bracing. This proposal worried the SHPO, as it had an effect on the historical character of the building. The problem was that some walls

in the building were damaged and needed urgent treatment to maintain public safety. To complicate matters further, the owner was trying to find a developer for the building and did not want to subject it to any permanent repair work. They felt that the developer, the party who would be using the building, would repair the building according to its intended use. Thus the owner had to take actions to prevent immediate public hazard, and at the same time make such actions temporary.

The owner believed that demolition might be a better investment since the building was half-empty at the time of the earthquake. The desirability of the location increased the potential for such an investment.

- The high cost of the requested temporary strengthening was an issue. FEMA tried to minimize the cost as it attempted to maximize efficiency of disaster funding, so suggesting a two-million-dollar scheme for temporary bracing was problematic. FEMA proposed spending $27,000 to repair the cracks. The owner insisted that the building was not safe and that retrofit was needed.

This phase involved much deliberation among the parties that were directly involved: the owner, FEMA, and SHPO. The public was invited for input and participation, as required by Section 106. Historic preservationists were involved in the meetings and the correspondence, and they pushed for solutions that could save the building with minimal intervention into its historic fabric. Yet as preservationists were pushing for saving the building, FEMA was concerned about saving cost, and the owner wanted an easier solution.

- Maintaining the integrity of the historic fabric, in addition to the historic character, are two issues that emerged as discussions continued. Retrofit work can affect the integrity of the architectural systems of the building (cf. Look 1997), and the bracing had an impact on its historic character. Since no one knew exactly how long it would be before a developer was found, such bracing could stay longer than anticipated. Such issues were of importance for the SHPO and historic preservationists, but the owner and the consultants believed that their suggested scheme would not have any adverse effect. This was a moot point in discussions, as each side insisted on its perspective.

In 1993, four years after the earthquake, the owner received warning from the Department of Public Works pointing out that the building was hazardous to public safety in its current condition. The owner decided to demolish the building in spite of the ongoing consultation with the SHPO, leading to the withdrawal of the SHPO from Section 106 review as a reaction to this decision. Still, FEMA would not give the owner the funds needed for the demolition, as the required Section 106 review was not yet completed.

2. *1993-1996: Primary decisions.* After the SHPO withdrew from the consultations, the Advisory Council on Historic Preservation (ACHP) became involved. The involvement of the ACHP resulted in a Programmatic Agreement between them, FEMA, and the owner that required the latter not to demolish the building unless it was shown that repairing it was unfeasible. It was agreed that the owner would brace it temporarily. The estimated total cost for the bracing, the retrofit, and repairs was more than six million dollars. Two million dollars of the estimated cost were for the temporary bracing, and the rest was redirected to other projects by the owner.[5] This, however, did not provide a solution for the building, which was awaiting a developer to do the final repair work.
3. *1996-around 1998. Unresolved.* In this period, work was continued on the building to provide the temporary strengthening as planned, but the building was standing empty without use or repair. In a publication by the United States General Accounting Office (1996: 46), the building was cited as an example of buildings that should not have received earthquake funding since it was vacant.
4. *1998-2002: Final decisions.* A developer was found and the building became part of a development project for the empty lot beside it. At first the developer considered the demolition of the building, arguing that it was deteriorated. The owner stated that it preferred not to demolish it due to the agreement with the ACHP and FEMA, unless it was proven that repairs were unfeasible (Gordon 1999). It was finally decided to keep the building. In a hearing before the San Francisco Landmarks Preservation Advisory Board (San Francisco Government 1999: item 7), the owner proposed a project that included the adaptive reuse and seismic upgrade of the Williams Building next to a new tower of 430 feet in height for a mixed-use development featuring hotel rooms, a museum/cultural center, and associated parking.

With the eight-floor historic building cornered at the base, the project is controversial in terms of the appropriateness of such a solution in relation to the historic character of the building and its scale. The Williams Building was preserved as a facade while its interior was completely removed. Such a result demonstrates how cultural values are challenged after earthquakes.

---

5   It is a common strategy to use funds attained from FEMA for the repair of a damaged building for an alternate project.

Roots of the conflict

Before the conflict developed there were dormant differences between the involved parties. The values of the groups involved were different. SHPO and historic preservationists took cultural values into consideration, the owner focused on economic factors, and FEMA considered related federal laws and regulations.

The different values of the parties involved affected the goals they had:
- The owner was focused on limiting effort and maximizing return. The building was damaged and demolition could have brought development opportunities. The feasibility of repairs was important; thus, the owner wanted to leave the repair work for the future developer.
- The SHPO and historic preservationists valued saving the building, especially since many other buildings were unnecessarily lost after the earthquake. They both cared about its historic character and fabric. The SHPO also valued regulations and was interested, as a public agency, in fulfilling the laws related to the situation.
- FEMA was mainly focused on implementing related procedures and regulations, in addition to reducing the cost. The building was historic; therefore Section 106 was triggered. The correspondence documents indicate that FEMA had no specific position on the discussions between historic preservationists and the owner, and that FEMA was merely following procedure. This continued until tensions escalated in 1993; at that point FEMA adopted a proactive role and sent the owner a letter indicating other options.

Even when groups had similar goals, conflict existed due to differences of values. This was the case with SHPO and FEMA, who seemed to be working together to facilitate recovery, although they sometimes pulled in different directions. Some respondents identified that as a "hidden conflict." FEMA was pushing for a cost reduction, while the SHPO was pushing for treatments that were sensitive to the historic fabric on the one hand, but increased cost on the other. This complicated matters for the owner, who had to satisfy both sides.

The regulatory context provided an environment in which such groups should have been able to negotiate, as the Section 106 process encouraged stakeholders to communicate. Yet negotiations failed when, due to safety concerns, the owner decided to demolish regardless of the other groups involved. While Section 106 allowed for an alternative when such negotiations fail by involving the ACHP, this does indicate that such negotiations could be managed differently to prevent similar conflicts. What seems to be missing from the process is the conflict management approach, which could have helped during the early years before the negotiations stopped. Having an outside party play the role of mediator could help in identifying common ground.

For preservationists, the building was another cultural property that they were about to lose. Some respondents pointed out that saving the building gained heightened importance as a reaction to the many demolitions that took place in a short time, leaving the historic preservation community with feelings of loss. Thus, many arguments were presented on the significance of the building, the importance of keeping it, and the possibility of reusing it. This also led to historic preservationists pulling together to provide alternatives for the use of the building, and working with other culture-related groups toward that end. This provides an example of how different groups cooperate in a post-earthquake situation for a specific goal.

The value differences explain the initial stance each group had, but the conflict escalated, leading to failure of the consultation. The respondents identified the roots of such a negative development in three main categories:

1. The building itself: the previous neglect and archaic construction materials led the owner to feel that repairs would not be feasible, and the reusability of the building was in question.
2. The people involved: the owner, professionals, preservationists, and representatives of government bodies had different roles to play in the recovery. The most prominent issues were as follows:
    - Lack of sufficient knowledge about historic preservation and related laws. Literature has pointed this out, focusing on the importance of education (Eichenfield 1996: 12–28).
    - Lack of knowledge about disaster recovery and FEMA process. This was cited by literature as well as a cause of complications. Many people are unaware that FEMA has a specific process for obtaining funding, which leads to incorrect assumptions (Eichenfield 1996: 29–30; Mader 1994: 222, 229).
    - The institutional culture of the owner, a public body, was identified by some respondents as a major cause for the conflict. The management approach was cited as the reason for the neglect of the building before the earthquake, and was also a reason why an agreement on how to repair the building was not achieved with the SHPO.
    - The perception of the other groups is important in terms of trust. The consultation is undermined when any side believes that the other side has hidden intentions or is not trying to find a solution.
    - Attitude of the individuals involved.

3. The context: This point includes all aspects that create the environment in which the recovery was taking place. The points below do not cover all the categories that usually play a role, but they reflect the points that the respondents identified as important in this case.
   - Regulatory context. Laws and regulations create a context defined by their objectives and processes. There were federal, state, and local regulatory contexts within which different groups had to function. In this case three points were made:
     – Clarity of related laws and codes: for example, the question of whether the San Francisco Section 104 (f) code was triggered. The issue of the codes was also raised in literature in relation to acceptable risk levels, functionality, codes, and ordinances (cf. Fratessa 1994).
     – Clarity of the meaning of the red tag: The owner and the general public assumed that it meant that the building should be demolished. This is cited as a source of conflict for many buildings after earthquakes (Nelson 1991: 47–49; Spangle Associates 1999: 18).
     – The process in the local government was separated from the state and federal government, which complicated getting approvals and permits, as each side had its own requirements.
   - The technological context: This reflected the knowledge available to professionals on archaic construction materials, their strength, and ways of retrofit.
   - The political context: The relationship between the public agencies involved and their responsibilities creates questions about why the same project that was initially rejected was eventually approved. The fact that the building was still standing damaged four years after the earthquake might have created pressures on the parties involved, leading to compromises. The politics of how government agencies relate to each other on different levels (local, state, and federal) and with different roles (redevelopment, historic preservation, disaster recovery) is worth further investigation.
   - The economic context: The feasibility of the repair was in doubt many times during the many years of negotiations. Literature has pointed out that more demolitions happen in historic downtown areas that suffer economic depressions than in areas with good economic status, as the community assumes that demolitions would bring new development (Eichenfield 1996:11).
   - The social context: Respondents identified the strong preservation culture in the local community and the existence of preservation activists as important for post-earthquake recovery of such buildings.

This primary categorization, however, is of the perceptions of the interviewees. It is of interest because it shows how professionals in the field perceive the issue. It is clear that their experience indicated that the building itself was of limited effect in comparison to the people and the context, both of which had more input in creating the conflict. Both these categories, the people and the context, can be improved through education and recovery planning. This indicates the importance of preparedness for future earthquakes.

Conclusion

As literature has pointed out, historic buildings face challenges after earthquakes. The interviews indicate that the context and the people involved have greater importance as conflict generators than the building itself. Understanding the recovery process is important, as it helps in saving effort, time, and cost. Longer time in recovery leads to higher cost (Al-Nammari 2005).

This study indicates that conflict develops in post-earthquake recovery in stages. Immediately after an earthquake, individuals involved are interested in repair and recovery, yet an initial tension exists between stakeholders due to their different goals and values. Such tension can develop into conflict in later phases if it is not managed through consultation and arbitration. Such management should take place early in the recovery period, before conflict escalates. Most of the conflict takes place in relation to funding and financial aid, which corresponds with Geipel's findings about conflict during recovery (Geipel 1982: 171).

As a social process, this study shows how historic buildings can be a contested space in post-earthquake situations. As different groups pull in different directions for the management of available resources, historic properties acquire different values for different groups.

The objective of this pilot study was to investigate how such conflicts occur in relation to publicly-owned historic buildings. Further inquiry is needed to understand the dynamics of conflicts for private buildings. Such investigations would inform future recovery planning and preparedness, thus reducing future complications and providing a better understanding of the process and its players. Also, more research is needed on the value of historic resources in post-disaster situations, and whether their significance is affected by the damage.

I would like to thank David Look, FAIA, the National Park Service, Oakland, California for his unlimited advice, guidance, and support. I extend my thanks to Steade Craigo, FAIA, the State Office of Historic Preservation, Sacramento, California and David Gardner, the Department of Homeland Security's Federal Emergency Management Agency, Oakland, California for help in attaining the necessary documents and files and answering my many questions. I am also grateful to all the individuals who helped either by being interviewed or by providing guidance and information.

References

Al-Nammari, Fatima M. (2005) *Sustainable Disaster Recovery of Historic Buildings: Learning from San Francisco after the Loma Prieta Earthquake.* Lecture at the American Institute of Architects, San Francisco Chapter, 22 February, co-sponsored by Western Chapter of the Association for Preservation Technology, Earthquake Engineering Research Institute Northern California Chapter Historic Building Committee, and National Park Service Pacific West Region.

Anstey, Mark (1999) *Managing Change, Negotiating Conflict*, Cape Town: Juta & Co.

Australian International Council on Monuments and Sites (1999) *"The Burra Charter: The Australia ICOMOS Charter for the Conservation of Places of Cultural Significance"*. http://www.nsw.nationaltrust.org.au/burracharter.html [July 30, 2005].

Berke, Philip R./Beatley, Timothy (1997) *After the Hurricane: Linking Recovery to Sustainable Development in the Caribbean*, Baltimore: John Hopkins University Press.

Bolin, Robert/ Stanford, Lois (1990) "Shelter and Housing Issues in Santa Cruz County". In Robert Bolin (ed.) *The Loma Prieta Earthquake: Studies of Short-Term Impacts*, Program for Environment and Behavior Monograph#50, Colorado: University of Colorado, pp. 99–108.

Craigo, Steade (1998) "A Helping Hand". In Dirk Spennemann/David Look (eds.) *Disaster Management Programs for Historic Sites*, San Francisco: U.S.A National Park Service, pp. 17–24.

Comerio, Mary (1997) *Housing Repair and Reconstruction after Loma Prieta.* National Information Service for Earthquake Engineering, University of California Berkeley, http://nisee.berkeley.edu/loma_prieta/comerio.html [August 24, 2005].

Eadie, Charles (1991) *Phases of Earthquake Response and Recovery Planning*, Santa Cruz, California: Santa Cruz Redevelopment Agency.

Eichenfield, Jeffrey (1996) *26 Tools That Protect Historic Resources after an Earthquake: Lessons learned from the Northridge Earthquake*, Oakland: California Preservation Foundation.

Feilden, Bernard (1987) *Between Two Earthquakes, Cultural property is Seismic Zones*, Rome: International Centre for the Study of the Preservation and Restoration of Cultural Property (ICCROM).

Fratessa, Paul F. (1994) "Buildings". In National Research Council *Practical Lessons from the Loma Prieta Earthquake*. Report from a Symposium Sponsored by the Geotechnical Board and the Board on Natural Disasters of the National Research Council. National Academy Press. http://www.nap.edu/openbook/0309050308/html/ [April 12, 2004].

Geipel, Robert (1991) *Long-term Consequences of Disasters: The Reconstruction of Friuli, Italy, in its International Context, 1976–1988*, New York: Springer-Verlag.

Geipel, Robert (1982) *Disaster and Reconstruction: the Friuli, Italy, Earthquakes of 1976*, Translated from German by Philip Wagner and George Allen, London.

Geva, Anat/Al-Nammari, Fatima M. (2002) "Nature or Terror Disaster? Church or City Hall? The Interactive Effect of Building Type and Disaster Agent on the Public Approach to Preserving their Historic Buildings". The Association for Preservation Technology *International Annual Conference: Extreme Impacts: Measured Response*, (September) Toronto, Canada.

Gordon, Rachel. "Historic Building May End Up Demolished". *The Examiner*, April 5 1999, via San Francisco Gate http://www.sfgate.com/cgi-bin/article.cgi?file=/examiner/archive/1999/04/05/NEWS10685.dtl [August 30, 2005].

Haas, J. Eugene et al. (1977) *Reconstruction Following Disaster*. Cambridge: The MIT Press.

International Council on Monuments and Sites (ICOMOS) (1987) *Charter for the Conservation of Historic Towns and Urban Areas (Washington Charter)*, [updated 05/06/2003] http://www.international.icomos.org/charters/towns_e.htm [Sept 5, 2005]

International Council on Monuments and Sites (ICOMOS) (1982) "Declaration of Tlaxcala". In *The Third Inter-American Symposium on the Conservation of the Building Heritage: The Revitalization of Small Settlements*, Trinidad, Tlaxcala, 25-28 October. [Revised 15 April 1996] http://www.icomos.org/docs/tlaxcala.html [4/14/2002].

International Council on Monuments and Sites (ICOMOS) (1999) *The ICOMOS International Cultural Tourism Charter*, http://www.icomos.org/tourism/ charter.html [4/14/2002].

Jones, Barclay G. (ed.) (1986) *Protecting Historic Architecture and Museum Collections from Natural Disasters*, Boston: Butterworths.

Kariotis, John (1998) "The Tendency to Demolish Repairable Structures in the Name of 'Life Safety'". In Dirk Spennemann/David Look (eds.) *Disaster Management Programs for Historic Sites*, San Francisco: U.S National Park Service, pp. 55–60.

Lindell, Michael /Prater, Carla (2003) "Assessing Community Impacts of Natural Disasters". In *Natural Hazards Review* (4): 176–185.

Look, David et al. (1997) "The Seismic Retrofit of Historic Buildings: Keeping preservation in the Forefront". *Preservation Briefs* 41, The National Park Service, Washington D.C.

Look, David/Spennemann, Dirk (eds.) (2000) *Disaster Management*, CRM 23/06.

Look, David/Spennemann, Dirk (eds.) (2001) *Cultural Resources Protection and Emergency Preparedness*, CRM 24/08.

Mader, G. (1994) "Recovery, Mitigation, and Planning." In National Research Council *Practical Lessons from the Loma Prieta Earthquake*. Report from a Symposium Sponsored by the Geotechnical Board and the Board on Natural Disasters of the National Research Council. National Academy Press. http://www.nap.edu/openbook/0309050308/html/ [April 12, 2004].

Miles, Mattew B./Huberman A. Michael (1994) *Qualitative Data Analysis: An expanded Sourcebook*, Thousand Oaks: Sage Publications.

Merritt, John (1990) *History At Risk, Loma Prieta: Seismic Safety and Historic Buildings,* Oakland: California Preservation Foundation.

Nelson, Carl (1991) *Protecting the Past from Natural Disasters,* Washington D.C: The National Trust for Historic Preservation.

Phillips, Brenda/Ephraim, Mindy (1992) *Living in the Aftermath: Blaming Processes in the Loma Prieta Earthquake*. Working Paper #80, National Hazards Research and Applications Information Center, Colorado: University of Colorado.

San Francisco Government (1999) *Landmarks Preservation Advisory Board (LPAB) Minutes,* May 1999. http://sfgov.org/site/uploadedfiles/planning/1pmn0599.htm [May 2005].

Schwab, Jim et al. (1998) *Planning for Post-Disaster Recovery and Reconstruction*. Chicago: American Planning Association.

Spennemann, Dirk/Look, David (1998) "Managing Disasters and Managing Disaster Responses: an introduction". In: Spennemann Dirk/Look David (eds.) *Disaster Management Programs for Historic Sites*. San Francisco: U.S National Park Service, pp. 1–6.

Spangle Associates (1999) *Decision to Demolish, Case Studies of the Fate of Earthquake-Damaged Buildings*, Portola Valley, California: Spangle Associates.

The United States General Accounting Office (1996) *Disaster Assistance: Improvements Needed in Determining Eligibility for Public Assistance*. Reports and Testimony: April 1996. Report to the Chairman, Subcommittee on VA, HUD and Independent Agencies, Committee on Appropriations, U.S. Senate. *May 1996.* http://www.gao.gov/archive/1996/rc96113.pdf [July 2003].

Warner, Michael (2001) *Complex Problems, Negotiated Solutions. Tools to Reduce Conflict in Community Development.* London: ITDG Publishing.

Wu, J. W./Lindell, Michael (2004) "Housing Reconstruction after Two Major Earthquakes: The 1994 Northridge Earthquake in the United States and the 1999 Chi-Chi Earthquake in Taiwan". *Disasters* 28/1, pp. 63–82.

IV. Exclusion, Security and Surveillance

The Phenomenon of Exclusion

HEINZ BUDE

This article aims to elucidate the concept of social exclusion from a phenomenological approach. Exclusion is distinguished from the mere problem of poverty, based on the three dichotomies: agony and agency, disparity and cohesion, and the self and the other. Moreover, exclusion denotes a shift in social responsibility. In analyzing social exclusion as a process of individual drift, four structural elements are significant—work, family, institutions, and the human body.

It was the discourse on the new urban underclass that emphatically showed that social inequality is not only a question of ups and downs but also, and with more existential relevance, a question of being-in or moving-out. Before outlining the elements and the dynamics of the vicious circle that takes one out of society and into a kind of social no-man's land, some conceptual questions must be considered. What does the concept of social exclusion mean and what is meant by a phenomenological approach to it?

In much of Europe in recent years, the discourse on poverty within the analysis of social problems has been replaced by attention to the broader, obviously more diffuse problem of social exclusion.[1] The socially excluded, according to this notion, are usually poor, but they suffer from more than just a shortage of money or material transfer pay; they endure other kinds of deprivation and deficits, the cumulative impact of which leaves them detached

---

1 An International Labour Organisation Report suggests that the concept of social exclusion can be seen as a replacement for poverty, which provides a multidimensional view of the processes of impoverishment (International Institute for Labour Studies 1996).

from the mainstream of our society. Some scholars see the problem as implying exclusion from the labor market, from education, from security, from health, or at least from human rights (cf. Badelt 1999). Other aspects of social exclusion involve a lack of participation in community life and insufficient access to social benefits (cf. Atkinson/Hills 1998). So, this is the conclusion, social exclusion is a problem that requires more than a public transfer to those in need (cf. Hills/Le Grand/Piachaud 2002).

We seem to know what poverty is about. Poverty is a question of shortage, lack, and deficiencies in relation to what the majority has, earns, and requires. It is something relative and nothing absolute (cf. Hauser 1997). But, nevertheless, there are a lot of findings that absolutely prove that poor people lead less healthy lives, experience more stress, and die earlier. So one could conclude that all it takes is to provide them with financial aid in order to change the relationship of those who have and those who have not. But what is exclusion about? And what does it mean to regard social exclusion as a phenomenon? There are three aspects that constitute a social fact as a social phenomenon (Herzog/Graumann 1991).

The first aspect means that we are "addressed" by a phenomenon. We are captured by experiences that create a rupture in our normal construction of the world. Let us take the situation at a party where you meet an old friend who appears set apart from all the others' way of living. He or she drinks too much and complains too much. Instinctively, you distance yourself from him or her because you do not want to be affected by those bad vibrations. In phenomenological philosophy, there is the term "fatality," which is assigned to this experience of being addressed or struck by a phenomenon.

The second aspect is that we see a phenomenon as a totality in itself. A phenomenon cannot be reduced to a certain element without destroying its whole structure. In this sense social exclusion has an effect on all of the dimensions of the personal life of an individual: not only on how you consume or on how you work, but also on how you love and on how you trust. That is the "totality" of a phenomenon.

Thirdly, a phenomenon implies a certain reflexive effect. The moment we are captured by it and see it as a whole, we are confronted with ourselves. We aim to distance ourselves from that friend at the party because there is the possibility that we could be in his or her place. He or she shows us the threshold of shame that rules out the possibility of being integrated into the community of belonging. In the vocabulary of phenomenological philosophy, this is the idea of "fundamentality." Faced with someone who is excluded, we are confronted with the question of what counts as a livable life and as a grievous death. Obviously, there is a shift in attitude when one replaces the concept of poverty with that of social exclusion. Through this phenomenological approach, the following three implications of the concept of exclusion become evident:

The first implication involves the difference between agony and agency. The excluded suffer, as the classical investigation on *The Unemployed of Marienthal* shows (Jahoda/Lazarsfeld/Zeisel 1975): they are in some kind of agony. They have lost or they are losing their focus, their control over the world. They no longer stand on their own feet. Inclusion therefore, means to reconstruct agency. The rhetoric of empowerment, activation, and responsibility are concentrated in the idea of agency; this concept changed social welfare politics from the principle of income maintenance to that of preventing social exclusion. This marked a shift from passive to active policies, from an emphasis on responsibilities to rights, a shift from protection to inclusion. In order to reconstruct agency, the enabling state that follows the welfare state aims no longer to protect labor, but to promote work (cf. Gilbert 2004).

The second difference involved in the concept of exclusion is that of disparity and cohesion. Especially in France, responses to the problem of social exclusion are embedded in the discussion about the republican nation. Those who are socially excluded are the pariah of the nation and thus mark a limit for liberal society. The community of the republican nation cannot bear the fact that significant parts of the population are on the outside. In this case, exclusion is connected with the notion of a division between the included and the excluded (cf. Nasse 1992).[2]

The third difference implied in the concept of exclusion is that of the self and the other. In the face of an excluded other, we are confronted with the question: Who cares (cf. Göttle 2000)? Who cares for those who are losing control and are being thrown into a state of distrust and hopelessness? It is obviously inadequate if the state alone, which functions according to the requirements of formal rights and standardized measures, takes on this task. The concept of social exclusion appeals to a "we" that cannot delegate its responsibility for the other to someone else. Who or what this "we" is, however, is highly disputed. Is it the nation, the neighborhood, civil society (cf. Walzer 1983), or is it, as Judith Butler would say in the words of Levinas, each of us as a human being (Butler 2003)?

At this point it becomes apparent how the concept of social exclusion leads to a shift in the grounds for social responsibility away from the state towards something else. In sociological terms, this is a shift from Marshallian citizenship to Durkheimian membership.[3]

---

2 For a general discussion, cf. Silver 1994.
3 As a widely discussed position inbetween, cf. Margalit 1997.

What can we do, how can we deal with this concept of social exclusion, that is, on the one hand, normalized and, on the other hand, dramatized? Is it more than an intuitive shortcut elaborated in philosophical dimensions?

There are different frames of reference from which studies about social exclusion typically operate: that of individual drift and that of chronic social contexts (cf. Mingione 1996). Studies of the second type look at mechanisms of institutional discrimination and territorial signation. They examine urban poverty, racial division, and gender relations. What I would like to present in the following are some results from our analysis of processes of individual drift. Normally, four structural elements play a role in the processes of social exclusion: work, family, institution, and the human body (cf. Bude 1998).

To begin with the end: It is the body that the everyday struggle for recognition seems to be focused on. We have this debate about "white trash" on the one hand, and the emerging beauty culture on the other: mere bodily appearance as a sign of an individual's lack of responsibility, flexibility, mobility. You see, smell, and feel someone moving from the zone of precariousness to that of exclusion. Robert Castel (2000) has promoted the model of social zooming in order to understand the micro-processes of social inclusion and exclusion. His main idea is that social exclusion is becoming a possibility that bridges the center and the edges of society. It could happen to everybody because of the change not only in the regimes of labor and employment, but also in the regimes of the family, the state, and the self. Things are getting more heterogeneous and precarious in all respects. You cannot project the excluded into a certain social place; they are among us and affect us. For this reason, the body is of social importance for the determination of one's position in the social world.

Of course, a certain kind of job experience is normally the starting point for a disastrous career. What is less important is the loss of the job itself; what counts more is experiencing a long period of failure in trying to get back into employment, which tends to condition people to continue to fail. There is a type of person, who could be called the "active loser," who is characterized by doing everything right at the wrong moment. He or she invests too much into a certain situation and therefore cuts off all paths of return.

A different type of person shows an inability to adapt to an "alternative role" that is supposed to secure a socially acceptable way of leaving gainful employment. A traditional example could be the change of status for a person who takes on the role of a housewife. Recently, extra "communitarian" bonuses have been awarded for "third sector" activities. But if people are not successful at regarding loss as a sacrifice, or feel exposed when the neighbors look at them rather contemptuously, they start to have doubts about the justification for their own existence.

A third negative experience regarding work would be a person dropping out of contingent work as a result of an "unusual life-event." Sudden illness or an unfortunate accident can pull the rug out from under an attempt to juggle with different sources of income. The whole economy of a household then breaks down.

The crisis in the family represents a second decisive factor. In principle, the crisis engendered by unemployment can lead to the re-establishment of family solidarity. On the one hand, the "extended family" often proves to be a secure environment, offering the final point of stability. But this, on the other hand, increases the vulnerability of people sticking together. Men in particular suffer from the fear of losing their "normative competence" because of their employment problems, and this can plunge the whole family system into a state of vague unrest, which causes everything to become a problem. If the family support system finally cracks under the strain, the individual who is left alone has taken a further step down the road towards believing he or she is superfluous.

Coupled with problems associated with work and family, a third factor of social exclusion must be considered. The social welfare institutions react decisively when confronted with obvious symptoms of social malaise. Personnel dealing with unemployment and poverty have their own ideas and theories on how to treat these people, and such opinions often play a most significant role. People who appear to be socially unstable will quickly lose their rights to full benefits in the eyes of officials. This battle for recognition between those seeking benefits and those awarding them is played out in the micro-situation of contact within the institution. There has been little research on how claim limits are defined in everyday situations like these. Whatever the situation, dependent people experience institutional classification and administrative assignments as degrading procedures that mark them as dependent beggars. In extreme cases, they can lose their ability to conform to the institution's expectations because they end up playing the role the institution expects of them, and this can lead to ongoing "institutional isolation" (Gans 1995).

The final and most important indication seen in processes of social exclusion is, as mentioned above, the human body. The road to superfluity, the road out of society is often marked by one type of addiction taken from the entire available spectrum. Physical dependence can be seen as the final closure mechanism initiated by a person to seal the break with the legitimate social link, with work, the family, and institutions.

What we have in the end is the logic of failure in terms of work, the logic of break-up in terms of the family, the logic of registration in terms of the institution, and the logic of stigma in terms of the human body. When these four components act together, a pattern of feeling superfluous can cumulatively build up and finally close people to all outside influence. Analysis of these processes shows an irreversible pattern of exclusion based on a loss of resources, bewilderment in the face of imposed sanctions, and the anticipation of being stigmatized.

If we pursue this analysis, we can distinguish at least three groups: the unemployed, the poor, and the excluded. There are links between all three, but no exact congruence. Normally, unemployment is a pre-condition for exclusion, but it is not the only factor. You can be included while being unemployed. Poverty usually is an additional factor, but to be marginalized does not mean to be excluded. It is possible for a person to come to the end of the social road despite a personal history that offered adequate provision for material needs.

One can see whether a person is excluded. One can see his or her weariness, indifference, or apathy. One is addressed by the other, imagines the totality of his or her life, and feels the urge to ask oneself: Who cares?

References

Atkinson, Anthony/Hills, John (eds., 1998) *Exclusion, Employment and Opportunity*, London: Centre for Analysis of Social Exclusion, London School of Economics.

Badelt, Christoph (1999) *The Role of NPOs in Policies to Combat Social Exclusion*; Social Protection Discussion Paper 9912, Washington, D.C.: World Bank.

Bude, Heinz (1998) "Die Überflüssigen als transversale Kategorie". In: Peter A. Berger/Michael Vester (eds.) *Alte Ungleichheiten – Neue Spaltungen*, Opladen: Leske + Budrich, pp. 363–382.

Butler, Judith (2003) *Kritik der ethischen Gewalt*, Frankfurt am Main: Suhrkamp.

Castel, Robert (2000) *Die Metamorphosen der sozialen Frage*, Konstanz: UVK.

Gans, Herbert J. (1995) *The War Against the Poor. The Underclass and Antipoverty Policy*. New York: Basic Books.

Gilbert, Neil (2004) *Transformation of the Welfare State. The Silent Surrender of Public Responsibility*, Oxford: Oxford University Press.

Göttle, Gabriele (2000) *Die Ärmsten! Wahre Geschichten aus dem arbeitslosen Leben*, Frankfurt am Main: Eichborn.

Hauser, Richard (1997) *Armut, Armutsgefährdung und Armutsbekämpfung in der Bundesrepublik Deutschland*. Jahrbücher für Nationalökonomie und Statistik 216, Stuttgart: Lucius & Lucius, pp. 524–548.

Herzog, Max/Graumann, Carl F. (1991, eds.) *Sinn und Erfahrung. Phänomenologische Methoden in den Humanwissenschaften*, Heidelberg: Asanger 1991.

Hills, John/Le Grand, Julian/Piachaud, David (eds., 2002) *Understanding Social Exclusion*, Oxford: Oxford University Press.

International Institute for Labour Studies (ed., 1996) *Social Exclusion and Anti-Poverty Strategies*, Geneva: International Labour Organisation.

Jahoda, Marie/Lazarsfeld, Paul/Zeisel, Hans (1975/1933) *Die Arbeitslosen von Marienthal. Ein soziographischer Versuch über die Wirkungen langandauernder Arbeitslosigkeit.* Frankfurt am Main: Suhrkamp.

Margalit, Avishai (1997) *Politik der Würde. Über Achtung und Verachtung*, Berlin: Fest.

Mingione, Enzo (1996) "Preface". In Enzo Migione (ed.) *Urban Poverty and The Underclass*, Cambridge, Mass.: Blackwell, pp. XII–XIX.

Nasse, Philippe (1992) *Exclus et exclusion: Connaitre les Populations, Comprendre les Processus,* Paris: Commissariat Général du Plan.

Silver, Hilary (1994) "National Conceptions of the New Urban Poverty: Structural Change in Britain, France and the United States". International Journal of Urban and Regional Research 17, pp. 336–354.

Walzer, Michael (1983) *Spheres of Justice: A Defense of Pluralism and Equality*, New York: Basis Books.

Orbit Palace.
Locations and Cultures of Redundant Time

SILKE STEETS

In eastern Germany, we currently observe how traditional forms of European urbanity degenerate through dramatic shrinkage. My contribution starts from empirical observations collected within an art project, "Orbit Palace," which deals with the complex structures of space against the background of redundant time in shrinking cities. On the basis of three heterogeneous case studies, I will analyze the underlying spatial micro politics and conclude with possibilities of urbanity today.

Having time, the journalist Verena Mayer argued in July 2003, no longer determines whether we do something or not (Mayer 2003: 17). The polite phrase "I don't have time!" has lost some of its argumentative power, because in our society people tend to have too much time. For German standards, the unemployment rate has been consistently high for years, and Mayer claims that this fact, as well as the fear of those who (still) earn an income, but are afraid of losing their job, are the reasons for this development. She concludes that having "spare time has been stigmatized" (ibid). In contrast to the 1980s, when the reduction of working hours and the observance of Sunday as a day of rest were eagerly contested issues, the worth of disposable free time seems to be diminishing, and the value of work is increasing progressively. The distribution of labor and spare time has once again become an indicator of class difference. But today the signs are reversed: jobs are scarce and greatly desired, and time is something for those without a job.

The following thoughts deal with the unequal distribution of time and labor in the context of Germany's shrinking cities, as well as with strategies that individuals have developed to cope with little work, little money, and much time. The process of urban shrinking creates not only space but also time. In part the result of radical deindustrialization, space and spare time are widely available in these shrinking cities, but labor is not. In order to explore this issue, I will turn to Leipzig, a city whose population decreased by 63,000, or 11.2 percent, between 1990 and 2003 (Statistisches Landesamt des Freistaates Sachsen 2005). Currently about 20 percent of the city's working population is unemployed (Stadt Leipzig-Amt für Statistik und Wahlen 2005). In reference to the postcolonial perspective, which confronts the normative model of the European City with the urban reality of the rapidly growing mega-cities of the south, I will investigate the opposite of growth: shrinkage. I will assume that the rapid shrinkage of cities questions notions of European urbanity just as rapidly as growth does. The key question I will explore is: How does a city shrink? Where can we observe this process and what exactly happens at these locations? I hope to find answers to these questions by means of micro-sociological case studies. More specifically: how do people spend their time when their days are not—or rather, are no longer—determined by the rigid timetable of Fordist production methods and they live in regions that are characterized by deindustrialization and a lot of redundant space? And: What spaces do they create—often unintentionally—to pursue their activities, or as a result of them?

The artistic research project "Orbit Palace," which I conceived together with an architect, two artists, and a photographer in Leipzig, and which was part of the exhibition "Shrinking Cities" at KW-Institute for Contemporary Art in Berlin in 2004,[1] explores similar questions. We used the title "Orbit Palace" as a search word for those locations that have become the home for redundant time. They are spaces that are no longer, or not yet, part of economic and social memories as the result of complex transformational processes. They are locations that signify a breach with the past and whose future appears similarly vague: derelict buildings, fallow land, abandoned infrastructures, ruins, and new cityscapes. At first glance these locations give the impression of being post-urban leftovers or holes in European cities. As part of the project, we documented in great detail how seven such locations are used today and discovered that those using them employ very different practices in doing so. I will now look in greater detail at two locations featured in the "Orbit Palace" project. Subsequently, I will tie the project and related findings into the context of current research on poverty, and will conclude my article by speculating on possibilities relating to the creation of urbanity in shrinking cities.

---

1 The full title of the project, which was done by Jens Fischer, Katja Heinecke, Reinhard Krehl, Silke Steets, and Nils Emde is: "Orbit Palace. Time Pioneers in Space," Schrumpfende Städte // Shrinking Cities, KW-Institute for Contemporary Art, Berlin (Sept. 4 to Nov. 7, 2004).

The spontaneous angler

Leipzig North, triangular junction, rainwater storage facility (*Figure 1*). He can organize his day as he pleases, because the construction companies hire him according to demand. Whenever the weather is right and the construction company does not call him, he goes fishing—sometimes as long as half a day. He travels by bike. In his bag he carries some snacks and canned sweet corn, which he uses as bait. He always crosses the railroad tracks and climbs down the embankment. He always casts his line into the wind because, as he claims, "carps can smell you."

Figure 1: Spontaneous angler (Photo: © Nils Emde, 2003)

He is very alert and knows where to find a shoal of fish. He returns every single fish he catches back to the lake. He only likes salt-water fish and the only carp he ever took home he brought back to the lake the following day.

He calls this place "paradise." It is peaceful at the lake, and once he has turned off his cell phone he is all by himself. He hates having to stand in line and wait. While fishing he only waits for himself. He needs nobody's assistance to do so. He refuses to have anything to do with fishing clubs and he has no fishing permit. He does not need one anyhow because the lake is outside anyone's jurisdiction. It is the product of a coincidence that was created in the course of the great modifications that were applied to the infrastructure of Leipzig North. A rainwater storage pond located in the midst of a triangular junction—found between the exhibition center, the highway, and the new manufacturing plants of Porsche and BMW. As a result of the development of certain parts of Leipzig, a new landscape is emerging.

Fernando S. is forty-two years old, divorced, and lives together with his girlfriend. He came to the GDR from Cuba at the age of twenty-two. Upon his arrival he trained as a railroad builder. Later on he was an engine driver at an opencast mine—always in the better-paid three-shift system. He has been unemployed since 1992. Today he gets by with the help of welfare and the occasional small construction job. He claims he is a good handyman. He has renovated and modernized several apartments already. Fernando says he did such a good job renovating one apartment that even the West German landlord was impressed with it. The neighbors in the allotment colony were equally impressed. Initially they were skeptical when a foreigner moved into the summerhouse next to theirs. After he renovated it for a whole summer he invited everyone over, and from that moment on his neighbors accepted him. He likes it in Germany. But if it should get too cold one day, he will return to Cuba. In terms of his private life this would not be a problem. His girlfriend speaks perfect Spanish.

The in-between trader

Leipzig West, a residential area built during the late nineteenth century, empty buildings. The lobby (*Figure 2*). The sweatshirts, which advertise the wastepaper collection facility, read, "Money is lying in the streets." He and his wife appreciate the value of trash and they are still familiar with the GDR's SERO system, the secondary raw material recycling system. Today's massive recycling industry inspired their business idea, which will hopefully enable them to break out of the job brokerage cycle of the unemployment agency. Their clients collect wastepaper for them and deliver it to their facility, they pay them at the current rate and, after having separated paper from cardboard, they resell it. The price their buyer pays is not guaranteed. They know that "the price for a kilogram of wastepaper fluctuates like that for pork." The prices arrive via fax in their "office," which is the telephone in their apartment. The profit margin is approximately 4 cents per kilogram. They have monthly expenses—including accounting, rent, public liability insurance, and the transportation of the paper—a minimum of 120 euros. This means: They make a profit if they sell more than 3 tons of wastepaper a month. Most of their clients live in the immediate vicinity of the collection facility. Many of them are superintendents, who collect the wastepaper in the lobbies of the buildings they work in and then drop it off.

Figure 2: In-between trader (Photo: © Nils Emde, 2003)

But private individuals, neighbors, and friends are also among their clients, even many children, who seem to enjoy collecting wastepaper. Their opening hours depend on two factors: the season and the job center. Their business is located in a house that awaits demolition. Their landlord has given them permission to use the building's lobby as a shop until the building is demolished. But there is no electricity, and therefore no electric lighting, which greatly restricts winter opening hours. The second factor that influences their business is the job center. They are only allowed to work fifteen hours a week. Anything else is illegal. But according to *him*, there is so much to do that they could work around the clock.

Günter P. is forty years old and a trained bricklayer. Due to back pain, he has been unable to work since the early 1990s. He is married to Ursula, who is thirty-seven years old and a trained nursery school teacher. She lost her job in 1992, and in the years that followed she gave birth to two sons. Since then she has been on maternity leave, received unemployment benefits, and been on welfare. During the nineties her husband held countless jobs, ranging from "maid" in a hotel to a forest ranger. In 2003 both of them had had enough. Something had to change, and one day they saw an advertisement for a wastepaper collection facility. "We can do what others can do, too!" Many visits to the social security office and the unemployment agency followed, then a useless seminar for people interested in founding a small business, until *he* finally founded a so-called *Ich-AG*, a one-man business. They will receive support from the state for a period of three years. All net profits go directly to the social security office. During the period that they receive support they must succeed in turning their company into a viable business. This is why *she* too started to work fifteen hours per week—the amount approved by the unemployment agency—for the company.

Leipzig PlusMinus

Leipzig is located on the edge of Germany's most intensively industrialized region east of the Harz Mountains, and much of the region's brown coal mining, energy-generation industries, and chemical industries have been located here since the late nineteenth century. For that reason, the number of plant closures and the massive layoffs that took place in the region after East-West reunification have been unrivaled. Between 1990 and 1993 more than eighty percent of industrial jobs were cut. In Leipzig alone this amounted to roughly 90,000 factory jobs (Rink 2004: 636). It was impossible to compensate for this loss by creating jobs in the third sector. However, the economic decline of the region is only one reason for the population decline that Leipzig subsequently suffered. A second factor is the declining birth rate, and a third factor is the West German, or rather US-style, suburbanization of living and working. Nevertheless, it should be stressed that Leipzig holds a special place in the discourse on urban shrinkage, because the city is shrinking and growing at the same time. At least that is the conclusion drawn by authors of the research project "Leipzig 2030" (Lütke Daldrup/Doehler-Behzadi 2004). This research projects the development of the city for the two decades to come, and according to the authors the product of this bipolar process is the "perforated city." Leipzig is characterized both by empty apartment houses and extensive decay as well as by selective growth and the successful renovation of the city's historic district that dates back to the late nineteenth century. This explains why, especially in northern Leipzig—the area around the highway, the airport, the exhibition center, the brand-new DHL logistics center, and the plants of the automobile manufacturers Porsche and BMW—is booming. The simultaneity of growth and shrinkage produces a spatial dynamic, and the significant structural changes make this most visible. Borders are redefined, territories are used differently—and therefore their relevance for society is changing as well—and many spaces appear barren. As a result, locations emerge that do not correspond to the traditional image of European urbanity but are nonetheless part of the everyday lives of people living in the European city of Leipzig. The two places I am talking about serve as examples to illustrate this process. The lake frequented by the spontaneous angler is located in the midst of the economic growth zone in Leipzig North and it is a by-product of infrastructural construction measures. The late nineteenth-century building awaiting demolition used by the in-between trader is located in Leipzig West, a borough that is affected by decay and urban shrinkage. Yet, contrary to what one might be inclined to assume neither transitory location is fallow. The activities that take place in these locations might just as well symbolize that urban space is used in new and different ways. But how can we comment on spending time in these places?

Autonomists, entrepreneurs, and creative people

In case he does not receive a call from the construction company, the spontaneous angler spends his day as he pleases. He considers spare time to be a gain in personal freedom. No clock determines his day. For him, fishing is a contemplative activity, something like meditation. While at the lake, he disconnects his personal time from society's macro-time—for as long as he wants. Yet despite his spontaneity, his life does not lack temporal structures. He very clearly differentiates between, for example, those workdays during which he goes fishing and the weekend, which he prefers to spend with his girlfriend. The in-between trader organizes his time much more around external influences. The wastepaper collection facility determines the rhythm of his day and its opening hours depend on factors over which he has no control: the season and the stipulations of the unemployment agency. Yet there is also plenty to do after the store has closed. He must collect, sort, and separate paper and cardboard. He never has much time and this requires him to be very organized. He has no time for hobbies such as tending a garden plot or going on excursions with his children, not even on the weekend. These two examples illustrate how different people, for whom the early 1990s marked a decisive point in their biographies because they lost their jobs, experience and design time. The spontaneous angler uses the surplus of spare time, the result of his unemployment, to his advantage and thinks of the benefits caused by a slow-paced life and greater freedom. By founding an *Ich-AG* that deals with waste paper, the in-between trader created a new job for himself and he feels —also in terms of time—the economic pressure that comes with being self-employed.

Four Dutch researchers had already established a similar spectrum of micro-social time cultures among long-term unemployed and illegal migrants (Engbersen/Schuyt et al. 1993). It should be emphasized that their study concludes that people without work experience and spend time very differently, because this result stands in stark contrast to the findings published during the 1930s in the so-called Marienthal Study (Jahoda/Lazarsfeld et al. 1975). The Marienthal Study called attention to the different attitudes towards unemployment, but—with regards to how these people spend their time—it paints a very homogenous picture. The Dutch study "Cultures of Unemployment," which uses the concept "culture" in an anthropological way, differs: "Culture pertains to the social environment in which people function, but [it] also pertains to the symbols, ideas and convictions that regulate and justify their actions and serve as a basis and justification for their social relations" (Engbersen/Schuyt et al. 1993: 158). Mental representations, as well as individually created structures of time, may thus be seen as a part of culture. And where the Marienthal Study only determined four types of long-term unemployed people, the Dutch study identifies six different ones: the conformists (36 %), the ritualists (9 %), the retreatists (25 %), the enterprising types (10 %), the calculating types (9 %), and the autonomists (10 %) (Engbersen 1993: 157).

Significantly, the characterization of the autonomists resembles what we have already heard about the spontaneous angler. According to the study, the so-called autonomists

> have neither a problem with spending nor structuring their time. Being able to determine how they spend their time is the most precious good for autonomists. While retreatists, conformists and ritualists often capitulate in the face of a surplus of time and the enterprising ones as well as calculating types complain about the lack of time, the autonomists assume a totally different position: they shape time according to their will and they do not experience it as a threat or obstacle to their social life. The autonomists claim that they are hardly ever bored. Instead they greatly value their freedom and spare time, which come along with unemployment. The autonomists spend their time according to their ideas, and they use it to grow in character independently. They ignore social pressure exerted on them by other people, groups and institutions (Engbersen 2004: 110f.).

In contrast, the in-between trader is perhaps best described as an enterprising type, who tries to augment his welfare benefits by taking on formal and informal jobs. Enterprising types often (65 percent) keep a calendar, which suggests that they try to structure their time effectively. They cannot complain about a lack of meaningful activities in their lives, and, as a result, they are integrated into a network of intense social contacts—clientele in the case of the in-between trader.

Describing further protagonists of "Orbit Palace" could expand the spectrum of micro-social *Zeitkulturen*, or, time cultures. In addition to the figures described above, it includes the figures of the club maker, the free riders, the cat's mummy, the snack bar family, and the football partisans. At this point I would like to cite one more brief example. The location I am going to talk about is a former stove-fitter's shop, located near unhitched railroad tracks.

Figure 3: Club maker (Photo: © Nils Emde, 2003)

During my interview with the main activist at this site, I showed him a photo of the site (*Figure 3*) and asked him to tell me what he saw. Simon P. replied:

(Laughing) it's an interesting photo, for sure. Because at first glance you don't suspect anything. You only see this sign, which is broken anyhow. We're going to get a new sign, too. So, you just don't expect anything further. Behind the door. You're thinking, dunno, basically nothing. Because if you want your gig to be a commercial success you normally would have to advertise it properly. Somethin' like that (laughing) (Interview Distillery, Fall 2003).

The photo showed the entrance to a quite well-known techno club in Leipzig. Between 1992 and 1994, ten students ran the place without a permit, but now the club has a lease and a liquor license. Legality brought a number of administrative obligations, but also the ability to plan ahead when, for example,

243

making a deal with a brewery or booking artists. Today the club is no longer run by the ten students, and the person whose name is on the trading license is chiefly responsible. This man spends ten to fourteen hours every day booking artists, creating the program, accounting, paying bills, organizing volunteers to help with the renovation of the club, taking care of press relations, ordering beverages, maintaining the club's website, and organizing the graphic design for the flyers, the visuals, and, not least, the music. The club is open for business Friday through Sunday from 10pm until 6am. As a former member of Leipzig's subculture, the club owner has learned that you cannot separate work and leisure. He is one of the protagonists of the local culture industry, people who were once "flexible rebels and girlies" (Holert/Terkessidis 1996: 9). Today many of them are flexible entrepreneurs who work in fields that promise a high degree of identification, but also bring great economic insecurity with them. Angela McRobbie explored the fashion and club scene in London and discovered that the commodification of cultural activities gave rise to an exciting mixture of self-realization and coolness on the one hand, and consistent poverty on the other (McRobbie 1999).

Conclusion: In-between spaces

The idea of the European city has long been considered a guiding model for worldwide urbanization. Urbanists only spoke of cities when the following characteristics applied: The physical body of the city had to be dense, heterogeneously used, and clearly defined, public trade had to flourish, civil society needed to be committed, and the public and private realm had to be clearly separated. In recent years it looked as if this model had become obsolete. Walter Siebel, for example, called the European city a "backwardly oriented utopia" and a leftover "shell of nineteenth-century society" (Siebel 29.07.2000: 7). Yet lately, the model has been regaining popularity:

> It seems like the "European city" and the myth that goes with the concept radiate imaginary powers that affect not only the nostalgic but various analytical and political theories also perceive it as a possible anchor that might offer protection against the trials of "globalization" and the unpleasantries that stem from it: A social division on a global scale, for example, which would manifest itself in the urban sphere as fortified gated communities for the affluent and marginalized slums and boroughs for losers, could be juxtaposed with the model of the European city, which tried in vain to integrate all social groups. In addition, the futile but unconditional mixture of and encounters between members of all social strata and the blend of the unfamiliar within the realm of the bourgeois-European city can be pitted against the commercial privatization and repressive surveillance of urban space (Becker/Burbaum et al. 2003: 8).

I would like to propose a perspective that differs from this line of argument, which complains about current urban developments and considers the (backward) utopia of the European city a way out. For this purpose it is useful to recall the discourse on the postcolonial city, which systematically undermines the geographic unambiguity of "the West and the rest" as well as ideas of a civil Europe and a chaotic South. If we assume a postcolonial perspective when looking at a European city like Leipzig, it is possible to articulate the variety of current urban products "from the outside in.' Furthermore, it so happens that the "perforated city" does not have holes: it only has them if the European urban model serves as a backdrop for their discussion. However, these holes are actually sites where what Hartmut Häußermann and Walter Siebel call "placeless urbanity" is emerging. Häußermann and Siebel argue that:

> Urbanity has [...] not disappeared but like modern labor it has become placeless [...] You cannot build urbanity because it rejects being purposefully staged, and it does not emerge overnight. But it is connected to locations, where it both takes shape and can be experienced. Such locations result from the city's aging and decaying, which create gaps inside which urban life may unfold [...] Because the retiring industrial society abandons empty factories and leaves outmoded infrastructure behind, cities age much faster again and, as a result, urban spaces may emerge. [...] Urban planning may only influence these processes by tolerating them but most times they build on top of them. In order to preserve urban cities, planning must allow for in-between spaces and transition zones, and build architecture that has the capacity to age and survive gaps, decay and misuse (Häußermann/Siebel 2000).

And perhaps these "placeless locations" will—due to the activities of club maker, spontaneous angler, in-between trader, and others—give rise to new forms of economic activities and social actions. These sites could serve as the nucleus for an economy of solidarity: an economy that does not only include the affluent and is not exclusively based on commerce. In short, an economy that constitutes a counterweight to the destructive tendencies of neo-liberalism. Looking at the informal sectors in African, Asian, and eastern European countries, Elmar Altvater and Birgit Mahnkopf report on local forms of economic and societal cooperation that seek to transcend direct dependence on the market: cooperative consortia in Chile, barter trade in Romania, or so called "orçamento participativo," a democratic instrument of city planning and budget participation in Brazil, are examples of such emancipative projects (Altvater/Mahnkopf 2003). If local initiatives were supported and networked on a global level—through NGOs for instance—Altvater/Mahnkopf believe that "new forms of socio-economic security that will prevent a possible 'globalization of insecurities' will emerge" (ibid: 29). In this sense, the title of the "Orbit Palace" project symbolizes the utopian spark, which—despite all inhospitableness—is inherent in all the locations about which I have spoken.

References

Altvater, Elmar/Mahnkopf, Birgit (2003) "Die Informalisierung des urbanen Raums". In Jochen Becker/Claudia Burbaum/Martin Kaltwasser, et al. (eds.) *Learning from*—Städte von Welt, Phantasmen der Zivilgesellschaft, informelle Organisation*, Berlin: b_books, pp. 17-30.

Becker, Jochen/Burbaum, Claudia/Kaltwasser, Martin, et al. (eds.) (2003) *Learning from*—Städte von Welt, Phantasmen der Zivilgesellschaft, informelle Organisation*, Berlin: b_books.

Engbersen, Godfried (2004) "Zwei Formen der sozialen Ausgrenzung: Langfristige Arbeitslosigkeit und illegale Immigration in den Niederlanden". In Hartmut Häußermann/Martin Kronauer/Walter Siebel (eds.) *An den Rändern der Städte. Armut und Ausgrenzung*, Frankfurt am Main: Suhrkamp, pp. 99-121.

Engbersen, Godfried/Schuyt, Kees/Timmer, Jaap, et al. (1993) *Cultures of Unemployment. A Comparative Look at Long-Term Unemployment and Urban Poverty*, Boulder, San Francisco & Oxford: Westview Press.

Holert, Tom/Terkessidis, Mark (eds.) (1996) *Mainstream der Minderheiten. Pop in der Kontrollgesellschaft*, Berlin: Edition ID-Archiv.

Häußermann, Hartmut/Siebel, Walter (2000) *Stadt und Urbanität*, http://www.kommunale-info.de/Themen/Stadtplanung/urban.htm, (accesed: 14.03.2003).

Jahoda, Marie/Lazarsfeld, Paul F./Zeisel, Hans (1975) *Die Arbeitslosen von Marienthal*, Frankfurt am Main: Suhrkamp.

Lütke Daldrup, Engelbert/Doehler-Behzadi, Marta (eds.) (2004) *Plusminus Leipzig 2030. Stadt in Transformation*, Wuppertal: Verlag Müller + Busmann KG.

Mayer, Verena (08.07.2003) "Freizeit für alle!" Frankfurter Rundschau, pp. 17.

McRobbie, Angela (1999) "Kunst, Mode und Musik in der Kulturgesellschaft". In Justin Hoffmann/Marion von Osten (eds.) *Das Phantom sucht seinen Mörder. Ein Reader zur Kulturalisierung der Ökonomie*, Berlin: b_books, pp. 15-42.

Rink, Dieter (2004) "Aufbau und Verfall einer Industrieregion". In Philipp Oswalt (eds.) *Schrumpfende Städte. Band 1: Internationale Untersuchungen*, Ostfildern-Ruit: Hatje Cantz Verlag, pp. 632-639.

Siebel, Walter (29.07.2000) "Urbanität als Lebensweise ist ortlos geworden". Frankfurter Rundschau, pp. 7.

Stadt Leipzig—Amt für Statistik und Wahlen, (31.12.2004): http://www.leipzig.de/business/wistandort/zahlen/arbeitsmarkt/arbeitslose/, (accessed: 15.08.2005).

Statistisches Landesamt des Freistaates Sachsen: *Kreisstatistik 2004 für Leipzig, Stadt*, (01.01.2004): htttp://www.statistik.sachsen.de/Index/22kreis/unterseite 22. htm, (accessed: 15.08.2005).

Pacification by Design:
An Ethnography of Normalization Techniques

LARS FRERS

Conflicts are produced in specific spatial and material settings. The placement of things, the way visibility is established, the accessibility of areas—all of these aspects of built space participate in the production of human action in the city. Drawing on ethnographies of Potsdamer Platz, Berlin, and of railway stations and ferry terminals in Germany and Scandinavia, this text analyzes the processes by which normalities are produced in tangible socio-spatial constellations.

The design of urban places is an integral aspect of the conflicts emerging or taking place in urban space. In cases of open conflict, the spatial and material aspects of the situation configure its development, while at the same time, the action might reconfigure the spatial and material setup. Cobblestones present themselves as thrown weapons, cars become barricades, dead ends become traps, and, in the streets of Beijing, bicycles can become effective messenger vehicles (cf. Dingxin 1998). However, space and materiality usually play more subtle roles in urban life. They are silent participants in everyday life, nudging people in certain directions, hiding things or exposing them; they can induce pain and uneasiness, comfort and pleasure. Taken together, space and materiality participate in the production of localized normalities that have a regulating influence on the behavior of people in these localities. In this paper, I will reconstruct the ways in which these normalities are produced in publicly accessible spaces like plazas and terminals, focusing on the mostly silent and successful evasion of conflicts: pacification by design.[1]

Although I will analyze digital video recordings, I will only be able to present them as stills, loosing what is most important about this valuable source: its temporal or dynamic character and the recorded sound.[2] This material is then enriched by my perceptions both of the surroundings and of myself, of how I feel and how I react to certain situations. An advantage of systematically analyzing your own perceptions and feelings is the privileged access one has to one's own sensual perception. I deal with these perceptions in a phenomenologically informed way, mostly based on Merleau-Ponty's "Phenomenology of Perception" (1962). In this perspective, sensual perceptions are not seen as a set of instruments that split the world into different parts. The act of perceiving is a process that unfolds in a specific context.

Working from this perspective means to focus less on meaning as it is ascribed in language, addressing concrete experience instead. In the context of this study, discourse about places is therefore ignored; Lefèbvre's "spatial practice" occupies my attention (Lefèbvre 1991: 33–46). This certainly does not mean that the representational or the discursive is unimportant—it is, by definition, more visible and more explicit than the subtle behavioral adjustments that are required to produce and reproduce the spatial and social urban order. Exactly because of the fact that this subtlety is so easily overlooked and yet extremely effective, I want to make it stand out more clearly.

The photograph on the right side, taken with a digital camcorder during the early afternoon of a pleasant day in June, can be used as an introduction into the spatial relations and material aspects that permeate situated social behavior. The photo was taken in the main railway station of Leipzig. People using this terminal experience its architecture, the things inside the building, the distances, the volume. Entrances allow access into the building, opening a horizon of activities. Entering the station with the escalator from the shopping mall that lies below, one is confronted with more than forty paces of open space directly in the foreground, a distance that has to be crossed to reach whatever goal one is looking for. To get to where they are, the young couple on the photo had to turn left, passing between the trashcan and the signpost. Continuing on to the escalator, the man with the backpack had to make a sharp right turn around the trashcan. Others walk through the enormous hall that stretches itself over a length of more than 200 meters. The privileged po-

---

1 I have been inspired to both this study and this terminology by Sharon Zukin, who talks about "domestication by cappuccino" (Zukin 1995: xiv), and by Lyn Lofland's chapter on "Control by Design" in her book on the public realm (Lofland 1998: 179-227).

2 Video clips are available on my website: http://userpage.fu-berlin.de/~frers/pacification.html.

lice officers in the central background of the photo entered the station with their car, only walking the short distance from its doors to the entrance of the terminal's police station.

Figure 1: Spatial relations and materiality. Main hall, Leipzig Hauptbahnhof, June 2004 (Photo: © Lars Frers)

All of these people are in viewing and shouting distance of each other, not necessarily taking note, but potentially being aware of each other—the boy, for example, is looking straight at the observer while he passes by. These are a few of the socio-spatial relations that can be discerned in this printed photograph. Let us take a look at the materiality of the place. The floor is made of polished stone tiles in light colors with darker stripes sweeping through the hall. Most of the time, this kind of floor is too cool to sit on. It also reflects the light that is shining in through the milk glass roof and through the train hall in the back of the figure. Opacity is of great importance; both the railing of the escalator and the wall that separates the terminal hall from the train hall are made of glass, exposing the things that happen behind them visible to the eyes of others. The signpost and the trashcan are anchored to the ground; even though they might be in the way, they will resist being moved without the use of tools.

In the following part of the paper, I will analyze the spatial and material aspects of social settings along the lines offered by distinct experiences: those of the eye, of the moving body, of the eyes and ears in conjunction, and those of the lingering body.

Visibility—self-regulation

In built spaces, walls are the main devices that establish visual separation. Depending on the opacity of these walls, seeing through is either impossible, reduced to shapes, or allows full view. Usually, these walls are static, rigid barriers that necessitate circumvention. Examples for exceptions to these rules are walls that are made up of plants or trees, or curtains that can be pulled aside. The specific materiality of the wall produces different kinds of visibility. However, visibility is also established through lighting. The way in which shadows fall, the placement, power, and color of lamps, the angle of the sun, or the fullness of the moon expose or hide things and people.

Figure 2: Visibility. Waiting booth, Leipzig Hauptbahnhof, June 2004 (Photo: © Lars Frers)

In the case shown in *Figure 2*, opacity is a carefully implemented feature of the glass walls surrounding the waiting booth on a railway platform. The waiting booth is a place that serves several purposes that are potentially conflicting. For many people, one of the most important aspects of waiting for their trains is the fear of missing their train. Having a view of the track on which the train will roll in is the best way to provide a sense of security and control to waiting passengers (cf. Radlbeck 1981: 14). At the same time, a relaxed waiting atmosphere also requires both protection from unpleasant environmental influences, and some degree of intimacy for those waiting. The glass walls of this booth are adapted to these requirements, allowing a view of the tracks on both sides of the platform, and providing some protection from harmful micro-climatic effects. Their most outstanding feature is probably the way in which the opaque stripes provide more protection from sight for the lower part of the body, especially when sitting, while allowing a view out of the booth (and into it for people on the outside). It is opaque enough to reduce the exposedness of those inside, while at the same time the gaze can pass into and out of the booth. Due to this specific arrangement, another effect is achieved: the waiting booth is a place in which many kinds of deviance could be observed from the outside. Vagrants and homeless have a hard time hiding here, if one was singing or playing music on a boom box, one would be heard; a fight would be seen and heard too. The design of this booth manages visibility in such a way that people using this place are made aware of their partial visibility. They are made aware of the fact that they are supposed to regulate a significant part of their conduct according to the expectations of others.[3] Gestures and movements that are big enough and/or that take place on a sufficient height should comply with the rules of the house and, even more so, with the unspoken rules of conduct in a terminal.

This self-regulation according to the expectations of others works particularly well in that it does not require the presence of dedicated personnel or technical devices that exert more or less open control. Architecture that offers many niches and corners, on the other hand, is inviting shady activities. As can be seen in *Figure 3*, in the local context of a niche these activities might even be openly displayed—the adolescent in the center of the group of five is smoking a cigarette and puffing the smoke in my direction.

Figure 3: Niches. Linksstraße, Potsdamer Platz in Berlin, May 2001
(Photo: © Lars Frers)

---

3 The classic studies of symbolic interactionists, and ethnomethodologists in general, are important references in this context (cf. Goffman 1971; Garfinkel 1984, and others).

These corners and niches might therefore require the installation of one-way seeing devices like surveillance cameras or windows that act as one-way mirrors. These devices serve to establish a sense of, at least potentially, permanent observation according to which people should behave. If the installation of these devices is problematic, the presence of security personnel becomes more relevant—in the course of a guided tour through the security facilities of the main railway station in Frankfurt,[4] the responsible manager, for example, was quite explicit about how quickly vagrants discover dead ends or blind corners and how it is one of the main duties of the terminal's security patrols to cover these spots.

Finally, I want to mention one other important factor that determines how visibility is constituted: the density of people moving through or spending time at a place. This case is most obvious for crowds; during the time I spent in the Potsdamer Platz area I often witnessed several hundred people leaving the local musical theater in a short time span. They gathered at the exits, talking more loudly with growing numbers. When they walked away they left traces: the normally well-cleaned ground would be littered by debris. In a crowd, individuals are not as distinct as they are in less dense social situations, the level of observation sinks, dropping stuff and pick pocketing will often go unnoticed.

Movement—channeling

Regarding crowds, control of individual behavior is difficult to attain. Other aspects of the environment come into play. The movement of people through space, the crossing of streets, passing through halls, walking into open spaces, happens according to the material setup of the locale. Again, walls are probably the most effective obstacles. Depending on their mass, structural stability, height, and texture, they are the prototypical, rigid material obstacle that people won't challenge, instead adapting themselves with regard to their position and direction.

The map (*Figure 4*) shows the layout of the surroundings of the Marlene-Dietrich-Platz (marked with a star), the width of the arrows indicates how many people come and go into which direction. The musical theater to the left also serves as the "Berlinale Palace" during the annual film festival, when large crowds are common in this area. The setup of water around the Marlene-Dietrich-Platz serves as a rather peculiar, and particularly efficient, crowd-management device. It blocks access to the entry of the Berlinale Palace with-

---

4 Organized in November 2004 by Sergej Stoetzer, Institute for Sociology, Darmstadt University of Technology.

out blocking sight, and it keeps the crowd from pressing into the fences that are set up for the span of the Berlinale. The water, along with fences and walls, blocks certain areas, channeling people into the remaining paths. Open spaces are organized into sections with specific uses, degrees of visibility, and more or less restricted access.

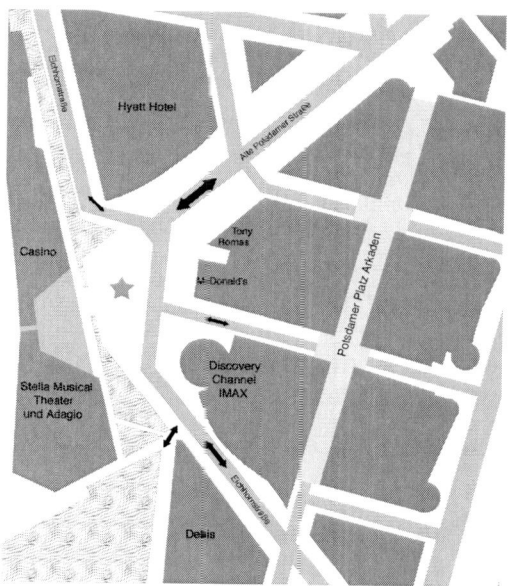

Figure 4: Water as an obstacle. Map of the Quartier DaimlerChrysler at Potsdamer Platz in Berlin (© Lars Frers)

Other ways to channel moving people into certain directions are bottlenecks. Entry gates at airport terminals, the gangway that leads to an entrance into the ferry's hull, and doors and portals in general necessitate that people collect and move through a small, easily observable and controllable opening. Often, this passage causes a reduction in speed, because the bottleneck will only allow a small number of people to pass through at a time—in situations where people want to flee from a place, these bottlenecks can become deadly traps; at other times, they might become mere annoyances. The stairways leading down to tracks in railway stations like those in Darmstadt and Berlin are overcrowded when commuter trains arrive and people spill out of the train, wanting to get home as quickly as possible. For frail people these situations can be dangerous; they might not be able to keep up with the crowd, forcing them to wait until the crowd has passed. In addition, the chance of coming into physical contact with others increases. Those that have to carry bulky items might become the target of unfriendly remarks or even shoving. In times of increased traffic, bottlenecks can produce hierarchies that center around physical power, recklessness, and male chauvinism—however, they are also places where beneficial social exchanges can take place, ranging from helping each other out to flirting and being explicitly polite.

The combination of obstacles, open spaces, and bottlenecks organizes places in a way that steers people along paths, keeping them out of certain areas, moving them past shops and advertisements, and allowing them to stay for an extended period of time in certain places. The order that is produced in this way is stable, because the spatial setup is not easily rearranged, and it is subtle, not becoming the center of attention or reflection, instead being taken as a granted feature of everyday routines. However, the spatial arrangement may also produce conflict when it does not accommodate the needs of people or when it creates opportunities for potentially risky contact that could be evaded under other circumstances.

Noise—atmosphere

Often, conflicts are heard before they are perceived with any of the other senses. Shouting or loud noise makes heads turn and gazes look around. The acoustical setup and local activities of a place determine how easily raised voices can be heard and how far a provocation or a cry for help carries. But there is much more to the acoustics of a place; it has a deep impact on the feeling or mood of the setting into which one is entering. Loud noise, especially industrial or shrill noise, or a mix of complex and different noises is stressful and creates a sense of chaos and irritation.

Figure 5: Organs and shouting. Main Hall, Leipzig Hauptbahnhof, September 2004 (Photo: © Lars Frers)

The still frame (*Figure 5*) offers a glimpse of a setting that irritated me when I encountered it. I recorded it during an arrival in Leipzig. As I left the train, I heard loud sounds that I couldn't immediately recognize. After a brief moment, my perception shifted and I realized that I was listening to music, probably barrel organs. Leaving the platform and walking up to the main hall of the station, I quickly realized that a throng of people was gathered around a group of barrel organ players who where playing their organs in synchrony, creating a loud and, at least for me, quite unusual musical experience. I quickly readied my digital camcorder and started recording the events.

The loud, hand barrel orchestra music combined with the general background noises of the train station in a confusing mixture that made it necessary for me to reorient myself and spend some effort in the interpretation of the situation at hand. However, as soon as I had made up my mind about what was going on, I was able to make use of the situation for my research. Others made use of this situation in different ways. As can be seen in the figure above, some people are standing around the ensemble in a loose semi-circle, watching the band and listening to the music. In the center of the figure, one might be able to discern two kids, who were dancing to the music. Many were just walking by—or being pushed by on a wheelchair by a member of the Bahnhofsmission (a Christian welfare organization for railway stations). Others changed their route and passed through on the other side of the hall, where no throng was making the passage difficult. The adolescents that are on the far left of the still frame, walking further leftwards, took this setting as an opportunity for a contrasting activity. While they were approaching the scene, one member of the group started to raise and shake his fist in time with the rhythm of the music. A few steps later the frontmost boy, who is carrying a bag over his shoulder, picked up on the characteristic of the setting itself: the music. He started to bawl to the rhythm. His shouting was acknowledged by visible consternation in the case of some of the bystanders and musicians, and grinning faces in the case of fellow members of his peer group. As I demonstrated with this example, music in this particular setting is used as an opportunity for more or less active entertainment and as an opportunity for provocation and the conflict-laden challenging of norms.

There are other aspects of the acoustic setup that frequently caused perceivable readjustments of people in the setting. One feature was particularly prominent in terminals during the less-dense traffic of evenings and during the night. People, both men and women, turned their heads or shifted their gaze when they heard the sound of footsteps, specifically the sound produced by women walking with high-heeled shoes. Most railway stations have stone or marble floors; this kind of floor material, when located in buildings with long halls and very few sound-absorbing surfaces, produces sounds that carry over long distances. Women with high heels adjust their behavior, taking particular care not to risk eye contact with strangers or appearing confused and disoriented—a brisk pace is best suited for this environment during a time when few people are present. The spectators are made aware of the arriving business-like person early, they can study him or her, look some other way, start talking about the person or even hollering something in his or her direction. The combination of soundscape, usage pattern, and outfit produces specific vulnerabilities and makes social hierarchies audible—both gender and class hierarchies, which in this particular case often run cross to each other.

Figure 6: Relative calm. Color Line Terminal, Oslo, December 2004 (Photo: © Lars Frers)

Soundscapes have a significant impact on the mood of a setting. People in the Western world have experiences with the implementation of sound in shops and warehouses. Depending on clientele, product, and season, music is played that supposedly improves sales and binds customers to a particular chain or brand. In terminals, the playing of music is not part of the usual setup. This does not mean that sound cannot participate in the creation of an atmosphere that fits the experience of traveling. In the case of the Color Line Terminal in Oslo, captured in the photo above, the low roof, which is tiled with pin-holed panels that muffle sound to a certain degree, helps to create a feeling of calm and orderliness that fits the rest of the setting: comfortable chairs, many benches with thick upholstery, plants, and models of Color Line's ships—sound, noise, music; all these are important participants in the creation of atmospheres (cf. Böhme 1995) that can be anywhere on the spectrum from calm to overstimulating to chaotic and even to outright aggressive.

Body—comfort and suffering

The comfortable upholstery in the ferry terminal makes it easier to use the waiting time for relaxation, idle chatter, or just watching others do the same until boarding time begins. During the last minutes before the gangway becomes accessible and the boarding gates are opened, the boarding area of the terminal rapidly fills with people, and many will leave their seats to join the queue. Those that remain seated—either because they do not want to squeeze themselves in with the rest or because extended periods of standing or slow shuffling are not convenient for them—will often be literally faced with a wall of human bodies that is thickening more and more before it starts seeping away through the boarding gates.

Figure 7: Edges. Railing in front of the Casino and Musical Theater. Marlene-Dietrich-Platz Berlin, May 2001 (Photo. © Lars Frers)

When an extended period of time is being spent in a single place, either in a ferry terminal lobby, in a waiting booth at a railway station, or in some other publicly accessible place, the need for some kind of seating or bodily support grows steadily. In the case of the Marlene-Dietrich-Platz (*Figure 7*), this may become a serious problem. As can be seen on the map in *Figure 4*, the Platz has characteristics of a dead end. When people arrive, they tend to slow down, look around, and finally stop. A decision has to be made: should I stay or should I go now? Staying will be trouble. There are no benches or "official" resting facilities at all. What about commonly used substitutes? The architecture here does not include stone slabs on which one could sit. There are stairs, though. The Marlene-Dietrich-Platz itself is lowered into the ground a bit, slightly reminiscent of an amphitheater. However, there is a significant difference from the steps of an amphitheater: the height of the steps is only about ten centimeters (four inches). Sitting on these steps is like sitting on the floor, making it an invalid option except for people who are fit enough and do not care about the stigma that is associated with sitting on the ground, i.e. adolescents and some younger adults.

One other option remains and is used by those who cannot or will not sit on the ground: the railing that runs along part of the water channels in front of the musical theater. Several times I observed elderly people, who were waiting for others at the Marlene-Dietrich-Platz, looking out for a spot where they could rest. Not finding anything suitable, they would lean against the railings visible in the figure. In one case an elderly women, after leaning on the railing for almost ten minutes, finally tried to squeeze herself into the railing to sit on the lower bar. However, sitting on either of the bars causes pain too. The bars are wide enough to offer some support, but they have sharp edges that quickly begin to hamper circulation and cause discomfort.[5] Spending more than a few minutes in this place is a problematic occupation.

Most people will quickly leave this place, those that remain will have to manage their corporality in a way that allows them either to ignore their physical discomfort and remain standing somewhere, or that allows them to ignore potential stigmatization as loiterers who sit on the ground.

Space and materiality—normalization

Regarding the evidence that I have presented about the Marlene-Dietrich-Platz, it can be argued that it is on the one hand a place that is secured and pacified by its design, exposing deviant behavior and preventing certain movements and activities. The behavior that establishes itself as normal is one of passing through, looking at the unusual architecture, and perhaps spending money in one of the local entertainment or food-consumption facilities. What

---

5   As I noticed recently, the situation got even worse: the water channels behind the railing now contain fountains that spray the railing with water, making it practically impossible to sit on them.

struck me as particularly interesting about this place is the fact that there is almost no visible presence of security personnel—very much opposed to the interior of the nearby Sony Center on the other side of the Neue Potsdamer Straße. The design of the Sony Center includes many corners, benches, and a fountain around which people gather to watch and talk. In this place, security personnel are patrolling regularly and openly. I would argue that the design of the Marlene-Dietrich-Platz makes this kind of policing mostly unnecessary. This does not mean that police or security personnel is not available—its visible presence is just not needed to establish a specific kind of self-controlled normality at this place: one of passing through, of consumption, of a tourists' place with unusual architecture and entertainment facilities. This orderly normality is based on the reduction of risk: encounters are brief and visible to everyone, extended stays are made difficult.

On the other hand, the design of this place produces a certain degree of uneasiness, discomfort, or even physical suffering for the people that want to use this place. A similar statement could be made about the halls and waiting facilities in train stations. The acoustic setup makes disturbances perceivable over long distances, this helps in securing the place to a certain degree, while at the same time this design could also make people more vulnerable and uneasy. Other places, like the lobby in the ferry terminal, or even the somewhat covered, lower part of the waiting booth, allow for a higher degree of relaxation. In both of these cases, hired staff is present and helping to keep up an orderly normality. Hired staff does not necessarily mean security personnel—other employees, in particular the members of the cleaning personnel, play an important part in the production of sanitary design. Places that offer hideaways that are somewhat shielded from sight and hearing make it possible to engage in other activities, be they as harmless as loitering or flirting, or extending into the realms of the criminal and unlawful.

One could say, therefore, that design can produce specific, highly controlled normalities that are based on spatial and material constellations in which principles of visibility or perceivability in general are governing. However, this kind of pacification by design has at least two limitations. First, this kind of design does not prohibit conflict and provocation per se. As has been demonstrated in the example of the adolescents who challenge the normality of the barrel organ entertainment setting, the design can also be a resource for the open display of deviance. Second, this kind of pacification by design also produces specific feelings of uneasiness, making it harder for some people to use these places, and causes specific vulnerabilities. The Marlene-Dietrich-Platz can make you feel uneasy, watched, and insecure about what you should actually do there; the non-existence of seats and benches and the unwieldy design of similar objects like stairs and railings can make it hard for frail people to spend time in a place, and the display of people can also make them vulnerable to harassment, especially if they belong to "weaker" groups like women, or to (ethnic) minorities.

The design of places, the spatial arrangement of walls, obstacles, and other objects, the channeling of people through a place, the opacity of barriers, the texture of surfaces, the acoustics of a place, and other features that did not fit into this text, like the micro-climate, the olfactory circumstances, and electro-magnetic design (wireless networks, radio, mobile phone networks etc.), all participate in the production of local normalities. These normalities are not completely stable and rigid, they may be challenged. Accordingly, I define these normalities as dynamic constellations. These constellations, however, contain spatio-material components that are of a greater stability and persistence than many social and situative ones. Temporary, even regularly occurring disturbances can happen, but the constellation quickly returns to the previous, stable setting.

References

Böhme, Gernot (1995) *Atmosphäre. Essays Zur Neuen Ästhetik*, Frankfurt am Main: Suhrkamp.

Dingxin, Zhao (1998) "Ecologies of Social Movements. Student Mobilization during the 1989 Prodemocracy Movement in Beijing". American Journal of Sociology 103/6, pp. 1493–1529.

Garfinkel, Harold (1984/1967) *Studies in Ethnomethodology*, Malden/MA: Polity Press/Blackwell Publishing.

Goffman, Erving (1971) *Relations in Public. Microstudies of the Public Order*, New York: Basic Books.

Lefèbvre, Henri (1991/1974) *The Production of Space*, Oxford/UK, Malden/MA: Blackwell.

Lofland, Lyn H. (1998) *The Public Realm. Exploring the City's Quintessential Social Territory*, New York: Aldine de Gruyter.

Merleau-Ponty, Maurice (1962/1945) *Phenomenology of Perception*, London/New York: Routledge & K. Paul Humanities Press.

Radlbeck, Karl (1981) *Bahnhof und Empfangsgebäude. Die Entwicklung vom Haus zum Verkehrswegekreuz*, Dissertation, Technische Universität München.

Zukin, Sharon (1995) *The Cultures of Cities*, Oxford/UK, Cambridge/MA: Blackwell.

Violence Prevention in a South African Township

KOSTA MATHÉY

South Africa's townships count amongst the places with the highest indices for violence and crime worldwide. The causes for this are complex and specific to the place; therefore attempts towards violence reduction necessarily need to be multi-dimensional, too. The paper describes the suggested approach for a German cooperation project for Khayelitsha Township near Cape Town. The project has recently started in the field.[1]

Increasing presence of violence has become a major concern in most big cities of the South. However, the actual threat still differs enormously from one country to another. Southern Africa belongs to the places of worst reputation, and within the country, and even within each city, the extent of violence can vary considerably. One rather remarkable example is Cape Town, where one may find some white bourgeois quarters where the fear of violence certainly is present—to tell by all the visible alarm and "armed response" signs outside of the houses—even if that fear might not be supported by police reports from that area. But then there are the townships, some of which present frightening violence statistics. Take Khayelitsha, with almost half a million inhabitants it is the biggest township of Cape Town, where two German cooperation pro-

---

[1] This article is based upon the feasibility study for the German-South African Financial Cooperation project "Violence Prevention through Urban Upgrading" that the author prepared as team leader of AHT International for the Kreditanstalt für Wiederaufbau (KfW) and the City of Cape Town. Co-authors of the quoted sections of the report are Ivan Jonker, Sean Tait, Jasmin Nordien, Einhard Schmidt-Kallert, and Nina Corsten.

jects are currently attempting to reduce urban violence.[2] In 2002 figures, the recorded yearly homicide rate for young black males amounted to 300 deaths per 100,000 inhabitants (almost one per day), whereas the national average was 48. In just one month (June 2002) there were more than 300 assaults reported to the police, 109 burglaries, almost 100 cases of robbery, 33 attempted murders, and 29 cases of rape. When interpreting these figures, one must keep in mind that (apart from murder, which is difficult to hide) only a fraction of violent incidents are reported to the police; realistic figures are estimated to be up to five times higher.

In order to reduce violence it is necessary to distinguish between different forms in which violence typically occurs in a particular place. This will help to understand its causes and circumstances, which is necessary to grab the evil by its roots. In Khayelitsha, these forms can be identified as follows.

Economic violence

Burglary and robbery are the most predominant incidents of economic violence in Khayelitsha. The prime targets of this type of violence are businesspeople, many of whom have already left the neighbourhood in fear of their lives. Though vibrant, the informal economy in Khayelitsha has limited infrastructure and is vulnerable to crime and robbery: there are only two banks and three ATMs in Khayelitsha, which makes people who earn or receive money easy prey for robbery, including old-age pensioners who often get assaulted after collecting their monthly pension. The other most vulnerable group are normal residents, whose belongings at home get stolen when nobody is home, or are robbed when only a woman or children are present. Particularly in the informal settlements, the makeshift houses cannot be securely locked.

According to police statistics, the level of economic violence has been rising since 1995; this has been connected to increasing poverty levels. While certain sectors of the Khayelitsha community are becoming more affluent, others nurse disappointed hopes of unfulfilled aspirations after the end of Apartheid. Also, the very poor conviction and punishment rates in the criminal justice system have been blamed for the increase: criminals have a sense of impunity, as the consequences of their activities will not be dire.

---

2   Urban Conflict Management Peace and Development Project (PDG) supported by the German Gesellschaft für technische Zusammenarbeit (http://www.gtz.de/de/weltweit/afrika/suedafrika/11629.htm) and "Violence Reduction through Urban Upgrading" by the Kreditanstalt für Wiederaufbau (http://www.kfw-entwicklungsbank. de /DE_Home/Laender_und_Projekte/).

Shebeen violence and substance abuse

Shebeens are informal taverns and are a very typical feature in townships. They belong to the most developed informal economic activities and have also generated the most violence in the community. Estimates suggest that there are approximately 1,500 shebeens in Khayelitsha, 200 of which are considered problematic. Shebeens are practically the only places where residents can meet or congregate and socialize in the dull township environment. People can dance, play billiards, and meet the members of the opposite sex without needing a pretext, opportunities that are almost unavoidably linked to the consumption of alcohol. But the lack of regulation of shebeens and taverns also intensifies social conflict, as there is no uniform closing time at night and loud juke box music is played until late at night without consideration for neighbours.

Most of the shebeen customers are youths from 12 years upwards. The landlords, known as Shebeen Kings and Queens, often start their businesses as a survival strategy, since only little investment is needed. Nonetheless, many of the shebeen landlords can generate some capital quite quickly, especially if they get involved in the business of marketing information and stolen goods.

The shebeens are considered to be the primary source of conflict and violence in Khayelitsha. There are many assaults that happen late at night when people leave the shebeens: Men rape women or go home drunk and abuse their partners. The police also believe in a strong link between shebeens and murder. The alcohol/drug and crime nexus is widely acknowledged. Statistical information notes a convincing correlation between the use of alcohol and drugs and crime. Fifty-five percent of unnatural deaths in Cape Town in 1998 involved people who had blood-alcohol concentrations greater than 0.08g/100ml, with the highest levels recorded in homicide-related deaths. Between 67 % and 76 % of domestic violence cases are alcohol-related. There is also a noted link between alcohol abuse and child abuse, with drinking parents more inclined to become negligent and abusive (Parry 2000).

Domestic violence

In a place where violence in public is part of everyday life, one is not surprised to discover that violence occurs just as much in the private sphere, namely, at home or in families where women and children experience abuse (Fisher et al. 2000). Women interviewed in Khayelitsha defined their experiences of violence against them in the following categories; economic, emotional, physical, and sexual abuse (Nedcor 1999). Alcohol abuse (mostly by men) results in women being battered weekend after weekend, as well as an increase in child abuse and incidences of rape.[3]

In a social climate of rapid urbanisation and enforced modernisation, poverty and stress often rule domestic life, and traditional forms of male-female division of labour prove to be incompatible with the modern reality of income earning: At least in parts of Khayelitsha, the majority of the households are headed by women. Other households have a female wage earner, while the husband is unemployed. Nevertheless, the man usually considers his wife as being fully in charge of children and household in addition to her job. About 80 % of the domestic violence cases reported are stirred up by disputes over the household budget.

Unlike public places, where individuals are protected—at least in theory—against violence, a victim at home finds it even more difficult to find assistance. Where maltreatment at home is evident, the police are often reluctant to take up the case and prefer not to interfere in "matrimonial matters," as they call it. During interviews some women indicated that the absence of suitable mechanisms of policing and justice has often meant that "*the most dangerous place for them is at home.*" The discrepancy between incidents of domestic violence and reported cases remains high for various reasons, in particular, because the women have no alternative places to go after reporting to the police, and women are also often afraid to lose their only wage earner if the man has a job. Even sexual abuse of children by their fathers over long periods of time is not seldom ignored by the mothers.

Gender-related violence

Gender-related violence in Khayelitsha includes various kinds of domestic violence, rape, indecent assault, and abuse of children and women, occasionally also of men, and neglect of children. Tensions and conflict between men and women are an integral part of life. In most cases, women and children become victims in one way or another. Sometimes they are physically hampered for life, sometimes also severely injured and infected with HIV; frequently, they are killed. In some cases, women and children live in a climate of extreme insecurity, with more reasons to be afraid than men.

A social study on Khayelitsha[4] revealed that two-thirds of interviewed women consider rape, violence, and abuse against women and children as major concerns, whilst the males prioritised theft and assault, drug trafficking, and political intolerance as major problems. According to data collected by assistant institutions, there is an average of three rape cases every day. Need-

---

3   Khayelitsha Development Project Summit, 2002.
4   Taylor study in Khayelitsha, Khayelitsha Development Project Summit, 2002.

less to say, especially for rape, only a tiny fraction of victims ever report the incidence to any institution at all. Children are frequently raped because of the myth that sex with a virgin is a cure for HIV infection.

Over six percent of known cases are gang rapes. When cases are reported, the case tends to be withdrawn by the victim at a later stage because of fears of revenge, or possibly even being beaten to death. Between ten and twenty percent of the victimised women are already HIV-positive. Around half the rape victims are between 14 and 19 years old.[5] The main time during which women and girls are attacked is the early evening or the night; about half the cases reported happen outside. Some places seem to be particularly prone, and residents sometimes try to make these places less dangerous, for example by cutting bushes and other greenery in publicly accessible areas.

School violence

Violence at schools has recently become a worrying issue in two respects. Firstly, secondary school pupils increasingly carry knives and even firearms at school, where they intimidate other children and staff. Theft or robbery of valuables, such as cell phones, and rape are frequent. Gang fights across school yards, while more common in certain other townships, are by no means unknown in Khayelitsha. Secondly, marketable goods such as computers, furniture, sanitary equipment, etc. may get stolen during break-ins.

Road and transport violence, gangs

Transportation generates a multitude of violence in Khayelitsha. There are conflicts between (minibus-) taxi associations, which flare up regularly: the taxi associations are in conflict with the buses, and commuters get caught in the crossfire of these conflicts, or are the victims of crime. Taxis were outlawed until deregulation in 1987. The taxi violence peaked in 1993, ceased in 1994, but has steadily been increasing since then. It is interesting to note that since 1997, injuries have not increased as much as deaths, suggesting that killings are becoming more focused and accurate.

Khayelitsha commuters who use public transport are incredibly vulnerable to crime and violence, as workers commute daily for approximately two hours —leaving home in the early hours of the morning and arriving home late at night. They travel using public transportation that is increasingly unsafe and unreliable. Buses are overcrowded, especially during peak hours, and taxis are

---

5 The rape of children under fourteen is not included in these figures.

not roadworthy. For example, it is a common sight to see a taxi without windscreen wipers on rainy days.[6] Taxi drivers have been reported to extort sexual services from women passengers who cannot pay their fare. According to the South African Police Service, buses in Khayelitsha have become prime targets for robbery. Most robberies and assaults reported occur en route to and/or at transportation junctions where people converge to commute to work, as they are carrying cash in order to pay for transport services. This risk can also be related to certain environmental factors:

- The lighting is poor, and commuters start travelling from as early as 4:00 a.m., when it is dark.
- There are some railway stations with no roads leading to the station, hence commuters have to walk between shacks or across bushy fields to get the station, making them vulnerable to being attacked.
- The buses, taxis, and trains are overcrowded.

Use of firearms

Gun violence is rife in Khayelitsha. Armed robbery tops the list of most-feared property crimes for residents. Serious crime such as murder, attempted murder, and aggravated robbery accounted for 42 % of crimes reported in 2001.[7] Death by firearm is listed as the second most common single cause of death (8.5 %) in Khayelitsha.[8] Gun violence is also highlighted as one of the biggest threats facing youth in the area today, both as offenders as well as victims.[9] As such, it impacts heavily on the social and economic lives of residents, and especially those of shopkeepers and street vendors–the entrepreneurs, and the self-employed, who tend to become the victims of shootings more than any other group. In addition, transport stations are particularly vulnerable to gun violence, being points of concentrated economic activity that become targets for crime. Clinics are robbed at gunpoint to access medicines which subsequently are resold to needy patients.

A key explanatory factor in armed violence is, in the first place, the ample availability of guns in the community. It is easy even for minors to buy such a weapon. One of the most important sources of illegal weapons is stolen legal fire arms, especially those stolen from the local police.[10]

---

6 Khaylitsha Development Project Summit, 2002.
7 SAPS, 2002. Statistics for Khayelitsha 1995 to 2001.
8 Khayelitsha Health Summit 2002.
9 Khayelitsha Violence Prevention through Urban Renewal Focus Group meeting 6 July 2002.
10 A practice not unusual was reported at the evaluation forum, whereby policemen on duty are offered free spirits at shebeens, and this, when they are drunk, makes it easy to grab their pistols.

Fear of violence

It is not surprising that exposure to high levels of violent crime directly, through common acquaintances and through the media, has an impact on residents' fear of crime. The Cape Town victim survey noted that there was little difference in fear of crime between people who had been victims of crime and those who had not personally suffered crime. Fear of crime was highest at night, when both victims and non-victims felt unsafe. Fear of crime and feelings of insecurity add considerably to the stress and tensions of life. This in turn impacts on productivity, with negative implications for the economy, and general feelings of well-being—eventually impacting political and social stability. In a survey conducted in Khayelitsha in 2002[11], the residents identified crime as their major concern and, in particular, referred to robbery, burglary, and gangsterism. Fifty-eight percent of all respondents said that they felt very unsafe in their homes, and 34 % felt very unsafe while walking in their neighbourhood areas during the day.[12]

An important factor contributing to the feeling of insecurity derives from the deficiencies of the social justice system. Considering the size of Khayelitsha, the assigned police compliment of 270 members (in 2002) is negligible, especially as this figure includes 50 % civilian and support staff. Allowing for shifts and leave, only less than 50 policemen are on duty at any one time. Furthermore, the shift patterns do not coincide with crime patterns: over the violent peak periods after hours and on weekends, the station is often depleted of personnel. The deplorable shortage of vehicles is further exacerbated by the absence of a driver's licenses among police staff. This situation implies that there are very remote chances that police will be able to interfere when and where violence occurs—or at least to secure evidence once it has happened. As a result, it is estimated that only a very few of all crimes are reported to the police and suspects are eventually arrested in only less than 25 % cases. Once in court, the conviction rate is around 75 %—less than 10 % of all the committed crimes. For certain types of crime the rate is even lower: For armed robbery, common assault, attempted murder, and theft between 80 % and 100 % of cases were also closed as undetected. Since only a fraction of cases taken to court lead to a conviction, conviction rates may drop as low as one percent!

---

11 Micro Cosmos Survey supervised by the author as part of the KfW feasibility study "Violence prevention through Urban Upgrading" in Khayelitsha.
12 While 74 % felt very unsafe while walking during the night.

An integrated approach towards violence reduction

As outlined above, high levels of violence in Khayelitsha occur in many different sectors, including different forms of economic violence, domestic and gender violence, social violence, transport violence, etc.[13] The causes of violence are highly complex and interlinked. To be effective, any attempt to reduce overall levels of violence in such a setting must take this into account. The analytical tool known as the "Triangle of Violence" (cf. Liebermann/Landmann 2000 and Kruger/Landmann/Liebermann 2001) can be helpful for developing suitable strategies for action. This tool refers to different factors that are always present in an act of violence and therefore imply the need to react on different fronts at a time: they must be directed towards discouraging a potential violator (offender), supporting the victim of violence, and to arrange the environment in a way suitable to reduce the opportunity for crime to happen. The following diagram illustrates the triangle for the example of rape:

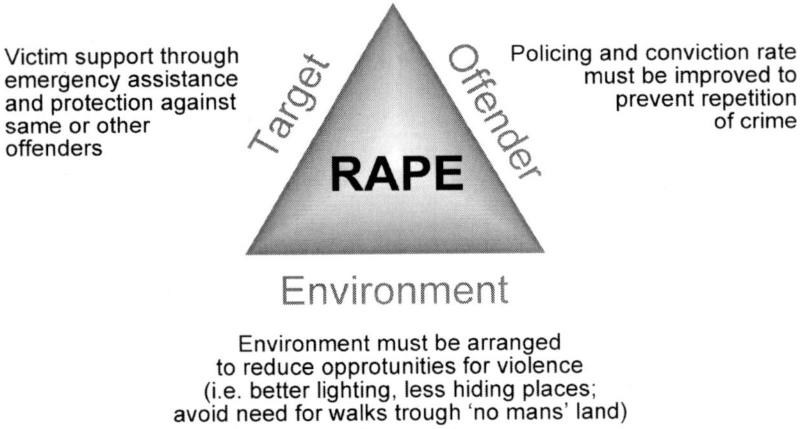

Victim support through emergency assistance and protection against same or other offenders

Policing and conviction rate must be improved to prevent repetition of crime

RAPE

Target — Offender

Environment

Environment must be arranged to reduce opprotunities for violence (i.e. better lighting, less hiding places; avoid need for walks trough 'no mans' land)

Figure 1: Triangle of Violence: Example 'Rape' © Kosta Mathéy

In other words: the triangle concept illustrates the need for an integrated programme to address violence in Khayelitsha, or any other township—and it leads to alternative options different from the "zero tolerance" approach adopted in certain other countries.

Considering the size of Khayelitsha, with its almost half a million inhabitants, a choice must be made about the geographic concentration of any intervention, since an equal spread of necessarily limited assistance over the entire township would not mean more than a drop in the ocean and have little perceivable impact. On the other hand, a limitation on only a few "hot spots"

---

13 Fortunately, gang and political violence are less prominent, but have been seen in the past and may show up again.

would probably not lead to the desired effect of violence reduction, but rather to the displacement of the same crimes to surrounding areas. Therefore, the definition of core zones of integrated action—including, for example, policing, infrastructure improvement, service provision, job creation measures, with a wider ring of "softer" measures, seems to be an adequate response to the given situation.

In the case of the Khayelitsha upgrading project, as it was conceived in the KfW feasibility study, this conclusion was the result of participatory analysis in the course of a "consultation forum" that drew together many different stakeholders, including a majority of residents apart from business people, local politicians and administration, the police, and NGOs. The same forum also gave an assessment on the most pressing security concerns, which should guide an anti-violence intervention:

- High vulnerability through the absence of police protection in cases of need, and conviction rates close to zero.
- Additional vulnerability through the need for long walks at awkward times because of the absence of facilities needed close to homes on a daily basis and due to a poorly functioning public transport system.
- Desperate material needs as a consequence of extremely high unemployment, poor education, and an alarmingly bad state of health.

Keeping this in mind, and referring to the above-mentioned need to concentrate interventions in a few selected locations, the "Safe Nodes" concept was formulated, which promises to have the best multiple impact on the complex causes and circumstantial nexus. This approach was equipped with two additional elements: a Social Development Fund and supporting complementary activities, as will be explained in the following section. A vector-impact prognosis shows how all three elements directly or indirectly contribute to the different predominant forms of violence in Khayelitsha.

The "Safe Nodes" concept

A "safe node" can be defined as a small urban sub-centre, principally catering to the residents living within easy walking distance, bringing together a combination of commercial, service, and work opportunities presently missing in the neighbourhood. Its contribution to the aim of violence prevention is achieved through:

- Proximity to a protective institutional policing body that will deter potential violators and criminals, and increase security for both shop and service operators and the public in general. With this improvement, business peo-

ple will thus flock to the centre rather than move out of Khayelitsha, which is happening at present.
- Better access to public transport, as each node will be supplied with bus stops and a taxi rank. The concentration of customers in these sub-centres will automatically imply a more readily available transport service.
- The availability of essential services to the residents within the neighbourhood will avoid the need for long walks through partially vacant land and thus reduce the exposure to risk of violence, especially assaults and rape.
- Additional local labour and education opportunities will contribute to better incomes and ultimately effect a drop in economic violence.

A safe node could be arranged around an open space, like a village square. This "place" would very soon become a social centre, and would be used, for example, for open-air public meetings and the popular music rallies that seem to occur especially on Sundays. In some densely built-up areas, a generous "Pedestrian Avenue" might be a more practical alternative to the square, and thereby create a "sense of place" in this otherwise very densely housed environment. Conversations with residents have also shown a surprising preparedness by many of them to give up their plots if needed for the benefit and general good of the community. For this reason a partial clearance and proposed relocation of some dwellings to the second-floor level of any new development or into overspill areas is a possibility when vacant land is not available for rehousing.

In greater detail, a safe node would offer the following facilities, of which the first three correspond to the three concerns in the "triangle" concept, and thus directly address violence, whereas the remainder indirectly contribute to lessen violence in the township:

- *Security through better policing*
  The need for physical protection through some kind of policing has been explained, but obviously it will not be possible to place a police station in every neighbourhood. Therefore the installation of other institutions that can offer refuge, protection, and can at least enable contact to the police is an essential asset of the safe node. In the case of Khayelitsha, such institutions could be, for example, offices for the PDP[14] or the city police,[15] a fire

---

14 The Peace and Development Project (PDP) was started in 1997 in the townships of Crossroads and Nyanga with the support of the GTZ. Its central elements are patrols of voluntary and unarmed peace workers recruited from the same neighbourhood, who also receive training and thus improve their job opportunities after this service.
15 The city police supplement the National Police Service and mostly look after traffic issues.

brigade, the Neighbourhood Watch,[16] or a Community Corrections Office.[17]

- *Victim Support*
  It has been criticised that the current policing and criminal justice system pays more (if not all) attention to the violator/offender than to the victim. Progressive anti-violence policies need to correct this, and one way of achieving it is through the provision of "Victim Support Centres." Different expressions of violence cause a variety of individual needs and call for a larger number of specialized support centres. Equally needed are "safe houses," which can offer refuge for battered/ raped women and children. There are NGOs that operate in this field but lack the necessary facilities and accommodations. In general, such institutions may receive financial support from the Province, among other donors.

- *Safer environment*
  Acts of violence are facilitated in certain types of environment, or may be discouraged through certain design principles for a "safer city." Examples include the provision of better street lighting, possibly a CCTV system (if connection to a central monitoring station and quick response in cases of emergency can be assured), good visibility, refuge and alarm systems, etc. Segments of the safe node, such as a courtyard, can be gated with metal detectors and transformed into gun-free zones. It must be emphasized, however, that the environment is one of many contributing factors. The notion of "designing out crime" cannot be considered a realistic perspective.

- *Decentralised service facilities*
  In order to reduce travelling need, those services required by the citizens on a day-to-day basis, such as a post office, cash-withdrawal and payment facilities, a surgery or clinic, information and counselling services, a library and internet access point, coin-operated laundromats, etc. should exist within walking distance from home and will be included in the safe node. Minority group-oriented installations, like pre-schools, old age homes, and special-needs schools should be considered wherever the subsequent operation of the same can be assured—interviews with relevant NGOs in Cape Town indicate a realistic perspective to attract more services of that kind in Khayelitsha. A very demanding need has appeared over the last years in catering for the AIDS orphans, who may exceed 100,000 within less than ten years. This urgent and complex problem will be dealt with in a different paper.[18]

---

16 Neighbourhood watches consist of specially trained and accredited civilians who act in extension of the national police SAPS.
17 Community correction offers assistance to reintegration of convicted law offenders as an alternative to imprisonment.
18 Research project on housing needs of AIDS orphans in South Africa at PAT/Technical University Darmstadt, cf. www.par-darmstadt.de.

- *Neighbourhood training and income opportunities*
  Whilst there apparently is an over-supply of primary and secondary schools (although not always of the desired standard) in Khayelitsha, opportunities for professional training and adult education are rare. As up-to-date skills are essential for any income-earning job, education is the best possible investment. Both NGOs and businesses provide a number of courses already, but the lack of suitable accommodations creates a bottleneck for extending the service. Adult classrooms and offices for continuous education should therefore be part of the accommodations provided in node development. Equipment and computers could be provided via donations.
  Direct income-earning opportunities will be created through a small market with lockable stalls, in order to provide a safer and more comfortable operational base to the vulnerable street vendors. Workshop space for rent will be provided for artisans and small industries, as there is a proven demand for it. Commercial retail shops would be included in the nodes as well, and the resulting rent income at market price could cross-subsidise social facilities, which, by definition, cannot be run on a profit-making basis.
- *Leisure facilities*
  Presently, shebeens are about the only available venues where residents can socialise in the township, but they have also been identified as a major factor in the spread of crime and violence, especially for adolescents. Special efforts are therefore needed towards the provision of alternative and competitive leisure facilities. Multi-functional youth clubs would be the first choice, apart from video-cinemas, licensed taverns and coffee shops, community halls, sports facilities, etc.
- *Replacement dwellings*
  Some parts of the township, which are older and offer better transport, may get quite crowded and do not contain empty land needed for creating a safe node. Therefore it may be necessary to clear a piece of land and to relocate a limited number of existing dwellings. The upper floors of a safe node can accommodate such replacement units and simultaneously inhibit a desertion of the node at night.

Community cohesion through a Social Development Fund

The creation of an island situation where violence is kept under control implies a serious risk that violence will just move out of the areas into to the immediate neighbourhoods. Therefore the neighbouring environment of a safe node and its residents needs to be included in the programme. Ample participation of the population is essential, but experience shows that this can only be achieved and sustained over a longer period if the residents have some power over decision making. The Social Development Fund is a very good instrument to reach this goal: The fund will be at the exclusive disposal of a neighbourhood and may be invested for the benefit of the community according to its own preferences. The target group may choose from a menu of typical investments, or can elaborate their own proposals. A better value from the allocated budget may be obtained through self-help inputs.

Self-organisation is required for the operation of these parochial projects, and this will help to stimulate and build up a strong and supportive community that is better prepared to put a stop to violence. Furthermore, it will foster the growth of collective self-esteem among the residents, and teach them the skills needed to obtain subsequent funding for community needs from third-party sources. Investments to be provided basically fall into three categories, namely technical infrastructure, measures directed towards a safer environment, and income generation:

- *Technical infrastructure*
  Townships were originally planned by the Apartheid government and commonly contain basic infrastructure. Allocation of residence was controlled by the authorities. However, with the fall of the Apartheid regime also came the freedom of residence, and may people arrived in the townships from the countryside and from the homelands. Many of them settled on the plots of friends and family, or squatted on empty land in and around the townships.
  The existing infrastructure could cope with the unplanned population increase, and the squatter areas still lack most basic facilities such as water, sanitation, footpaths, and storm water drainage. The Social Development Fund can provide for an economic infrastructure in the eligible settlements, like shallow sewer systems (10 % of normal cost), plastic piping for water connections, additional bucket-system toilets, and street lighting.
- *Safer environment*
  The environment can be improved and made safer through community efforts. Examples include playgrounds to keep children off the streets, peace gardens, safer pedestrian walkways and road crossings, the relocation of shebeens, and establishing an address system for the easy location of homes by police or other authorities.

- *Income generation and education*
  Provisions from the Fund can be invested directly in community-based income producing projects, like urban farming, or a waste recycling scheme. Neighbourhood-based pre-schools or other educational initiatives could receive special training. Cultural identity workshops and courses or a local history room could be funded. Special attention may be paid to arts and music projects (e.g. "township jazz"), as these provide a real opportunity for black, low-income residents to enter the national and even international stage.

Logistical support and complementary activities

"Invisible" development efforts, many of them logistical or educational, are at least as important as "hard" physical investments that can be visited and photographed. In this context, "Supporting Activities" may be defined as soft project elements that are essential for the safe nodes and the Development Fund to function, but also peace building, conflict management, and assistance to community self-administration would fall into this category, even if they could be directed towards the whole township of Khayelitsha, and not only to the residents living close to a secure node. Examples for Supporting Activities, as they were already identified in participatory workshops, include:

- Civil peace-building workshops dealing especially with female victims of violence and with conflict management.
- Awareness-raising campaigns on domestic rights and facilities for family conflict resolution.
- Conflict management and development programmes to avoid possible outbreaks of violence.
- Introductory civil rights training for members of Community Safety Forums.
- Training and internal administration support for Street Committees.
- Staff training for (especially informal) pre-schools.
- Training for KDF/KDT organs and delegates in preparation of safe node administration.
- Teacher training in adult education and preparation for self-employment and market-related skills in support of provided facilities.
- Training of staff for advice and counselling facilities to be provided.
- "Trusty taxi driver" and "Recognized shebeen" programmes.
- Housing design and finance management for replacement housing.
- Participatory design for community open space and housing.
- Cultural roots development (arts, collective memory, and history).

Part of the success of an improvement and development programme lies in the capability to detect and facilitate synergies with existing activities and possible projects by other stakeholders and development agencies—which is the role of urban management and governance. Particularly when considering the complexity of violence-prevention issues, complementary efforts should be well-coordinated and synchronised in order to produce a visible outcome and thus maintain the support of residents. After all, what was repeatedly criticised both by the population and by the experts is the lack of coordination of efforts by the municipality and private and voluntary stakeholders in their recent development efforts. Typical fields in which those complementary activities might be placed include:[19]

- Improvements to the criminal justice system.
- Improvements to the youth justice system.
- Technical infrastructure provision.
- Management support for infrastructure.
- Environmental improvements.
- Social Services (initiation camps, orphans hospices, old age homes, cemeteries).
- Business and job creation.
- Support to the projected Central Business District.
- Improvement of the transportation system.

From theory to practice

The Feasibility Study for a possible German Cooperation Project, on which this paper is based, has been prepared for the German Bank for Reconstruction and Development in 2002. The contract for the execution of the project was finally signed in 2005, and implementation will hopefully start in the same year. In the meantime, some circumstances have changed. Most staff and community leaders, who cooperated in the initial project formulation, have changed jobs and may have moved elsewhere. The business situation seem to have improved after the construction of a number of supermarkets, which does not necessarily create much employment, but improves shopping facilities and reduces the distance that residents have to walk carrying either money or goods. But violence remains a central concern, like elsewhere in South Africa—this is why another upgrading project with a focus on violence prevention with KfW support is already in the conception phase in Buffalo City, in the Eastern Cape Province.[20]

---

19 The Feasibility Study prepared for the KfW project recommended some 130 complementary projects and identified adequate third-party funding for most of them.
20 Another research project on urban violence in Southern Africa has been formulated at the PAR institute, Darmstadt University (www.par-darmstadt.de).

References

Dugard, Jackie (2001) "From Low Intensity War to Mafia War: Taxi violence in South Africa (1987–2000)". Violence and Transition Series 4. CSVR.

Fisher et al. (2000) *Working with Conflict: Skills and Strategies for Action*, London: ZED Books.

Kruger, Tinus/Landmann, Karina/Liebermann, Susan (2001) *A Manual for Crime Prevention through Planning and Design*, Pretoria: SCIR.

Liebermann, Susan/Landmann, Karina (2000) *A Manual for Community Based Crime Prevention*, Pretoria: CSIR/National Crime Prevention Centre.

Nedcor ISS (1999) Vol. 3– May to June.

Parry, CDH (2000) *Alcohol Abuse and Crime in the Western Cape*, Cape Town: SA Medical Research Council.

Homeland/Target:
Cities and the "War on Terror"

STEPHEN GRAHAM

Programmes of organized, political violence have always been legitimized and sustained through complex imaginative geographies. This chapter demonstrates that the Bush Administration's "war on terror" rests fundamentally on such dialectical constructions of (particularly urban) place. The essay argues that the discursive construction of the "war on terror" since September 11th 2001 has been deeply marked by attempts to rework imaginative geographies separating the urban places of the US "homeland" and those Arab cities purported to be the sources of "terrorist" threats against US national interests.[1]

Introduction

Programmes of organised, political violence are always sustained through imaginations of place and of geography. Whilst the places of the "homeland," which are purportedly defended tend to be sentimentalised and romanticised within such imaginations, those of the purported "enemy" are often simultaneously dehumanised and demonised. Crucially, such imaginative constructions of the "home" places, or territory to be protected, and the enemy places to be assaulted and turned into military targets, are therefore always manufactured together. The highly charged attachment to the homeland places works in parallel with calls to violence against a demonised, "foreign" place. Both of these constructions, moreover, often rest on homogenous imaginations of the

---

1 Some material in this chapter draws on an article published in the *International Journal of Urban and Regional Research* (2006).

two communities. Any sense that home or enemy places are actually diverse and made up of many diasporic, ethnic, and political groups tends to be lost in the recourse to absolute ideas of what is good, what is evil, and who is the righteous victim.

In what follows, I seek to demonstrate that George Bush's "war on terror" rests centrally on such a parallel sentimentalisation of US cities and the demonisation of Arab ones. In particular, the "war on terror" rests centrally on Bush's "with us or against us" rhetoric, which pits the "turf" and "homeland" of the continental US—spaces of intrinsic "freedom" to be "secured"—against the demonised and dehumanised cities of the Middle East. These are cast as intrinsically evil or barbarian places, labyrinthine and structureless cities that are, essentially, "nests" of terrorism to be assaulted and cleansed in order to save Freedom. Because of the inseparability of the imagination of homeland and target places in the "war on terror," it is inadequate to address the programme of "homeland security" or the US invasions of Iraq and Afghanistan in separation. Rather, the way places are represented within both these programmes needs to be looked at together.

This contribution does just this. It explores the two sides of place construction in the war on terror in an integrated way. On the one hand, then, an analysis is undertaken of the way in which the cities of the US homeland are, post 9/11, being represented as intensely vulnerable places requiring massive state effort at "homeland security." On the other, attention turns to the way in which the cities of Iraq are being widely represented by US politicians, US military commentators, the media, and in popular cultural spaces, as little but "nests of terrorism" to be assaulted through massive US military fire power.

As Edward Said's (1978) book, *Orientalism*, demonstrated, this two-sided construction of places is the latest in a centuries-old story. Ever since the dawn of Western colonial power, Arab cities have been represented by Western powers as dark, exotic, labyrinthine places that need to be "unveiled" for the production of "order" through the superior scientific and military technologies of the occupying West.

The Bush Administration's language of moral absolutism is, in particular, deeply Orientalist. It works by separating "the civilised world"—the "homeland" cities that must be "defended"—from the "dark forces," the "axis of evil," and the "terrorists nests" of Islamic cities, which are alleged to sustain the "evildoers" who threaten the health, prosperity, and democracy of the whole of the "free" world. The result of such geographical imaginations is an ahistorical and deeply Orientalist projection of Arab civilization that is very easily worked to recycle what Said called, just before his death, "the same unverifiable fictions and vast generalizations to stir up 'America' against the foreign devil" (Said, 2003: vi).

Discourses of "terrorism" are crucially important in sustaining such binaried notions of place, and the highly different values accorded to human lives in each zone that result. Central here is the principle of the absolute eternality of the "terrorist"—the inviolable inhumanity and shadowy, monster-like status of those deemed to be actual or dormant "terrorists," or those sympathetic to them. The unbound diffusion of terrorist labeling within the rhetoric of the "war on terror," moreover, works to allow virtually any political opposition to the sovereign power of the US and its allies to be condemned as "terrorist" or addressed through emergency "anti-terrorist" legislation. Protagonists of such opposition are thus dehumanized, demonized, and, above all, delegitimised.

Securitising "homeland" cities

The first element in the geographical imaginations that fuel the "war on terror" is an appeal by the Bush Administration to "securitise" the everyday urban spaces and infrastructures of the US "homeland." This is paralleled with endless cycles of manufactured fear, from the famous colour-coded warnings of the risk of terrorist threats, to a wide range of political adverts and media outputs carefully describing what a "dirty bomb" or vials or "anthrax" could do to a major US city. Paradoxically, the programme for "homeland security" relies, then, on the manufacture and endless extension of pervasive feelings of insecurity.

Here, endless discussions of "security" emphasize a virtually infinite range of threats from a limitless range of people, places, and technologies—all to justify a massive process of state building. The basic spaces and systems of everyday life in US cities—airport immigration points, the Internet, the postal system, subway and train networks, the electricity grid, street grids, public spaces, the water systems—are portrayed as geographical or technological borders through which a potentially threatening "Other" might leap at any time or place. Vast efforts are being made by US political, military, and media elites, in particular, to spread what Jonathon Raban (2004 3) recently called a "generalized promiscuous anxiety through the American populace, a sense of imminent but inexact catastrophe" lurking just beneath the surface of normal, technologised, (sub)urbanised, everyday life in the US.

This reimagining of "homeland" cities involves four related areas of work. First, a massive process of "re-bordering" is underway. This has involved a reimagination of the nature of US civil society as a bounded, national space whose flows and connections elsewhere—of people, information, commodities, and money—can be demarcated, surveilled, and carefully filtered. Most obviously, this involves the militarisation of national borders, the insistence of

279

biometric passports for all nations who have a visa waiver agreement with the US, and the installation of a wide range of "smart" sniffing and detection devices through the technological fabric of US cities. Radiation sniffers now straddle the entrances to container ports. Anthrax detectors inhabit the innards of the postal system. New York police officers carry portable devices for detecting "dirty bombs". And so on. Jonathan Raban captures the palpable transformation of US urban landscapes well. "To live in America now," he writes:

> at least to live in a port city like Seattle – is to be surrounded by the machinery and rhetoric of covert war, in which everyone must be treated as a potential enemy until they can prove themselves a friend. Surveillance and security devices are everywhere: the spreading epidemic of razor wire, the warnings in public libraries that the FBI can demand to know what books you're borrowing, the Humvee laden with troops in combat fatigues, the Coast Guard gun boats patrolling the bay, the pat-down searches and X-ray machines, the nondescript grey boxes equipped with radar antennae, that are meant to sniff pathogens in the air (2004: 4).

Second, major crackdowns have occurred on diasporic social groups deemed potentially to harbour, or provide sympathy to, terrorist groups. Arab-American communities, in particular, have faced the brunt of this escalation of state incarceration, profiling, and repression as McCarthyist obsessions with the "enemy within" have been Orientalised on the post 9/11 world. Tellingly, the largest Arab-American community in the US, the Detroit suburb of Dearborn, was the first city district to receive a local departmental office of Homeland Security.

In most mainstream US media discussions, such places have been portrayed unerringly as zones of threat. They are represented as homes to people who, whilst being US citizens, must, inevitably, be loyal to the "terrorists" who, as we shall see shortly, are judged by many neo-conservative commentators to be the sole inhabitants of the enemy zone (Middle Eastern cities like Fallujah). Consequently, "Arab" and "American" are widely portrayed as antithetical adjectives in the mainstream US media since 9/11.

Third, a broader chill on dissent has been notable in post-9/11 USA, as anyone deemed to be insufficiently patriotic within the escalating militaristic fervour has been increasingly vulnerable to accusations that they, too, have sympathy with "terrorists." Notable here has been the campuswatch.org campaign, where Middle Eastern scholars across the US who have been espousing the work of Said or other postcolonial scholars have been publicly "exposed" and students attending their sessions have been urged to denounce their professors in class.

Finally, the very language of "homeland security" invoked by the new state apparatus has played a vital role. Crucially, it has worked to problematise the sorts of cosmopolitan and diasporic mixing which is now the dominant feature of most US cities. This language, which uses "folksy" words like "turf," as well as the endless use of the word "homeland" itself, is intrinsically anti-cosmopolitan, anti-urban, and anti-immigrant. Paul Gilroy (2003: 274) recently argued that the widespread invocation by the Bush Administration, following Samuel Huntingdon, of the idea of a "clash of civilizations," necessarily "requires that cosmopolitan consciousness is ridiculed" in the pronouncements of the US state and the mainstream media.

This geographical reimagination of the US "homeland," in a world of intensifying connection, mobility, and porosity, means that a sort of homogeneous community within US cities of authentic, patriotic US citizens is being suggested. Such an imagination undermines the legitimacy of large swathes of the social fabric of the nation. First Tom Ridge, the Homeland Security Secretary, for example, has widely argued that, post-9/11, "the only turf is the turf we stand on." This suggests that the US nation is a singular, almost ruralised and domestic community that is tied closely to the "turf" of the land.

This geographically fixed imaginary, with its strong borders separating the US "turf" from the outside world, contrasts starkly with the language of previous generations of US politicians who widely celebrated the boundless sense of mobility, possibility, immigration, and assimilation within US nation building. As Amy Kaplan (2003) has argued, the reality of an urban, multi-ethnic USA, with many competing turfs and multiple points of view—a reality which was, ironically, demonstrated by the large number of nationalities represented on the lists of dead on September 11th 2001—is therefore denied. Instead, the language and programme of "homeland security" hints that a privileged, singular community exists of those settled and authentic US social groups whose deep connections with their "turf" mean that they can be relied upon to be sufficiently patriotic.

The positions of more recent waves of immigrants, meanwhile—especially "illegal" ones—become dramatically more perilous. This is especially so as such groups have been widely linked in the media with "terrorist" groups, allowing many of their members have been incarcerated, both within the US and in the extra-territorial "camp" at Guanttánamo Bay, without trial and with the possibility of remaining in captivity until death. As with the civilians of Iraq and Afghanistan who have died in the wars, then, the reimagining of the geography of the US "homeland" has played a crucial role of stripping demonised groups of both life chances and even the right to life.

Constructing Arab cities as military targets

Inseparable from such reimaginations of the geographies of the US national space, a many-stranded effort has been underway since 9/11 to portray certain Middle Eastern cities as intrinsically barbarian and terroristic spaces. This has been necessary to legitimise their assault by massive US fire power, allegedly to protect the "freedom" of the sentimentalised places of the US homeland. These two parallel discourses have worked powerfully to establish the absolute separation of the "us" and the "them," a separation that allowed the huge violence against the everyday spaces of Iraq and Afghanistan to be legitimised.

This invocation of assaults of demonised places to protect the places of the "homeland," of course, is actually a very large part of the story of the legitimisation of the assault on Iraq. The WMD attack on European and US cities within 45 minutes is a crucial example here. But the pronouncements of Bush and Blair are only the tip of the iceberg here. Much less discussed, but perhaps more powerful still, have been the way in which Iraqi and Afghani cities have been portrayed as little but targets for ordnance within a wide range of media, military, and computer-game environments. It is worth exploring a few examples of how this has been done.

First, the voyeuristic consumption by Western publics of the US urban bombing campaigns, which have been such a dominant feature of the "war on terror," is itself based on representations where cities are actually constructed as little more than receiving points for the dropping of murderous weaponry. Vertical web and newspaper maps, in particular, have routinely displayed cities like Baghdad as little more than a collection of impact points where GPS-targeted bombs and missiles are either envisaged to land, or have landed, are grouped along flat, cartographic surfaces viewed as if from space (Gregory 2004a). Meanwhile, the weapons' actual impacts on the everyday life for the tens of thousands of ordinary Iraqis or Afghanis who are caught up in the bombing, as "collateral damage," have been both marginalised and violently repressed by the US military. Most famously, this has involved the bombing of Al-Jazeera transmission facilities because they transmitted images of the dead civilians that resulted from the bombing. As Derek Gregory (2004b) has argued, in these representations, Arab "cities" are thus reduced to the "places and people you are about to bomb, to targets, to letters on a map or coordinates on a visual display."

Strikingly, the failure even to count the 100,000 or so dead Iraqi civilians that had resulted, by December 2004, from the war's bombing campaigns and urban battles (Roberts et al. 2004), reveals that the civilians of targeted cities are "cast out" so that they warrant no legal status or visual presence. In stark contrast to the inviolable lives lost on 9/11, because they are deemed to inhabit intrinsically "terrorist" places, their sacrifice can go largely unremarked; their bloody deaths can go blindly unrepresented.

Second, such casting out of the lives and suffering of ordinary civilians is legitimized and obscured in the "war on terror" by a wider discourse in which entire cities of such victims are portrayed as little more than "factories" or "nests" sustaining "terrorists" and "extremists." To achieve this, huge efforts are being made by both the US military and the mainstream US media to construct Islamic cities as dehumanized "terror cities"—nest-like environments whose very geography undermines the high-tech, orbital mastery of US forces. For example as a major battle raged there in April 2004 in which over 600 Iraqi civilians died, General Richard Myers, Chair of the US Joint Chiefs of Staff, labeled the whole of Fallujah a dehumanized "rat's nest" or "hornet's nest" of "terrorist resistance" against US occupation that needed to be "dealt with" (quoted by News24.com).

In the bloody urban battles of 2004 for Saddam City, Fallujah, and Najaf, the promulgations of the US military forces fighting in Iraq—and their leaders back in the US proper—have also routinely blended Islamophobic racism and crude Orientalism. Again, this worked continually to reinforce the perception that these cities are little but "nests" of terrorist violence that necessitate targeting by superior US surveillance technologies and military firepower which will somehow act to "cleanse" or redeem the intrinsically terroristic urban places of Iraq. "The Iraqis are sick people and we are the chemotherapy," boasted one US Marine to the New Statesman in April 2003.

Widespread pronouncements of the fighting US soldiers themselves illustrate these geographical imaginaries all too clearly. US Marine snipers, after the battle of Fallujah, for example, talked exultantly about their "kills" of "rag-heads" and "sand niggers" in Fallujah (Davis 2004). Shocked senior British officers in Iraq—whose forces are far from blameless in terms of brutality against Iraqi civilians—even alleged (anonymously) that American forces often viewed Iraqi civilians as *Untermenschen* (the Nazis' word for subhuman). This view, of course, has been reinforced by the extending list of prison torture scandals that have erupted since the end of the 2003.

Added to these street-level discourses, a large group of professional "urban warfare" commentators, writing regular columns in US newspapers, have routinely projected deeply racist notions implying that the inhabitants of targeted Iraqi cities are merely subhuman pests requiring extermination. An important example comes from the highly influential "urban warfare" commentator, Ralph Peters, writing in the neo-conservative *New York Post*.

To Peters and many like him, cities like Fallujah and Najaf are little more than killing zones that challenge the US military to harness its techno-scientific might to sustain hegemony. This must be done, he argues, by killing "terrorists" as rapidly and efficiently—and with as few US casualties—as possible. During the battle of Fallujah, Peters labeled the entire City a "terror-city" in his column. Praising the US Marines "for hammering the terrorists into the dirt" in the battle, he nevertheless castigated the cease-fire negotiations that, he argued, had allowed those "terrorists" left alive to melt back into the civilian population (2004a).

In a later *New York Post* article, Peters (2004b) concluded that a military, technological solution was available to US forces that would enable them to "win" such battles more conclusively in the future: killing faster, before any international media coverage is possible. "This is the new reality of combat," he wrote. "Not only in Iraq. But in every broken country, plague pit and terrorist refuge to which our troops have to go in the future." Arguing that the presence of "global media" meant that "a bonanza of terrorists and insurgents" were allowed to "escape" US forces in Fallujah, US forces, he argued "have to speed the kill." By "accelerating urban combat" to "fight within the 'media cycle' before journalists sympathetic to terrorists and murderers can twist the facts and portray us as the villains," new technologies were needed, Peters suggested. This was so that "our enemies are overwhelmed and destroyed before hostile cameras can defeat us. If we do not learn to kill very, very swiftly, we will continue to lose slowly." It is arguments like Peters' that have been central in constructing Fallujah as the crucial, symbolic space of resistance within the whole Iraqi insurgency. Such a symbolism has made the destruction of resistance in Fallujah a central objective of US forces.

Third, the construction of Arab cities as targets for US military firepower now sustains a large industry of computer gaming and simulation. Such simulations—which are created especially to create positive images for the US military amongst younger computer game users—propel the player into the world of the gaming industry's latest obsession: modern urban warfare. They work to further reinforce imaginary geographies equating Islamic cities with "terrorism" and US military intervention.

Such games serve to further blur the boundaries separating war from entertainment. Worse still, they demonstrate that the entertainment industry is actively collaborating in constructing a culture of permanent war. Within such games, Arab cities are represented merely as environments for participants to enter in search of animalised "terrorists" to kill repeatedly (without blood or screams). When people are represented, they are the shadowy, subhuman, racialised figures of absolutely external "terrorists" to be annihilated repeatedly in sanitized "action" as entertainment or military training (or both). Andrew Deck (2004), writing on the website *No Quarter*, argues that the proliferation of urban warfare games based on actual, ongoing, US military interventions in Arab cities, works to "call forth a cult of ultra-patriotic xenophobes whose greatest joy is to destroy, regardless of how racist, imperialistic, and flimsy the rationale" for the simulated battle.

These representations, of course, resonate strongly with the pronouncements of military urban warfare specialists in the wider media like those of Ralph Peters discussed above. They also blur with increasing seamlessness into news reports about the actual Iraq war. Kuma Reality Games, for example, which has actually sponsored Fox News' coverage of the "war on terror" in the US, uses this sponsorship to promote an urban combat game. In their words, this centres on US Marines fighting "militant followers of radical Shiite cleric Muqtaqa al-Sadr in the filthy urban slum that is Sadr city."

The US Army—which now brands itself as "the world's premier land force"—itself works hard and at many levels to demonize Arab urbanism per se through the medium of video games. In fact, it is now one of the world's biggest developers of video games, which it now deliberately deploys as aids to training and recreation amongst US soldiers and the generation of both recruits and revenue.

The US Army now gives urban warfare computer games such as *America's Army*—with its simulations of "counter terror" warfare in densely packed Islamic cities in the fictional country of "Zekistan"—free to millions over the Internet as an aid to recruitment. *America's Army* has been followed up by the even more elaborate game, *Full Spectrum Warrior*, another ex-military training video game in which US forces again wage urban warfare in simulations of Middle Eastern cities, whilst this time dispensing racist and Islamophobic expletives. Even some video game reviewers have criticised the racism of the game. One reviewer on the *GamingAge* website argued that "this game would have been fine without the tawdry 4 letter words and negative racist remarks" from the simulated US soldiers. Such racist remarks have done little to inhibit the game's popularity, however. Writing in a chat room on the neo-conservative *FreeRepublic.Com*, one reviewer of the game gushes that, "given the current state of the world, it's amazingly relevant, not to mention fun to fire on raghead terrorist wanna-be's."

Finally, to parallel such virtual, voyeuristic, "Othering" of Arab cities, US and Western military forces have constructed their own simulations of Islamic cities as targets—this time in physical space. A chain of 80 mock "Islamic" urban districts have been built across the world since 9/11 designed purely to hone the skills of US forces in fighting and killing in "urbanized terrain." Taking 18 months to construct, these simulated "cities" are then endlessly destroyed and remade in practice assaults that hone the US forces for the "real thing" in sieges such as those in Fallujah.

Replete with minarets, pyrotechnic systems, loop-tapes with calls to prayer, donkeys, hired "civilians" in Islamic dress wandering through narrow streets, and olfactory machines to create the smell of rotting corpses, this shadow urban system simulates not the complex cultural, social, or physical realities of real Middle Eastern urbanism. Rather, it reflects the imaginative geographies of the military and theme park designers that are brought in to design and construct it.

Conclusions

This brief essay has shown that Bush's "war on terror" rests fundamentally on imaginations of geography which necessarily represent both the cities of the United States and those of the Middle East in highly charged ways. Given the highly urbanised nature of both the USA and Iraq, highly contrasting and symbolically charged representations of cities are the central pivot of such imaginative geographies. Such geographical imaginations, far from being of mere academic curiosity, have done, and are doing, massive political and geopolitical work. Without their widespread acceptance and recycling, and their incessant symbolic violence, the war on Iraq, simply put, would have been impossible. Without the flowing of racist and incendiary representations of Arab urbanism as little more than a domain for the killing of "terrorists" in a wide swathe of US popular culture, the war could not have been sustained. And without the careful construction of imagined geographical zones of peace from those of war, the casting out of civilians who die as "collateral damage," or who are thrown into extraterritorial camps with no legal rights—potentially to the end their days—could not have occurred so effectively.

This is because the successful construction of the geographical imaginaries outlined in this essay has, very literally, worked to demarcate where death is of consequence and where it is not. It has provided the mental and psychic guidance for ethical decisions of where human beings have worth and must be protected and where they do not and can be killed with no recourse to visibility, ethical dilemma, or risk of illegality. More troubling still, these implicit, but all-important, distinctions have been routinely re-circulated in the "popular geopolitical" spaces of entertainment and the voyeuristic consumption of war.

The ultimately tragedy of the geographical imaginaries that are at the root of the "war on terror," however, is that they are almost indistinguishable from those invoked by Osama Bin Laden. Whilst the homeland and target places are obviously reversed in Bin Laden's rhetoric, the geographical imaginaries invoked by both Bush and Bin Laden are otherwise startlingly and depressingly alike. Both assert the power of righteous victimhood and the inviolate importance of homeland cities, whilst at the same time projecting a God-driven violence on the demonised Other—whether it be places or people. Both invoke homogenous notions of community and deligitimise, or demonise, the cosmopolitan and diasporic mixing in cities that is the very essence of contemporary social change. Both cast out the dehumanised civilians who inhabit targeted places, and who die as a result of the called-for violence, from any legal, ethical, or theological protection. And both benefit from the inevitable circle of atrocity, or terror and counter-terror, which results.

The challenge, then, is to collectively dismantle both these self-reinforcing fundamentalisms, along with their associated baggage of hate-filled geographical imaginaries, which together work to sustain this dance of death. Only by achieving this, and by pushing all such fundamentalisms to the lunatic fringes where they belong, might the possibility of building up tolerant, cosmopolitan, and transnational civil societies on our rapidly urbanising planet realistically emerge.

This is not to romanticise multicultural cities or to see them as panaceas. Far from it. All such mixing is necessarily ambivalent; hatred, tension, and misanthropy are inevitably leavened through all such cities. Rather, it is to stress that such cities are now the norm and to urge that all political and geographical imaginaries should only be considered legitimate when they take this as a basic starting point. In today's world, all calls to homogenous community, and all geographical imaginations based on them, can do little but end up being calls to violence.

References

Davis, Mike (2004) "The Pentagon as global slum lord". TomDispatch: http://www.tomdispatch.com/, 19 April, accessed June 10th.
Deck, Andy (2004) "Demilitarizing the playground". No Quarter: http://artcontext.net/crit/essays/noQuarter/.
Gilroy, Paul (2003) "'Where ignorant armies clash by night': Homogeneous community and the planetary aspect". International Journal of Cultural Studies 6, pp. 261–276.
Gregory, Derek (2004a) *The Colonial Present*, Oxford: Blackwell.
Gregory, Derek (2004b), "Who's responsible? Dangerous geography". ZNet: www.znet.org, 3 May, accessed May 10, 2004.
Kaplan, Amy (2003) "Homeland insecurities: Reflections on language and space". Radical History Review 85, pp. 82–93.
News24.com (2004) "Fallujah a 'rat's nest'". www.news24.com, 21 April, accessed 15 June 2004.
Peters, Ralph (2004a) "Getting Iraq right". New York Post, 29 April, www.nypost.com, accessed 10 June 2004.
Peters, Ralph (2004b) "He who hesitates". New York Post, 27 April, www.nypost.com, accessed 10 June 2004.
Raban, Jonathan (2004) "Running scared". The Guardian, 21 July, pp. 3–7.
Roberts, Les/Lafta, Riyah/Garfield, Richard/Khudhairi, Jamal/Burnham, Gilbert, (2004) "Mortality before and after the 2003 invasion of Iraq: Cluster sample survey". The Lancet 29 October, pp. 1–8.
Said, Edward (1978) *Orientalism*, London: Routledge and Kegan Paul.
Said, Edward (2003) *Orientalism*, 2003 Edition, London: Penguin.

Terrorism and the Right to the Secure City: Safety vs. Security in Public Spaces

Peter Marcuse

The threat of terrorism has been manipulated in the United States to achieve political results that reinforce the established power structure. This has been done by vastly expanding what is held out to be the threat, substituting false for legitimate responses, and making the issue one of ontological security rather than reasonable safety. The result has been a severe limitation on residents' right to the city, a limitation particularly visible in restrictions on their use of public spaces The threat of terrorism has thus been used to restrict democracy in cities and across the nation.

The argument

A great deal is at issue in the manipulation of the threat of terrorism in the United States today. While various abuses of civil liberties and common sense have been involved in the governmental responses to the threat of terrorism, the most serious may be the sale of the threat as a threat to existential security, instead of one threat among others to public safety. The result after 9/11 has been to reinforce the positions of those in power and to limit further the freedom that is at the heart of the right to the city. The current treatment of public space illustrates the process.

The argument proceeds as follows: The threat of terrorism includes both legitimate and false responses generated by government. The most damaging of the false responses is the manipulation of the threat to present it as a risk to existential security, rather than as a matter of public safety. The distinction between security and safety is crucial to understanding this situation.

False responses are damaging in three ways: they suppress analysis, inquiry, and criticism; they restrict and pervert the uses of public spaces, both directly limiting political uses and indirectly restricting popular functions. While the surveillance of public space is only a small part of what converts the threat of terrorism from an issue of safety to one of insecurity, it is part of an increasingly omnipresent imposition of awareness of the narrowing of the scope of the right to the city. But most pervasively, they limit fundamentally the right to the city, understood as the freedom of individuals to develop their capacities fully in a society of support and solidarity. Finally, I want to end with a somewhat tongue-in-cheek suggestion about a better way to handle the matter.

Two preliminary remarks:
The threat of terrorism is of course not unique historically in playing the role of legitimating existing power relations. Patriotism/chauvinism, at the extreme going to war; racism; responses to other catastrophes, including national disasters and individual tragedies, such as assassinations; fear of social unrest, have all been put to similar uses. As this is written, President Bush is calling for an expenditure of over $9 billion dollars to meet the threat of avian flu; political commentators see this as a public relations move to relegitimate a federal government whose standing has been severely damaged by its (failed) response to hurricane Katrina. But the threat of terrorism is not only the most current large case of this pattern, it also relies to an unusual degree on the replacement of concerns for public safety with a manipulation of causes of existential insecurity, a point taken up in detail below.

Further: aspects of what is described below as the response to terrorism seem unique to the United States: orange alerts, a Department of Homeland Security, and certainly the invasion of Iraq justified as a defense against terrorism. One notices the difference in daily conversations, in media reporting, in airport security, in reactions to the use of military force: for most Europeans, the risk of terrorism is a small risk and one risk among others, not a pervasive concern of government or political discourse.

There are several possible explanations for the difference: cultural ones that relate to attitudes towards violence; or prejudice against others (although the United States is a nation of immigrants and tolerance might be more expected here); racism, although terrorists are not African American or black—the traditional objects of racist prejudices; a higher level of insecurity in the absence of welfare-state guarantees of a respectable safety net.[1] Or it may be that, because the attack on the World Trade Center was the first incursion of an outside power on the territory of the United States since 1810, while whole European countries have historically seen multiple invasions, that the response has been so disproportionate here. Or it may be (the explanation that seems to me most satisfactory) that in Europe the legitimacy of the state has been, in different forms, that it serves a welfare function, true of authoritarian as well a democratic regimes, while in the United States that function has been in severe decline for at least the last decade. Thus extensive state action is not legitimated in the United States, and meets sharp resistance. Yet extensive state action is required to protect and extend its economic prosperity and international power. The portrayal of terrorism as a life-threatening danger can thus play the role of legitimating extensive government action. Other threats to public safety, e.g. epidemics or extreme poverty, might require welfare-type actions which the regime does not desire; hence the threat of terrorism must be distinguished from these threats, and is made into a threat to "security" of an over-riding nature, rather than just another threat to safety. Or it may simply be another example of a complex American exceptionalism.

The legitimacy of the responses to the threat of terrorism

Security in the face of a declared threat of terrorism dominates much of the discussion about city life in the United States today, with frequent reference to the events of September 11, 2001 (9/11). Does the government, and do the dominant institutions in the United States, give appropriate weight to the threat of terrorism after 9/11? How are responses to the threat related to the events of 9/11?

The basic argument of this paper is that a great deal has changed in what is done purportedly in response to the threat of terrorism since 9/11. I argue that there have been both legitimate and false responses to the perceived threat. The impact of the legitimate response is almost trivial, representing more of a continuation of trends already in place before 9/11 rather than something new. In contrast, the impact of the false response has been substantial. The false response has used the threat of terrorism as a pretext to bring about changes that have nothing to do with physical safety or protection against terrorism, but implement quite unrelated agendas. In New York City, those agendas have sometimes had to do with changes in real-estate values in

---

[1] I have argued elsewhere that this higher level of social insecurity explains the United States' preoccupation with crime generally, as well as with terrorism. (Marcuse, 2004).

lower Manhattan. In general, however, the implicit agenda has been to increase the political control of dissent, to limit debate about some general direction of policies, and to control the use of public space for democratic but dissident purposes. That implicit agenda has been advanced since 9/11 under the pretext of the threat of terrorism, not in legitimate response to it. I do not, however, claim that this political agenda and these limitations on the use of public space are new or solely related to 9/11; again, the pattern precedes 9/11, although it has intensified since then.

Let me begin by specifying what I mean by legitimate and false responses to terrorism:

	Type of Response	Impact	Examples
Legitimate	Targeted responses	Directed at grounded risks, regardless of costs	Efficient— metal detectors at airports Inefficient— shoe removal at airports
	Balanced responses	Attempting to balance risks against economic and civil rights costs	Surveillance cameras at entries to public buildings; inefficient targeted responses
False	Directly repressive responses	Curtailing activities or restricting individual rights unrelated to terrorism	Ethnic profiling, immigrant restrictions, "No Loitering" signs at train stations, Patriot Act
	Manipulated climate responses	Creating a pervasive atmosphere of fear about terrorism, substituting security for public safety as the goal	Orange alerts, election rhetoric, constrained assemblies, surveillance in public spaces, fortifying/ bunkering buildings

Table 1: False and legitimate responses to terrorism

Targeted responses are effective responses directed to eliminate grounded threats of terrorism. The goal of targeted responses is to eliminate essentially all risk from the targeted threat. Targeted responses share two characteristics: there is a substantial basis for the belief that the risks at which they are directed are real, and the measures aimed at guarding against those risks use the minimum resources and cause the minimum disruption needed to achieve their objectives. Metal detectors at airports fall into this category; other airport security measures (such as taking off one's shoes or having dogs sniff passengers or luggage) may be ineffective or inefficient. At the margin, some balancing (of what?) is also involved; a very complex security measure that reduces risk only to a trivial extent may not be appropriate. But the decision as to what measures are appropriate is, at least in the first instance, a technical one in which the capabilities of various technologies and the evaluation of intelligence information are key, and on which I claim no expertise, even though some measures in effect today seem, to me, to defy common sense.

Balanced responses take into account the absolute costs of eliminating grounded threats, and attempt to strike a balance between physical safety and economic or social cost. The harm that could be done at a crowded subway station in New York City, for instance, might be great, but the disruption caused by any serious measure to avoid the risk of that harm would be tremendous. As a result, no action is taken. For example, posting signs that say "If You See Something, Say Something" in train stations is not likely to eliminate much risk. Yet the importance of large numbers of people getting to work without a huge waste of time outbalances the protection that any further measures might provide against the risks involved.

False responses are actions not reasonably related to the threat of terrorism, but put forward as justified by that threat. Some, those that are directly *repressive responses*, limit conventional civil rights. They include bans on demonstrations, or their restriction in manners calculated to limit their effectiveness in gross disproportion to the dangers they might cause; and, in disregard of alternative, less restrictive measures, provisions of the Patriot Act punishing speech posing no clear and present danger, arrests and incarcerations without the normal protections of due process. *Manipulated climate responses* are less directly repressive. They create a climate of fear and insecurity in which normal and peaceful activities that may be critical of existing policies or practices are inhibited, in which a pervasive awareness of a superordinate power is created. They include yellow, orange, and red alerts; the stationing of National Guard troops in public spaces, transport facilities, and important buildings; jersey barriers and bollards around buildings; warning signs and loudspeaker messages suggesting the dangers of unattended packages or unusual behavior; the replacement of glass with concrete on the lower floors of new buildings (up to 20 stories, in the case of the planned "Freedom Tower" at the World Trade Center site); constantly reiterated references to the "war against terrorism" in public speeches, news articles, and media presentations; restricting access to public buildings and public spaces; random searches of bags and packages, etc. Their effect is to put questioning of dominant state practices out of bounds, and to produce informal reactions within civil society that stultify free speech.

Private and public responses to the threat of terrorism thus range from legitimate to false, from balanced to manipulated. The line between them is not always clear, but the extreme cases are. The stereotyping of what a terrorist looks like, with all its racial and religious overtones, clearly is a false response, as is stockpiling duct tape as a defense against biological terrorism.[2] And, it appears that individuals in suburban communities have been more likely to alter their habits in response to the threat of terrorism, to be suspicious of strangers, to post police in public spaces and at public events, and to guard their public buildings than individuals in far-denser urban centers, where presumably the threat is greater. Thus there is a subjective factor in the response, and one conditioned by characteristics of class, and likely of race, of gender, and of age. But our concern here is with the external and public aspects of the response, rather than variations in the subjective reactions to it.

And there are cross- and counter-currents to the manipulated response. On the one side, many people object to the intrusive character of many of the manipulated responses, and some planners and architects have devoted themselves to the search for forms that conceal the anti-terror aspects of some measures: making concrete barriers with flower planters on top, making bollards inconspicuous, finding social uses for extreme setbacks, etc.[3] And at some point people simply ignore the proclaimed threats: subway ridership in New York City remains the same whatever level of "threat" may be announced by the authorities. At the same time, other measures are taken solely for the purpose of giving publicity to the threat, hammering home its dangers: the stationing of police or National Guard troops at very visible public locations, where in fact their function is not to be prepared to take action but simply to raise consciousness of danger, the random search of bags on mass transit, etc., are all calculated to manipulate awareness of the threat of terrorism.

Buttressing power: security vs. safety

At the heart of the effectiveness of manipulated responses is a basic shift in the perspective on the threat of terrorism, a transformation of a threat to public safety to a threat to existential security. Thus, the threat of terrorism is presented as an issue of security rather than of safety, and used politically not only in the narrow sense of partisan politics but more broadly to justify major infringements on not only the use of public space, but also the rights to the city.

So what is the difference between security and safety? And what difference does it make? There are key differences between threats to safety and to security:

---

2 I would go further and argue that the election of George W. Bush was in large part a result of a false response to the threat of terrorism, but that brings us outside the scope of this article.

3 Cf. the Washington, D.C., Metropolitan Planning Agency's guidelines and citations in Vale (2005).

Existential insecurity
- Long-term unemployment
- Cancer
- Rejection in love

Acceptable unsafety—assessed risks
- Urban life
- Remote risks
- Involuntary risks
- Calculated hope of gain
- Gambling

Both involve risk, not in Beck's terms. In common usage, insecurity also describes uncertainty about minor details of everyday life: not knowing directions is referred to as being insecure when driving—which way to turn at an intersection, how not to get lost in a strange city—but that might simply be referred to as *unsureness,* and is not the concern here. Other examples of the difference between insecurity and unsafeness can be listed:

Other examples of insecurity
- Homelessness
- Generally uncertainty as to the availability of satisfaction of basic needs, including food, shelter, health care, old age support, and education (cf. Millennium list, UN Declaration of Human Rights)

Less dramatic examples
- Avoiding urban public spaces
- Retreating to gated communities in the suburbs
- Not leaving home after an extended youth
- Wanting to work behind Jersey barriers, fences, gates, and street setbacks to protect United States buildings
- Wanting to work in a tower with the elimination of windows up to the height of up to twenty stories. I proposed that Freedom Tower, planned for the World Trade Center site, be renamed the "high-rise bunker."

Examples of public actions positively increasing security
- Social security
- Anti-eviction legislation
- Universal free medical care
- An effective FEMA

Examples of activities involving safety and risk
- Generally understanding and acceptance of risk
- Jaywalking
- Driving normally
- Living in the city: no one expects to live in the city without risk, risk is accepted as part of the urban, part of what makes a city a city in the sense I impute to Lefebvre
- Courtship, perhaps love itself

Examples of unsafe activities
- Driving drunk
- Swimming with an unknown undertow

Examples of public actions increasing safety
- Warning signs
- Often, police presence
- Enforcement of traffic rules
- Some airport security measures (banning knives: yes, removing shoes: no).

A current example of the difference: In New Orleans, we know that the residents of low-lying areas were unsafe even before Katrina, but their experiences in the convention center and the Superdome and the mismanagement of the authorities produced, I would argue, a feeling of insecurity that was qualitatively different from the unsafety experienced before the storm.

Let me try a formal definition: Unsafety is the exposure to risk, but involves the recognition and acceptance of known risks and the decision to accept or avoid the risk remaining after it has been assessed and voluntarily chosen risk minimizations have been implemented. It assumes satisfaction that the risk and benefits of alternative courses of action are understood and taken into account, with confidence that the course of action decided on is right. Insecurity is existential. It involves doubt about risk, and fear of risk. It does not measure risk of harm or extent of benefit, but assumes risk is unknowable in its extent—it cannot be "assessed"—it is unavoidable in occurrence and beyond human control—there is no alternative to taking the risk and simply attempting to minimize its adverse consequences. It assumes that the understanding of risk is uncertain, both in probability and in scope, and involves no confidence that the course of action decided on is right, yet maintains that is must nevertheless be taken.

There is not an absolute division, and many cases are borderline, and there is certainly a subjective element involved. The responses of different individuals to different risks will vary. When the federal government declares an orange risk for the subways of New York City, the reaction of the New York City Police Department to put police very visibly, and with much publicity, on many (but a minority of) cars is calculated to increase insecurity, and will be seen by some as a reason to avoid the subway—but the overwhelming majority of New Yorkers will continue to use it. As indeed did the majority of train riders in Madrid and Underground riders in London—seeing the threat of further terrorism as simply another question of safety, assessing the risk, and riding.

The distinction between security and safety is key to understanding the true impact of the current manipulation of the threat of terrorism. Let me return to that argument.

The threat of terrorism as imposing insecurity

I argue, then, that the responses to terrorism of the character I have outlined earlier produce, and are manipulated to produce, an atmosphere of insecurity, one that goes far beyond a concern for public safety. And the threat is pushed as an issue of security for a specific political purpose: control. In a general discussion of the politics of fear—I take insecurity to be virtually synonymous with his usage—Frank Furedi says: "Today, the objective of the politics of fear is to gain consensus and to forge a measure of unity around an otherwise disconnected elite. [...] its main effect is to enforce the idea that there is no alternative." (The New York Times, 2005).[4] No alternative to the continuing maintenance in office of the present administration, and more generally, no alternative to the continued rule of the existing elite. Furedi speaks of "fear entrepreneurs" as the actors promoting the politics of fear. In the United States today, those fear entrepreneurs, those selling insecurity, can be rather readily identified, and the directly political results of their efforts may be the key explanation for the victory of George W. Bush in the 2004 election.

In the broader sense, the use of the threat of terrorism to promote a sense of insecurity, its formulation as an issue of security rather than safety, not only undergirds a particular political agenda but also limits freedom and restricts the right to the city in general. And we can see this manifest in the way the threat of terrorism and the insecurity it promotes is used to affect the use of public space—as in the Republican National Convention case.

---

4   He is explicit: "The politics of fear is a manipulative project that aims to immobilise public 'dissent.'"

Public space as a case in point

City planning is concerned with the physical space of cities. City planners believe that public spaces should be adequate, open, usable, and accessible to all. We see public spaces, in a sense, as the symbols of a democratic and open city. New York City has some great public spaces, including Central Park, Union Square, and much of the waterfront. The debate over the protests surrounding the Republican National Convention demonstrates that the presence of physically adequate public space is not enough to achieve that openness, that democracy, that urban planners want to see in cities. The management and control of space in the city, as well as its physical aspects, are at stake. New York has become a city of control; the political authorities, rather than the people, determine how the city and its public spaces are used. In the controlled city, rights can best be exercised at home, in private, not in public.

The impact of the threat of terrorism on public spaces in cities has been substantial. Henri Lefebvre, the French Marxist intellectual, viewed public space as representative of the physical nexus of a humane and urban life, as a form of lived space in which the right to the city could be exercised (cf. Lefebvre 1996).

Condoleezza Rice has lately taken to quoting the definition of democracy advanced by Nathan Sharansky: Can an individual say what he or she wishes, standing in the middle of the largest public square in town, without fear of arrest or harassment? In this view, which harks back to a view that sees public space, the agora, the forum, as central to democracy, the openness of pubic spaces becomes the essence of democracy. It is collective action, not individual action, communicative action, not self-expression, that is at the core of the democratic use of public space (cf. Habermas 1984).

I use the phrase "public space" in the lived sense, not in the legal sense. This view implies a broader conception of public space than a formal, legal one that looks at ownership as the defining criteria for publicness. I mean public space in its social sense, space that is lived as open and communicative, seen and felt and treated by most as public, without regard to any particular form of ownership or physical arrangement.

I am concerned with those spaces that traditionally might be considered available or suitable for public discussion of common concerns, and specifically for the expression of political opinions. One might argue that these are spaces in which the rights to free speech and freedom of assembly under the United States Constitution are guaranteed.[5] The complexities of formal defini-

---

5 One might thus conceive of six legal forms of ownership of public space: public ownership, public function, public use (streets); public ownership, public function, administrative use (city halls); public ownership, private function, private use (space leased to commercial establishments); private ownership, public func-

tion and legal interpretation are substantial, but I want to raise the issues of the use of public space as they affect both city planning and the uses of public space in cities in the United States today as matters of policy and political concern, not as legal matters.

The following are classic examples of the kind of public spaces to which I refer:

- The agora of Athens, as to its (limited range of) citizens[6]
- The squares of Rome, as that in which Mark Anthony denounced Brutus in Shakespeare's play
- The Plaza de Mayo in Buenos Aires in which the mothers of the disappeared protested the dictatorship
- The Capital grounds in Washington, D.C. at which Martin Luther King, Jr. gave his famous "I Have a Dream" speech
- The streets of Leipzig where protesters marched and helped precipitate the events that ultimately led to the downfall of the East German regime
- The streets of Seattle, where protesters raised discussions of globalization to a new level of awareness
- Most recently, the square in front of Parliament in Kiev, where masses of people camped to bring down a falsely elected president
- Genoa
- Tiananmen Square
- Prague
- Caracas, in the struggle around Chavez' presidency.

Not only public space, but also spatial arrangements in general are affected.

The impact of Homeland Security measures on the directly political use of public space is well known: the restrictions placed on various protest marches and demonstrations in the nation's capital, and similar measures elsewhere around the country, as for instance in limiting demonstrations to cordoned-off and remote locations at the time of the Republican National Convention in New York City (Marcuse, 2005). But this type of restriction is only the tip of the iceberg. What is even more serious is the manipulation of the threat of terrorism to justify

---

tion, public use (airports, gated communities, zoning bonus private plazas, community benefit facilities); private ownership, private function, public use (cafes, places of public accommodations); private ownership, private use (homes) (cf. Marcuse, 2003).

6 Slaves were excluded from the discussions. While publicness is rarely absolute in practice, here it was very limited.

- A broad level of surveillance
- Invasions of privacy
- The gathering of information about persons and activities by central governmental agencies
- The constant publicity given to the threat of terrorism by government agencies
- The color-coding of states of danger
- The "If you see something, say something" signs
- The use of security against terrorism as a justification for mammoth budgetary expenditures for policing and behavior control measures
- The presence of armed National Guard troops on subways, train stations, and places of public assembly.

Public space issues are at the center of many responses, and afford direct examples of the way the false threat of terrorism and the selling of security have been used to restrict rights to the city:
- Restrictions on the everyday use of public space
- Restrictions on access to public buildings
- Restrictions on political expression and assembly for political purposes
- Restrictions on the freedom of immigrants to use public facilities and services in the city
- Promoting flight from the density and diversity of the central city, including its public spaces, resulting in
- Increased segregation, exclusion, and concentrated deconcentration of residences and economic activities
- Restrictions on privacy and freedom from surveillance.

What is the situation in regard to such spaces today in a city like New York after 9/11? "Securing public space" often means, in Larry Vale's words, securing space from the public rather than for it. One concluding example may suffice: the use of the streets of New York City, Union Square, and Central Park—by anyone's definition of public spaces—during the recent Republican Convention.[7]

There were approximately 400,000 protestors wanting to demonstrate their objections to the Bush agenda in a public place where they could be heard. After long negotiations, the organizers of the protest and city officials finally agreed on a march-route up Seventh Avenue, and a permit was secured. The organizers hoped to end the march with a rally at the Great Meadow in Central Park, where hundreds of thousands had gathered on previous occasions for everything from rock concerts to anti-war protests. But

---

7 I was a participant in the events described below.

the City said no, asserting that such a rally would endanger the grass on the Meadow. Court appeals, perhaps too late—the city strung out the "negotiations" before a lawsuit was filed out skillfully—failed. Ultimately, there was no rally at all.

As the march proceeded up Seventh Avenue, protesters chanted "Whose Streets? Our Streets! Whose Streets? Our Streets!" Thousands of voices claiming their right to the city. This was the people energized, democracy in action. It felt good, at the time.

But was it really democracy in action? Reflecting on the march, I realized that what was being demonstrated was precisely that the streets were not "our" streets, that no "right to the city" had been exercised. The Mayor and the police could dictate where assembly could take place, how and when and where and by whom the streets could be used, whether the public parks could be used for the collective expression of political opinion or not. Whose streets? City officials' complete domination over the use of public space in New York City clarified that these were their streets, not "our" streets—and there was nothing that could be done about it. Polls showed a substantial majority of New Yorkers favored allowing a rally on the Great Meadow, but that did not matter. The message was that parks are for harmless picnics, not protests.

Yet a democratic use of public spaces requires the ability to organize in advance, to procure loudspeakers, to erect a platform, to permit collective communication among large numbers of people. There needs to be a balance between the use of a city's parks for recreation and streets for traffic, and their use for democratic, collective purposes. That balance, however, was tipped far in the private direction, for the benefit of the attendees at the well-organized indoor Republican Convention; it did not favor those protesting that convention outside.

The issues around the use of public space for public purposes, and the appropriate response to the threat of terrorism in regulating their use, are not confined to New York City or the United States. Around the Reichstag in Berlin is a "Bannmeile," an officially signposted "mile" of space in which demonstrations are prohibited (cf. Eick 2005). The grounds are clearly public, and the restriction is enforced supposedly only when parliament is in session. But in reality, the police determine whether or not the restriction is enforced. Similarly, in Washington, D.C., arrangements for demonstrations and marches and assemblies are subject to ever increasing restrictions of time, place, and manner. Of course legitimate concerns demand a balance between rights of use and protection against terrorism. But, as New York City's response to the Republican National Convention demonstrated, the line between legitimate balance on the one side and, on the other side, false use to limit the impact of actions unfavorable to the administration is increasingly suspect. A panel of the American Planning Association recently conceded that "[t]he fear of terrorism and the rush to protect against it has made the democracy of public space a victim" (quoted in Finucan 2005: 5). Good planners are doing what they can to make the restrictions on public space as inconspicuous and innocuous as possible. Planners, however, are told they must adhere to the guidelines provided by city officials. Those guidelines, if they come from the authorities in charge of security, are never open for discussion. Thus, the security authorities have unilateral authority to determine the balance of uses and rights.

And these limitations on public use are all legitimated in the name of "security." The term "security" has become a catch-all to be defined at the discretion of the police and the professionals in homeland security. Was anyone really at risk from terrorism in New York City while the Republican convention was there? Were the conventioneers, many of whom had not yet arrived, in any event ensconced within the fortress created around Madison Square Garden, with access to it and New York's second largest railroad station tightly controlled by police, dogs, metal detectors, cameras, helicopters? Hardly. Was there danger from a few anarchists? Certainly over-kill; there were not any on the march given to violence, and the extensive intelligence infiltration of protest groups would have shown that. But the word "security" has been cut off from its moorings in reality, and instead has become a mantra that citizens do not even think about questioning. In the controlled city, use is by permit, not by right. So much for public space.

But the Right to the City has been under siege since before 9/11, and the false use of the threat of terrorism is only an accentuation of already existing trends. The use of public authority to control the use of space in the city at the expense of its residents and the use of power to override the desires and needs of those with less power have a long history. Robert Moses ran roughshod over citizen opposition with his highway projects (cf. Caro 1974). Urban renewal displaced thousands against their will. Private urban renewal, gentrification, is supported by the city's leadership, despite its adverse impact on residents. Mega-projects, giant developments internalizing many aspects of city life (security, shopping, recreation facilities), are supported by the city as sources of tax revenue, regardless of the impact such projects have on the surrounding communities and the people they displace. The city uses taxes to subsidize global financial firms that will make the city "competitive," although such actions may help only a minority of the city's residents.

In broader terms, the situation is even worse. Not just the use of particular streets, or parks on particular days, is out of the control of the city's residents—city officials also control major changes in the city's form and structure, with only the most limited participation by the voters. One of the most recent examples is the rebuilding of lower Manhattan. The City is using billions of dollars allocated to it by the federal government to deal with the consequences of 9/11 to subsidize real estate in lower Manhattan and to build a "one-seat ride" direct rail link to lower Manhattan from JFK airport. But these funds would be better directed towards affordable housing, new schools, subway improvements, and job expansion. The majority of the city lives outside of Manhattan in the outer boroughs; they have crying development needs. If the matter were put to a vote, the money would likely be spent differently. But the issue is not put to a vote. Most recently, the state has moved jobs from state offices in Jamaica, Queens, where the residents had fought hard for investment, to lower Manhattan. These decisions are not made by the people of the city.

So, undemocratic political decisions have limited the use of public space, with the threat of terrorism being only the latest argument for a continuing narrowing of this aspect of the right to the city.

The ongoing shift from public to private sector control over, and provision of, "public" space is another piece of the same pattern.[8] In part, this is the simple privatization of existing public space: putting selected commercial uses in Bryant Park, giving Business Improvement Districts (BIDs) the right to police public spaces, selling air terminals to private corporations. Greater quantitative impact, however, is exerted by substituting private space to fulfill many of the functions of public space: the common areas of private shopping malls, for instance, have become the "streets" for passage and planned and random encounters, bookstore cafés have taken over some of the functions of public libraries, museums become private venues for weddings and fundraisers. In each of these cases, restriction on access is in private hands; there is no right to public use of these spaces.

The manipulation of the false threat of terrorism, one manifestation of which has been the events surrounding the Republican Convention protests, are perhaps only the most striking and the most directly political signs of the retreat from the right to the city. The cordoning off of large sections of central Washington, D.C. for the inauguration is another sign of this retreat. Even without massive arrests, the precautions taken in the name of security devalue the right to use public space in the city.

So, the threat of terrorism is used to limit the political use of public space, and is legitimated by the artificially induced insecurity that the present form of responses breeds.

---

8   Diane Davis of MIT has helped me see this point more clearly.

References

Caro, Robert A. (1974) *The Power Broker: Robert Moses and the Fall of New York,* New York: Alfred A. Knopf.
Eick, Volker (2001) "Städtische Politik zwischen Bürgergesellschaft und Polizeistaat". AK – Analyse & Kritik, Zeitung für linke Debatte und Praxis 453/20.
Finucan, Karen (2005) "Security that Works – Beautifully". Planning Magazine 71/3, pp. 4–5.
Habermas, Jürgen (1984/1981) *The Theory of Communicative Action,* McCarthy Boston: Beacon Press.
Lefebvre, Henri (1996/1967) "The Right to the City". In Eleonore Kofman and Elizabeth Lebas (eds.) *Writings on Cities,* London: Blackwell, pp. 63–184.
Marcuse, Peter (2003) "The Meaning of Public Space". Conference presentation, Conference on Public Space, University of Cottbus.
Marcuse, Peter (2004) "Die Manipulation der Kriminalitätsangst: Antiterrorismus als Verlagerung der Unsicherheit nach dem 11. September". In Sylke Nissen (ed.) *Kriminalität und Sicherheitspolitik: Analysen aus London, Paris, Berlin, und New York.* Opladen: Leske + Budrich, pp. 89–102.
Marcuse, Peter (2005b) "The 'Threat of Terrorism' and the Right to the City". Fordham Urban Law Journal XXXIII.
New York Times (2005) October 16, Section 4, p. 3. In http://www.spiked-online.com, October 18, 2005.
Vale, Lawrence (2005) "Securing Public Space". Typescript.

Authors

Al-Nammari, Fatima, is an architecture Ph.D. candidate at Texas A&M University. She came to the USA as a Fulbright scholar in 2001. She holds a B.S. in architectural engineering and an M.A. in archaeology from Jordan and has broad experience as an architect, faculty member, and historic preservationist.

Berking, Helmuth, is professor of sociology at Darmstadt University of Technology. His teaching and research areas include social theory, political sociology, and urban anthropology.

Bhatti, Anil, is professor at the Centre of German Studies and concurrently dean of the School of Arts and Aesthetics at Jawaharlal Nehru University, New Delhi, India. His main areas of interest are comparative literature and culture studies between Europe and India/Asia.

Bude, Heinz, Dr. phil., sociologist, is the Director of the Research Unit "The Society of the Federal Republic of Germany" at the Hamburg Institute for Social Research and has been Professor of Macrosociology at the University of Kassel since 2000.

De Koning, Anouk, is currently employed as a researcher at the Royal Netherlands Institute of Southeast Asian and Caribbean Studies (KITLV), Leiden. She recently completed her Ph.D. thesis at the University of Amsterdam, entitled *Global Dreams: Space, Class and Gender in Middle Class Cairo*.

Fenster, Tovi, is senior lecturer at the Department of Geography and Human Environment, Tel Aviv University. She publishes on ethnicity, citizenship, and gender in planning and development. Her most recent book is *The Global City and the Holy City: Narratives on Knowledge, Planning and Diversity* (2004).

Frank, Sybille, is a sociologist at Darmstadt University of Technology. She worked at the Wissenschaftszentrum Berlin für Sozialforschung (WZB) and lectured at the Free University Berlin. Her research areas are globalization, tourism, heritage industries, and the spatial politics of memory.

Frers, Lars, sociologist at Darmstadt University of Technology, studied at the universities of Kiel, Bloomington, and Berlin. His academic interests span urban studies, ethnomethodology, science and technology studies, social theory, and the interactions between space/materiality and human corporality.

Graham, Stephen, is professor of human geography at Durham University in the UK. He is the co-author of *Telecommunications and the City*, *Splintering Urbanism* (both with Simon Marvin), co-editor of *Managing Cities*, and editor of *Cybercities Reader* and *Cities, War and Terrorism*.

King, Anthony D., is Emeritus Professor of Art History and Sociology, State University of New York, Binghamton and lives in the UK. His most recent book is *Spaces of Global Cultures: Architecture, Urbanism, Identity* (2004). With Thomas A. Markus, he is co-editor of Routledge's *Architext* series on architecture and social/cultural theory.

Kong, Lily, is professor of geography at the National University of Singapore. Her research is broadly in social and cultural geography, and covers religion, national identity, and cultural policy and economy.

Law, Lisa, is a cultural geographer at the University of St Andrews. Her research focuses on the politics of sexual and national identities, especially in the context of intra-Asian migration. She is currently writing about expatriate life in Singapore, where she lived and worked before arriving in the UK.

Löw, Martina, is professor at the Institute for Sociology, Darmstadt University of Technology. She has been visiting professor at the TU Berlin and the Ecole des Hautes Etudes en Sciences Sociales Paris, and visiting fellow at the IFK, Vienna. Her areas of research are gender studies, sociology of space/cities, and sociological theory.

Marcuse, Peter, is a lawyer and planner, and professor of urban planning at Columbia University, New York. Peter has taught in Europe, Australia, Africa, and both Americas. He has written extensively on housing, urban development, the history and ethics of planning, racial segregation, and globalization.

Mathéy, Kosta, is professor for urban planning and building in non-European regions at Darmstadt University of Technology. His research fields include integrated and participatory development, urban ecology, and housing policies. He directed the feasibility study *Violence Reduction through Urban Upgrading*.

Meier, Lars, completed his studies at the universities of Trier and Göttingen with a diploma in geography and an M.A. in social sciences. Since April 2003 he has been a Ph.D. candidate in the post-graduate college Technology and Society, and he lectured in sociology at Darmstadt University of Technology.

Ries, Marc, Dr. phil., specializes in media and cultural theory. From 1989 onward he has taught in Austria and Germany, and was professor for comparative image theory at Friedrich Schiller University in Jena in 2000/2001. His projects and publications are in the fields of mass media, culture, architecture, and art.

Ruhne, Renate, Dr. phil., is a sociologist at Darmstadt University of Technology. She worked and lectured at the Universities of Bielefeld and Hamburg and at Braunschweig University of Technology. Her present research focuses on the social constructions of space and gender and on prostitution.

Steets, Silke, is a sociologist at Darmstadt University of Technology, and a member of the artist collective niko.31, Leipzig. She is working on her Ph.D. project about the production of urban spaces in cultural industries' networks. Her research areas are sociology of space, new urban ethnography, and transitional cities.

Stoetzer, Sergej, educationalist, is a research fellow at the Institute for Sociology, Darmstadt University of Technology. He worked at the Institute for Higher Education Research Wittenberg and studied in Halle and Berlin. His research areas are sociology of space/place, perception of (urban) space, surveillance and society, and visual methods.

Trubina, Elena, is professor of philosophy at Ural State University, Ekaterinburg, Russia. She is co-organizing the collective project *Diverse Cultures in Contemporary World*, sponsored by the Kennan Institute. Her areas of interest are social philosophy, urban and art theory, cultural studies, and audience research.

Venn, Couze, is professor of cultural theory at Nottingham Trent University. His publications include *Changing the Subject* (1984; 1998), *Occidentalism: Modernity and Subjectivity* (2000), and *The Postcolonial Challenge* (2005).